Comparative Studies in Asian and Latin American Philosophies

Also available from Bloomsbury

Comparative Philosophy Without Borders, edited by
Arindam Chakrabarti and Ralph Weber
Doing Philosophy Comparatively, by Tim Connolly
Landscape and Travelling East and West: A Philosophical Journey,
edited by Hans-Georg Muller and Andrew Whitehead
The Public Sphere From Outside the West,
edited by Divya Dwivedi and Sanil V

Comparative Studies in Asian and Latin American Philosophies

Cross-Cultural Theories and Methodologies

Edited by
Stephanie Rivera Berruz and Leah Kalmanson

BLOOMSBURY ACADEMIC
LONDON • NEW YORK • OXFORD • NEW DELHI • SYDNEY

BLOOMSBURY ACADEMIC
Bloomsbury Publishing Plc
50 Bedford Square, London, WC1B 3DP, UK

BLOOMSBURY, BLOOMSBURY ACADEMIC and the Diana logo are trademarks of
Bloomsbury Publishing Plc

First published 2018
This paperback edition published 2020

A catalogue record for this book is available from the British Library.

A catalog record for this book is available from the Library of Congress.

ISBN: HB: 978-1-3500-0788-8
PB: 978-1-3501-3673-1
ePDF: 978-1-3500-0790-1
eBook: 978-1-3500-0789-5

Typeset by RefineCatch Limited, Bungay, Suffolk

To find out more about our authors and books visit www.bloomsbury.com
and sign up for our newsletters.

Contents

Acknowledgments vi

1 Introduction *Stephanie Rivera Berruz and Leah Kalmanson* 1

Part I Coloniality and Orientalism in the Nineteenth and Twentieth Centuries

2 Occidentalism and Orientalism in the Late Writings of Antonio
Caso *Andrea J. Pitts* 13

3 The Indian Veil: The Metaphysics of Racial Origins in the
Americas *Adriana Novoa* 33

4 The Search for the Orient in Creole America: The
Nineteenth Century and its Paths *Hernán G. H. Taboada
(translated by Alba Lara Granero and Maria C. Vera)* 71

Part II New Directions in Asian-Latin American Comparative Philosophy

5 Breastfeeding in Between: A Lugonian Reading of Watsuji
Tetsurō's *Rinrigaku* *Allison B. Wolf* 105

6 Two Ideas of Education: Amano Teiyū and José Vasconcelos
Agustín Jacinto Zavala 129

7 Confucius and the Aztecs on The Mean *Sebastian Purcell* 155

Part III Comparative Philosophy from the Anti-colonial Perspective

8 Is Anarchy a False Hope? Latin American Revolutionaries Knew
Dhamma and *Saddha* *Susan E. Babbitt* 175

9 The Ants and the Elephant: Martial Arts and Liberation Philosophy
in the Americas *George Fourlas* 201

Legacies of Legitimacy and Resistance: Imperial and State Violence
ᵎn South Asia and Latin America *Namrata Mitra* 217

239

Acknowledgments

We would like to thank Drake University's Center for the Humanities and William Paterson University's Office of the Provost and Office of the Dean of the College of Humanities and Social Sciences for their financial support that made possible the Spanish-to-English translation of Hernán G. H. Taboada's contribution to this collection. We thank Alba Lara Granero and Maria C. Vera, the translators, for their thoughtful engagement with Taboada's Spanish-language original. We would like to further acknowledge the Midwest Society for Women in Philosophy's 2014 conference for providing the congenial space where we crossed paths and developed the ideas that led to our collaboration.

Stephanie Rivera Berruz is grateful to a number of people who have been supportive of her work. Above all, she would like thank Jorge J. E. Gracia, Tommy J. Curry, and Mariana Ortega for supporting her commitment to the idea that philosophy as a discipline benefits greatly when done in conversation with many traditions. She would further like to thank her community of Latinx scholars, some of whom are featured in this anthology, especially Andrea Pitts and Adriana Novoa, for their commitments to expanding the breadth of philosophy. She also wishes to share a very special thanks to her mother, Juanita Berruz, for always insisting that she could achieve anything she set out to do. And finally, she is grateful to her partner Jamilett Aguirre, for her enduring and unwavering support.

Leah Kalmanson would like to thank a wide network of supportive people, who have, in many different ways, encouraged the direction she has taken in comparative philosophy, including her friends at Drake University, her former professors in the Department of Philosophy at the University of Hawai'i, her community of fellow UH graduates, and her colleagues in the Comparative and Continental Philosophy Circle, the International Association of Japanese Philosophy, the International Society for Buddhist Philosophy, the Society for Asian and Comparative Philosophy, and the Society for Teaching Comparative Philosophy. She would especially like to thank Sarah Mattice and Amy Donahu for always making time to brainstorm ideas, read drafts, and give their invalua feedback.

1

Introduction

Stephanie Rivera Berruz and Leah Kalmanson

Comparative philosophy has long been an important site for the study of non-Western philosophical traditions, but it has also been associated almost exclusively with "East-West" dialogue. We seek to disrupt this trajectory. To borrow a phrase from Dipesh Chakrabarty, this collection aims to "provincialize"[1] the West within comparative philosophy and to focus explicit attention on conversations across Latin America and Asia. We take "provincialization" here to mean neither the erasure of Europe, nor of neocolonial political realities, nor of the Western philosophical heritage at large, but rather a strategic reorientation of comparative philosophy to self-critically navigate the hegemonic influence that Western theories and methods always potentially wield in any philosophical encounter. Our strategy, in this case, is to foreground an Asian-Latin American dialogue that reflects both the philosophical diversity of these regions and their shared concerns on issues of coloniality, globalization, and liberatory politics.

Chakrabarty's comment occurs not with reference to philosophy but in the context of the study of history. As he says,

> insofar as the academic discourse of history—that is, 'history' as a discourse produced at the institutional site of the university—is concerned, 'Europe' remains the sovereign, theoretical subject of all histories, including the ones we call 'Indian,' 'Chinese,' 'Kenyan,' and so on. There is a peculiar way in which all these other histories tend to become variations on a master narrative that could be called 'the history of Europe.'[2]

In other words, we might try to use the term "history"—or its component terms "ancient," "medieval," and "modern"—to refer neutrally to the chronological records of past events in various cultures across the globe. But this attempt at neutrality covers over the "master narrative" in which such terms carry evaluative weight, meaning the record of progress along an assumed path of cultural, social, and political development.

The discipline of history has perhaps taken many critical turns, even since the publication (in 1992) of Chakrabarty's above comment.[3] But his characterization of the academic study of history still sounds remarkably appropriate for philosophy as it is practiced today "at the institutional site of the university." As Peter K.J. Park shows in his 2013 book, *Africa, Asia, and the History of Philosophy: Racism in the Formation of the Philosophical Canon 1780–1830*, this so-called canon arose from the same Eurocentric teleology that produced now-standard historiographical terms. Prior to the late 1700s, African and Asian sources were commonly mentioned as members of, or contributors to, the discipline of philosophy. Then, around the same time that Europeans began developing dubious racial taxonomies to rank and characterize the peoples of the world, the notion of a purely Greek origin for philosophy gained currency. This, says Park, was no coincidence.[4] As he shows, two major theorizers of the history of philosophy—Immanuel Kant and G.W.F. Hegel— were informed heavily by the racial taxonomies of figures such as Christoph Meiners and Wilhelm Tenneman. Moreover, the philosophical narrative that Kant and Hegel promoted continues to shape the curriculum of most philosophy departments today, not to mention the identity of the profession at large.

One key point that Park makes during his study of philosophy is worth noting as we consider the emergence of comparative philosophy as a field in the twentieth century. Kant asserts that the history of philosophy unfolds according to rational, not necessarily chronological, stages. In other words, the stages of philosophical development are unquestionably evaluative, charting progress from so-called "ancient" (i.e., primitive) to "modern" (i.e., advanced) modes of thinking and being. Accordingly, the study of philosophical historiography requires not an empirical but a rational account of the "natural order of the ideas."[5] This basic claim about philosophy's "natural" progress influences Hegel and continues to mark the profession. Today, we may no longer teach students that the birth of spirit occurs with the Greeks, flowers in the modern period, and comes to fruition in contemporary times, but we might as well be—the structures of our departments, the programming of our curricula, and the presentation of our canon all work together to give precisely this effect.

Add to this image of philosophy the claim that being rational is a core feature of being human, and we see how easily philosophical progress is conflated with human progress and why the exclusion of Africans and Asians from the discipline also serves to deny them their full humanity. Comparative philosophy emerges in the twentieth century partly in response to these Eurocentric and colonialist attitudes informing philosophical practices. In his historical overview of comparative philosophy, Ronnie Littlejohn comments:

Partially as a result of the emergence of comparative studies in nineteenth-century Anglo-European intellectual history, the University of Hawaii sponsored the first in a sequence of East-West Philosophers' Conferences in 1939. Since that time comparative philosophy, area studies philosophy, and world philosophy have continued to grow and cross fertilize each other. Nevertheless, comparative philosophy as a field is only now becoming fully self-conscious, methodologically and substantively, about its role and function in the larger enterprises of philosophy and area studies.[6]

We contend that becoming self-conscious of its role within philosophy at large requires questioning why comparative philosophy, as a field, has been associated so closely with "East-West" dialogue. With this contention, we do not devalue the contributions of comparative philosophy to the decolonization of the discipline, but we do agree with David Kim's frank assessment of the conditions surrounding Asia's status in the field:

> Whatever may be the full story of classical Asian philosophy's unique reception, I think it cannot have as its center the apparently innocent idea that early Western proponents of classical Asian philosophy simply understood and appreciated the special philosophical character and potential contributions of this foreign system of thought. . . . Whatever the full story might be, it seems difficult to plausibly deny here the long-standing reign of the Hegelian world-historical hierarchy in which it is believed that only the expressions of Asian civilizations begin to approach those of Europe. The turn toward Asia, it seems, was also a turn away from Africa and the indigenous Americas, among other places. Incidentally, the entrenchment of this Hegelian structure might help explain why, once admitted into philosophy proper, classical Asian philosophy, presumably stagnant or immature, was so often relegated to the margins.[7]

Again, we see here the traces of a quasi-Hegelian view of world history, marking not only Europe's understanding of its own past, but also its characterization of its significance vis-à-vis other cultures. Asia's acceptance into philosophy proper, at the expense of Africa and the Americas, reflects not simply the philosophical import of Asia's scholarly traditions but also a Eurocentric worldview that ranked Asia "higher" than Africa and the Americas all along.

Our goal, as stated at the outset, is to provincialize the West within comparative philosophy, and yet so far we have discussed only the seeming intractability of Eurocentrism. However, we find hope and a little irony in Littlejohn's use of the term "provincial" to describe Europe's philosophical history in contrast to Asia's: "the earliest treatments of China by Western philosophers, such as that of Hegel, really cannot properly be called comparative philosophy because they lack any serious engagement from the Chinese side. The story is quite different in Asia, where cultural traditions mingled and clashed with considerably more frequency than in the relatively provincial West."[8] As this statement suggests, Eurocentrism is, ironically, an indicator of European provinciality—it is a symptom of the cultural chauvinism that has both produced and reinforced Europe's ignorance of other cultures for much of its history. Compare such provincialism with the centuries-long cross-cultural philosophical conversation that marks the reception of Sanskrit and Pāli Buddhist texts in China beginning as early as the Han dynasty (206 BCE–220 CE). For comparative philosophers from history who have worked entirely outside the orbit of the West, we need only look to the famed translators who facilitated this exchange, such as Kumārajīva (334–413) and Xuanzang (c. 602–664).

Europe's historical provinciality returns us to another of Chakrabarty's points, i.e., that the so-called West is indeed a "hyperreal" term whose apparent centrality is a figure of "the imaginary."[9] But, of course, as Chakrabarty also quickly reminds us,

> just as the phenomenon of orientalism does not disappear simply because some of us have now attained a critical awareness of it, similarly a certain version of 'Europe,' reified and celebrated in the phenomenal world of everyday relationships of power as the scene of the birth of the modern, continues to dominate … Analysis does not make it go away.[10]

Latin American philosophy has long confronted this dilemma of the simultaneous centrality and provinciality of the West. One of the most notable philosophical discussions in Latin American philosophy centers on the question: does a distinct Latin American philosophy exist? At the heart of this question is a claim about the identity of Latin America vis-à-vis Europe—it is important to note that the point of comparison is with European philosophy and not African philosophy or Asian philosophy. Hence, the sovereign master narrative that dictates what is distinctly philosophical about Latin America has been and continues to be centralized in the Western philosophical tradition.

Chakrabarty notes that one of the consequences of this situation is that at the level of theory Europe becomes the fundamental category of knowledge production.[11] As a result, all other histories are constructed as extensions from a European theoretical backbone. In considering the distinctness of Latin American philosophy, Augusto Salazar Bondy argues that to trace the history of Latin American philosophy is to find the importation of European doctrines throughout Latin America—it is not to tell the history of a distinct Latin

American thought.[12] He maintains that an authentic Latin American philosophy is not possible until the culture of domination imposed by Europe is overcome. In his claims about the identity of philosophy in Latin American, Salazar Bondy is tracking the impact of the sovereignty of Europe on the construction of Latin American philosophical identity, which as he notes has only been possible to the extent that it emanates from the theoretical skeleton of European thought.

This habit of questioning the legitimacy of Latin American philosophy reflects a tendency to read non-Western history in terms of lack and inadequacy. As Chakrabarty notes, the themes of failure, lack, and inadequacy ubiquitously characterize the narrative of Indian history.[13] In the Latin American context, the fact that the starting point of a discussion over philosophical identity is packaged in the form of a question already presumes that we have reason to doubt that a distinctive Latin American philosophy exists. It should not be surprising that some philosophers have answered the question negatively by claiming that philosophy in a strict sense cannot be geographically bound or provincialized; yet all the while they are deploying a Western notion of what it means to be philosophical. In other words, the question of authenticity or distinctness only makes sense when Western philosophy provides the standard with which to measure the discipline's possibilities.

By shifting the point of comparison across the axis of Latin America and Asia, we intervene on the centralization of the West as the anchor for all comparison. The comparative shift reveals the situated nature of "the West," thus invalidating its status as the epicenter of universal philosophical values. By looking at comparative philosophy through the Latin America-Asia lens and vice versa, we showcase how the concepts and ideas indebted to Western thought are themselves always already modified by the particularities of their circumstances. Through this work, we unsettle the hegemony of the East-West dialogue and foreground other approaches to comparative philosophical analysis.

In this process, the goal of "provincializing" the West is accomplished by drawing attention to the orientations of comparative philosophical analysis. Paying mind to the East-West axis as the presumed orientation of comparative philosophy highlights the history that has positioned certain geographical points as the standard points of comparative work. The "orient" in "orientation," as Sarah Ahmed has argued, brings to the fore the sense in which we think of finding one's way in the world as intimately related to the use of the East as a privileged direction over others.[14] Hence, what is eastward from one geographic region becomes *The East* through processes of normalization that take some peoples' views of cartography and geography as givens over others.[15] The dominant philosophical orientations are the result of normalizing processes that have constructed the Orient as that which is "not Europe" or "not Occidental" and hence a point of continuous orienting comparison.[16]

In order to interrupt the comparative trajectory of philosophy, this anthology takes disorientation as one of its central tasks. Ahmed's distinction between "orientation toward" and "orientation around" is useful in this context. To be oriented *toward* something implies that we face it, that it be in our field of vision. "Towardness" emerges as a mode of direction as it implies that I am facing an "other"—an "other" that is located where I am not.[17] In revealing where I am not, what I am oriented toward also illuminates where I am; that is the location that makes my "towardness" possible in the first place. The conditions that make "orientation toward" possible hinge on what we are "oriented around." Orientation around something entails that the thing in question is central to our being or action.[18] It draws attention to that which holds our center, making it binding and reflecting how we come to constitute ourselves as centers, as well.[19] In light of these distinctions, comparative philosophy has been oriented around the "West" for its sense of what counts as appropriately philosophical. As a result, the "East" emerges as the "orientation toward" of comparative philosophy to the extent that it has been the normalized direction of the Western gaze. Hence, Ahmed's distinctions help to account for the East-West trajectory of comparative philosophy even without resorting to the teleological historiography mentioned above. Being orientation *toward* the East and *around* the West speaks to the persistence of constructed cultural categories that are the legacies of colonialist cartographies.

By generating comparative conditions across Asia and Latin America, we unsettle the orientations of comparative philosophy and undermine the ground on which these categories have been constructed. The work of disorientation emerges in this anthology as moments that disrupt those trajectories of comparative analysis that would otherwise capitulate to Western centrality. We do not take this project to be exhausted by the contributions in this anthology, but rather we hope it will be a starting point upon which to continue reflecting on the orienting conditions of comparative philosophy. As Ahmed poignantly notes, disorientation is an inevitable part of life, but what is of most importance is how those experiences interrupt normative orientations of bodies and spaces.[20] What matters is what disorientation can do as the foundation for new lines of inquiry that may find their orientation in yet to be considered points on our horizons.

Chapter summaries

The collection begins with three chapters that provide critical context and historical background relevant to philosophical exchange between Latin America and Asia, focusing on the encounter with Asian traditions in the work of Latin American philosophers and theorists in the nineteenth and twentieth centuries. Although the phenomenon of Orientalism in Latin America has been analyzed through literary studies, less attention has been given to the role it plays in philosophical works of this time period. In "Occidentalism and Orientalism in the Late Writings of Antonio Caso," Andrea Pitts traces the effects of various engagements with Asian philosophy on questions of identity, race, and nationality in Mexican thought. She focuses on Antonio Caso (1883–1946), one of the founders of the humanistic and anti-positivist philosophical movement Ateneo de la Juventud ("Athenaeum of Youth"). Along with other Mexican intellectuals of the time, Caso's reaction against positivism was partly influenced by his study of non-Western philosophical traditions; yet, unlike some of his colleagues, he was perhaps more suspicious of the uncritical appropriation of supposed "Eastern" mysticism. Despite the obvious Orientalist tropes that mark Caso's descriptions of Asian thought and culture, his work stands today as a powerful critique of the West's fascination with Asian traditions through the lens of politics and power.

Adriana Novoa turns to the work of Caso's colleague and Ateneo co-founder José Vasconcelos (1882–1959) in the chapter "The Indian Veil: The Metaphysics of Racial Origins in the Americas." She situates the issue of Orientalism in Latin America in the context of philosophical debates between materialism and spiritualism, showing how Indian philosophical terms entered Latin American discourse through movements such as Theosophy. While remaining critical of the assumptions of Orientalism in nineteenth-century Mexico, Novoa examines how figures such as Vasconcelos appropriated Asian traditions as alternatives to the hegemonic presence of European thought in the philosophical debates of the day. Finally, the third chapter in this section charts a notable reaction against Asian influences, and a shift back toward European discourses, in Latin American philosophy later in the nineteenth century. In "The Search for the Orient in Creole America: The Nineteenth Century and Its Paths," Hernán G. H. Taboada attributes this shift to the rising popularity of liberalism as a political and philosophical movement and to Latin America's ambiguous position vis-à-vis Western identity. As he concludes, only in recent years—perhaps due in part to greater cultural contact facilitated by the Internet and other communication technologies—is exchange between Asia and Latin America possible without the "mediation of Europe."

The second section of this collection follows up on what such exchange might look like, with three chapters in the vein of comparative philosophy. In "Breastfeeding in Between: A Lugonian Reading of Watsuji Tetsurō's *Rinrigaku*" Allison Wolf makes two related claims: (1) the moral philosophy of Watsuji Tetsurō (1889–1960) gives us an appropriate framework for analyzing the political debates over breastfeeding, but (2) this framework only becomes visible when we read Watsuji though the lens of Latina feminist philosophy. Wolf accomplishes this through a comparative reading of Watsuji and the contemporary philosopher María Lugones on notions of betweenness and liminality. In the next chapter "Two Idea of Education: Amano Teiyū and José Vasconcelos," Agustín Jacinto Zavala compares the pedagogical philosophy of Vasconcelos with his contemporary in Japan, Amano Teiyū (1884–1980). Both Vasconcelos and Amano were not only philosophers but also policymakers, working in various capacities on education reform in their home countries. As Jacinto Zavala shows, their ideas on student creativity and holistic education remain relevant to ongoing discussions in the philosophy of education today. Next, in "Confucius and the Aztecs on The Mean," Sebastian Purcell compares early Confucian writings on moderation (*zhong*) with the "middle" way (*tlanepantla*) of Aztec philosophers. His work underscores the fact that the usual suspect—i.e., Aristotle's virtue ethics—need not set the terms for a comparative discussion of morality and moderation.

Although many of our contributors deal with political themes, the chapters in the final section focus more explicitly on political movements and activism. They explore the role of comparative philosophy in both theorizing and effecting political change, by engaging resources such as Buddhist anti-essentialism, liberation philosophy, and the intersection of postcolonial and decolonial studies. Susan Babbit examines the work of several nineteenth-century Cuban philosophers and political revolutionaries on the role of epistemology in socio-political life in "Is Anarchy a False Hope? Latin American Revolutionaries Knew *Dhamma* and *Saddha*." She argues that our understanding of their approach to epistemology is significantly deepened when we consider their aims and ideas not in light of the Western philosophical tradition but in terms of Theravadan Buddhist theories of knowledge. Next, in "The Ants and the Elephant: Martial Arts and Liberation Philosophy in the Americas," George Fourlas discusses the influence of Japanese martial arts in the Americas, and especially Brazil, with a focus on the relation between martial practice, liberation philosophy, and liberatory politics. He argues that the popularity of martial arts in Latin America has gone in two general directions—one liberatory and transformative; the other violent and indeed counter to the spirit of the martial traditions. With reference to Japanese philosophical writings on martial arts, Fourlas defends an ideal notion of martial theory and practice and its relevance for Latin American politics. Finally, in a chapter that brings together many of the concerns of the entire collection, Namrata Mitra compares and contrasts anti-colonial philosophy in South Asian and Latin American contexts in "Legacies of Legitimacy and Resistance: Imperial and State Violence in South Asia and Latin America." As she shows, subaltern and/or indigenous resistance is theorized differently in the postcolonial (South Asian) and decolonial (Latin American) literatures; however, increased conversation across these fields opens up multiple points of disruption in the colonizing discourses surrounding historiography, epistemologies of political thought, and literary theory in academia today.

Notes

1 Dipesh Chakrabarty, "Postcoloniality and the Artifice of History," *Representations* 37 (Winter 1992): 22–23.

2 Ibid., 1.

3 The essay on which we rely here, "Postcoloniality and the Artifice of History," was later republished as the first chapter of Chakrabarty's book *Provincializing Europe: Postcolonial Thought and Historical Difference* (Princeton: Princeton University Press, 2000).

4 Peter K. J. Park, *Africa, Asia, and the History of Philosophy* (Albany: SUNY Press, 2013), xiii.

5 Qtd. in ibid., 22–23. Park quotes from *Kants gesammelte Schriften*, Vol. 12: 36.

6 Ronnie Littlejohn, "Comparative Philosophy," *Internet Encyclopedia of Philosophy*, http://www.iep.utm.edu/comparat/.

7 David Kim, "What is Asian American Philosophy?" in *Philosophy in Multiple Voices*, edited by George Yancy (Lanham, MD: Rowman and Littlefield, 2007), 222–224.

8 Littlejohn, "Comparative Philosophy."

9 Chakrabarty, "Postcoloniality and the Artifice of History," 1.

10 Ibid., 1–2.

11 Ibid., 29.

12 Salazar Bondy, *The Meaning and Problem of Hispanic American Thought*, edited by John P. Augelli (Kansas City: Lawrence Center for Latin American Studies of the University of Kansas, 1969), 388.

13 Chakrabarty, "Postcoloniality and the Artifice of History," 34.
14 Sarah Ahmed, *Queer Phenomenology* (Durham, NC: Duke University Press, 2006), 113.
15 Ibid., 113.
16 Ibid.
17 Ibid., 115.
18 Ibid., 116.
19 Ibid., 116.
20 Ibid., 158.

References

Ahmed, Sarah. *Queer Phenomenology: Orientations, Objects, Others.* Durham, NC: Duke University Press, 2006.

Bondy, Augusto Salazar. *The Meaning and Problem of Hispanic American Thought,* edited by John P. Augelli. Kansas City: Lawrence Center for Latin American Studies of the University of Kansas, 1969.

Chakrabarty, Dipesh. "Postcoloniality and the Artifice of History." *Representations* 37 (Winter 1992): 1–26.

Kim, David Haekwon. "What is Asian American Philosophy?" In *Philosophy in Multiple Voices,* edited by George Yancy, 219–271. Lanham, MD: Rowman and Littlefield, 2007.

Littlejohn, Ronnie. "Comparative Philosophy." *Internet Encyclopedia of Philosophy.* Accessed March 31, 2017. http://www.iep.utm.edu/comparat/.

Park, Peter K. J. *Africa, Asia, and the History of Philosophy.* Albany: SUNY Press, 2013.

Part I

Coloniality and Orientalism in the Nineteenth and Twentieth Centuries

Occidentalism and Orientalism in the Late Writings of Antonio Caso

Andrea J. Pitts

In recent decades, scholars studying the philosophical and literary contributions of post-revolutionary Mexican thought have noted that a form of what Edward Said has described as "Orientalism" can be located among the writings of prominent authors in the first half of the twentieth century.[1] Recent scholarship in this area of study has explored the reception of Indian, Japanese, and Arabic writings, imagery, and ideas in the work of authors such as Francisco I. Madero, José Vasconcelos, and Octavio Paz.[2] These debates are centered on Said's articulation of the relationship between knowledge production and power that operates through the representation and circulation of writings about "the Orient" and "the Occident." In Julia Kushington's framing of what she describes as "Hispanic Orientalism," she cites Said's use of the term "Orientalism" as a "Western style for dominating, restructuring, and having authority over the Orient."[3] This form of domination, she proposes, persists through a "series of irreconcilable binary oppositions ... East/West, domination/subordination, Christian/non-Christian."[4] In the context of Latin American postcolonial theory, Kushington's work is part of a set of debates about whether the construction of archives and discursive trajectories about non-Western cultures, histories, and religions is distinctive from that of French and British iterations of Orientalist knowledge production. Theorists such as Silvia Nagy-Zekmi propose, for example, that Latin American iterations of Orientalism are continuous with these other forms of Orientalism, and they "indirectly demonstrate the hierarchy established by the colonial discourse in favor of Europe."[5] Kushington's view is that Hispanic Orientalism, unlike its British and French counterparts, is "political in the sense that it is opening a dialogue and exchange with the East."[6]

However, recent work by Laura J. Torres-Rodríguez has intervened in these debates by arguing that the construction of "the Orient" by Mexican intellectuals during the late-nineteenth and early-twentieth centuries was neither wholly distinct from European iterations of Orientalism nor wholly subsumable under the goals and representational practices of French and British imperialism. Instead, Torres-Rodríguez argues that the "Mexican Orientalist archive adapts itself to the political purposes of Mexican intellectuals whose awareness of their 'eccentric' position relative to the centers of cultural knowledge is very keen."[7] In this vein, Torres-Rodríguez offers a way to interpret the political and philosophical aims of post-revolutionary Mexican theorists as bearing significant relations of power and knowledge production to European writers and traditions, while also recognizing that some authors at the time were themselves critical of the emerging dominance of European and U.S. forms of cultural imperialism.

Torres-Rodríguez's recent work analyzes the writings of José Vasconcelos and, in particular, his 1919 work *Estudios indostánicos* (*Hindustani Studies*). Her framing of post-revolutionary Mexico and the reception of Francisco I. Madero's commentaries on the *Bhagavad Gītā* offers an important context through which this essay will analyze the writings of Antonio Caso, a colleague of Vasconcelos and fellow member of the post-revolutionary group of intellectuals, politicians, and writers known as the *Ateneo de la Juventud*. In what follows, I first discuss the context of the *Ateneístas* and the philosophical and political goals of the *Ateneo*. Then, I turn to Caso's chapter titled *"El Oriente y el Occidente"* ("The Orient and the Occident") in his 1941 work *La persona humana y el estado totalitario* (*The Human Person and the Totalitarian State*). I argue that, in that piece, Caso demonstrates an oppositional stance toward the conflation of Hindu and Buddhist writings with liberal individualist traditions stemming from specifically Christian tenets within Occidental philosophy. In the final section, I conclude by demonstrating how Caso's analysis of the distinctions between "Occidental and Oriental" systems of thought defers to the conceptions of history and progress that support the dynamics of what Walter Mignolo and others have called the *colonial matrix of power*.[8] My interest in this final section is to articulate the extent to which Caso's work contributes to the Orientalism created by French, German, and British philosophy, and how the nationalist and philosophical questions circulating throughout Mexico during his life impacted his depiction of religions such as Hinduism and Buddhism and their relevance for Mexican nationalism.

Before turning to this material, a brief caveat is in order regarding my analytic focus in this chapter. The contemporary debate regarding Orientalism in Mexico endorses Said's principle claim that discourses of Orientalism are not themselves about cultures and nations in Asia per se. Rather, following Said's articulation of the concern, Orientalism "deals principally, not with a correspondence between Orientalism and the Orient, but with the internal consistency of Orientalism and its ideas about the Orient despite or beyond any correspondence, or lack thereof, with a 'real' Orient."[9] Thus, in this sense, this chapter and the following analysis will not be an examination of whether any post-revolutionary Mexican writers were *accurately* depicting specific cultures or religious traditions. Rather, my concern is the creation of forms of literary and cultural placement for discourses about "the Orient" and "the Occident" within the writings of these thinkers.

1. The emergence of Orientalism after the Mexican Revolution

A significant historical and literary feature of the Orientalist writings of Latin America is the long-standing relationship between the geopolitical regions that would eventually become known as Spain, Northern Africa, and the Asian continent. As Kushington notes, the dominance of the Moors in Al-Andalus for over seven centuries gave rise to a tremendous impact on Iberian languages and cultures, an historical feature of which authors of Latin America have been well aware.[10] In the context of Mexico in particular, Torres-Rodríguez writes that "Between 1565 and 1815 Spanish trading ships sailed twice a year from the ports of Acapulco to Manila. This commercial route represented more than two centuries of direct contact between the Viceroyalty of New Spain and the Asian continent."[11] In addition, authors and policymakers of various modernization movements in Mexico were examining the political strategies of Japan and India, including the Meiji Restoration and decolonization struggles in India.[12]

In Mexico City, Mauricio Tenorio-Trillo argues that the period from the 1860s to the 1940s was an era of "Odalisque-Mania," i.e. a period of exoticization and fetishization of Indian and Japanese religion, art, and philosophy in the urban history of the city.[13] These discursive and representational interests helped give rise to the modernist self-image of Mexico City as the intersecting urban center between "the East" and "the West." As such, several overlapping concerns among the writers, artists, and politicians of this period of Mexico City's history help explain the cultural obsession with India and Japan. Namely, "the allure of the alien, the wisdom of what is ancient, the sensuality of a variant sexuality, and the sublimity of longevity and authenticity" were among the concerns that led writers and other intelligentsia of Mexico City to examine "the Orient" in relation to Mexico.

In addition, the significance of the newly emerging national identity of Mexico during the early 1900s helps clarify why authors of the period were creating an Orientalist archive. The Mexican Revolution from roughly 1910 to 1920 was a period of political and cultural significance for Mexican intellectuals in terms of reimagining the trajectory and values of the nation. Philosophically, the *Científicos*, or the technocratic intellectuals that supported Porfirio Díaz's modernization doctrine and efforts, were central interlocutors for members of the *Ateneo de la Juventud*. The *Porfiriato*, as Díaz's reign was called, preceded the Mexican Revolution and was characterized by a number of philosophically distinct features that reflected the aims of Mexico's bourgeois ruling class. Moreover, the policies of the Porfiriato led to the further detriment of rural and indigenous communities throughout the country.

Eduardo Mendieta notes that the philosophical ideals of this regime—i.e. European variants of positivism—were derived in part from Auguste Comte's reading of the social utopian literature that followed the French Revolution.[14] Comte's view was a reworking of G.W.F. Hegel's philosophy of history wherein the development of human civilization is marked by three distinct stages: the theological, the metaphysical, and lastly, the positive or scientific.[15] The scientific stage of humanity thus required that human social and moral organization would be handled via a "physics of the social."[16] The eventual publication of Charles Darwin's *Origin of Species* and Herbert Spencer's *Principles of Biology* would help explicitly frame the trajectory of human progress in organic terms. As Mendieta writes, positivism became the view that "Society itself could be and should be seen as a living organism that grows, decays and dies in accordance with the laws of organic evolution."[17] In this sense, the struggle for survival that characterized the continuance of a species would and should be conceptually used, according to this view, to explain the growth and decline of social groups.

With respect to Mexico, Mendieta outlines several prominent features of Díaz's thirty-four-year rule. Among these, several are important for this study. Mendieta states of Díaz that his regime was "instrumental in the emergence of a Mexican, mestizo, bourgeoisie that linked their own wealth to the development of industry, railroads, and an educated elite."[18] This mestizo ruling elite, according to Mendieta, "concentrated all wealth and development in the capital city, to the detriment and impoverishment of most of the country".[19] Thus, growing inequalities and uneven wealth distribution across the nation began to give rise to various forms of social and political discontent, which themselves became seeds of the revolution.

Historians of the Mexican Revolution, Gilbert Joseph and Jürgen Buchenau state that 1876 to 1905 marks a "first phrase" of the Porfiriato in which the nation underwent a dramatic economic boom. During this period, Díaz opened up the nation to foreign investment and expanded transportation networks across the northern border to facilitate trade.[20] Regarding these changes, they write, "Foreign capital and technology helped restore the silver mines, U.S. investments unlocked the vast copper deposits of the northwestern state of Sonora, and foreign investment in oil and plantation crops (cotton, rubber, henequen, and coffee) also soared."[21] In addition, French, British, German, and U.S. cultural influences became prominent during this period. Architecture in the nation's major urban centers, food products, and department stores from Europe and the U.S. became fashionable, as did intellectual trends from these geopolitical regions.

Alongside this consolidation of wealth and urbanization in Mexico, a number of foreign travelers and investors were also fascinated by what Tenorio-Trillo calls the "search for the Brown Atlantis."[22] A sought-after authentic past, much like the mythic and moralizing images of Atlantis in Plato's writings, was prevalent throughout this period of Mexican history. Among those who sought this new Atlantis were artists, writers, and photographers interested in discovering an ancient, racialized, and "purely Indian" Other who survived the poverty and degradation of the rapidly transforming late-nineteenth century. For example, Mayan peoples and cultures were described as the "Atlantes," and noted writers in Theosophy such as Konstantin Balmont understood Mayan civilization to be part of a singular thread of spiritual significance that connected ancient Egyptian and Hindu traditions with indigenous cultures of the Americas.[23]

The "second phase" of the Porfiriato from 1905 to 1910 came as a result of the increasing socio-economic inequalities between the elite mestizo and foreign business class and the urban and rural working class.[24] The economic boom of the business elites of the nation had become possible only through the harsh exploitation of laborers in plantations that had spread throughout the southern regions of Yucatán, Chiapas, and the Valle Nacional de Oaxaca, and through the mining and transportation industries of the northern states of Chihuahua and Coahuila.

The beginning of the revolutionary stirrings was the 1906 labor protest of the Cananea miners of Sonora, which helped spark the subsequent textile, railway, and plantation worker strikes that followed throughout the next decade and a half. However, the labor protests that began during this second phase of the Porfiriato were also bolstered by an emerging middle class comprised of university-trained intellectuals who brought with them a philosophical clash of ideas with the *Científicos* (scientists) of Díaz's regime. Leading intellectual voices of this movement were members of the *Ateneo de la Juventud*, a group that formed in 1909. The *Ateneo* explicitly situated itself as opponents to the specific brand of Porfirian positivism that marked Díaz's modernization efforts in the nation. Among the scholars and educators in this group was Antonio Caso, who, in fact, helped fund the *Ateneo* and the faculty of philosophy at the National University of Mexico.[25]

The leading philosophical trajectory of the *Ateneo* was to turn away from the influences of Auguste Comte, Herbert Spencer, and Gabino Barreda, and instead to embrace threads of vitalism and aesthetics from figures such as Henri Bergson, Friedrich Nietzsche, Arthur Schopenhauer, and José Enrique Rodó.[26] This turn, in Caso's work, involved a complicated series of debates about the method and content of positivism. Namely, as Alexander Stehn argues, Caso appears to seek to supplement or supersede positivism, rather than merely negate it.[27] For example, Caso's interests in the limits of the rational human intellect distinguish him from previous generations of philosophical influence in Mexico, including his previous mentor at the Escuela Nacional Preparatoria, Justo Sierra. In this sense, rather than merely reject a figure like Comte, Caso adapts tenets of Comtean positivism—i.e. interpreting altruistic acts as the highest stage of moral development—to defend an aesthetic turn to intuition as a founding component of moral personhood.[28] Art and aesthetic intuition become the limit cases that mark the inability of the biological sciences to explain the social, political, and moral behaviors of the human being. Caso interprets the natural sciences, and so too the positivists, as mistakenly focusing on particular objects of experiences as the means to generalize about human beings. Instead, through reference to figures like Edmund Husserl and Bergson, Caso argues that there are pure objects of intuition, divorced from the empirical constraints of the biological animal. Moreover, as Stehn states, Caso proposed that "the unity of humanity is not a metaphysical reality; it is a moral ideal."[29] In this sense, the *Científicos* and their search for social order through the natural sciences presupposes a metaphysical reality that comprises the human biological animal. Against this view, Caso proposes a moral ideal that gives primacy to human freedom and social responsibility. National culture, as Mario de la Cueva writes of the post-revolutionary period in which Caso constructed his philosophical works, was in the "service of liberty and justice."[30]

These metaphysical and moral positions were also importantly connected to Caso's interests in Buddhism and Hinduism. As I argue below, in his 1941 book *La persona humana y el estado totalitario* (*The Human Person and the Totalitarian State*), Caso asks why there has been a fascination with Buddhism and Hinduism in the context of Occidental philosophy. While Caso's earlier text *La existencia como economía, como desinterés y como caridad* demonstrated Caso's moral and aesthetic articulations of personhood, *La persona humana y el estado totalitario*, as well as his 1942 work *El peligro del hombre* (*The Peril of Man*) brought his earlier philosophical views to bear on socio-political issues, including legal personhood, freedom, statehood, and Marxism. Also, as John Haddox has noted, in these works Caso brings to full maturity his conception of personalism, a view regarding the centrality of personhood and the metaphilosophical primacy of persons as a category of analysis. Caso's emphasis on personhood develops throughout his corpus, and culminates in his 1940s writings. Put briefly, the moral and metaphysical endeavors that he pursued throughout his career regarding the relationship between the biological and non-biological aspects of the human animal become the means whereby he critiques both *laissez faire* individualist capitalism and totalitarian conceptions of communism in his later works.[31]

In this vein, his emphasis on the "peril" of humankind and the threat of totalitarianism can be read as a warning regarding the function of egoism in the human person. For example, Haddox argues that Caso was a critic of both capitalism and communism because each endorsed an incipient individualism that neglected the charitable and disinterested acts that constitute moral personhood.[32] Laissez faire capitalism treats the human being as a purely self-interested organic unity, and not, as Caso would propose, a fully creative and moral being. Moreover, personhood, for Caso, entailed the creation of culture, which was unique to human personhood. Communism, however, also failed to preserve human personhood, because, according to Caso, Marxist-Leninism is a "new religion" that offers an inadequate social ontology. Caso interprets historical materialism as reducing all products of culture to class struggle.[33] Arguing this point, he writes in *La persona humana* (*The Human Person*) that "the dogma of Marxism is the false selection of the foundation of the social."[34] Here, Caso cites Marxism as inadequately attending to the complexity of "human collective efforts."[35] Caso writes later in this same work that the community under Marxism becomes egoistic by denying the dignity of the individual.[36] Instead, the individual "must be subordinated to the community" and its own needs.[37] In this sense, the whole of the community takes on the character of an egoistic entity that denies the flourishing of human personhood.

Against these views Caso defends a conception of society based on justice, which, according to him, is the moral union of humankind.[38] A true community, in the sense in which Caso describes it, recognizes human persons as "spiritual centers of cultural action," and culture "reflects the historical continuity of [its] generations and the moral solidarity of [its] people."[39] This conception of the human person in relation to society is thereby the means by which Caso comes to examine "el Oriente en la mentalidad occidental" ["the East in the Western mind"].

2. "El Oriente en la mentalidad de Caso"

Caso dedicates a significant middle section of *La persona humana* to "El Oriente y el Occidente" ("The East and the West"), and the subsections contained therein extend his analysis of personhood and the role of the state in the context of "Western" perceptions of "Eastern" religions. Of particular interest for this paper is the first subsection titled "El Oriente en la mentalidad occidental" wherein Caso outlines the concerted interests of Western philosophers in "Brahmanism, Taoism, and Buddhism."[40] As I mention above, Caso's interest in "el Oriente" was not new to the Spanish-speaking world. The *Bhagavad Gītā*, for example, had been translated into Spanish by José Roviralta Borrell in 1896. Also, Francisco I. Madero, a major figure involved in the political overthrow of the Porfiriato and the president of Mexico from 1911 until his assassination in 1913, read and published commentaries on the *Bhagavad Gītā* from 1912 to 1913.[41] Madero's writings developed a view called *el espíritismo* (*spiritism*), which was, in his words, "the child of modern positivism and owes its advent to the methodical observation of phenomena that in previous epochs were declared supernatural."[42] A recent analysis of Madero's commentaries on the *Bhagavad Gītā* and *el espíritismo* by José Ricardo Chaves describes spiritism as a defense of metaphysical individualism, democratic principles such as equality and freedom, and the social contributions of women.[43]

Madero came into contact with spiritism during his studies in France in 1891 and it was there that he encountered the ideas of Allan Kardec, the pseudonym of Hippolyte Léon Denizard Rivail.[44] Kardecist or *kardecista* spiritists included a number of religious and philosophical influences, including, as David Hess has discussed:

> hermetic and esoteric traditions (the astral body, vital fluids, and spirit communication through mediums), Indic philosophy (reincarnation and karma), highly reformed protestant theology (a Unitarian doctrine and the interpretation of heaven and hell as psychological states), Catholicism (the

emphasis on spiritual hierarchies and the mediating role of an extrabiblical doctrine), social reformism (the emphasis on equality, progress, freedom of thought, and education), as well as modern science (what Kardec called the "experimental" side of spiritism, which later became known as psychical research and still later as parapsychology).[45]

Madero's writings, using pseudonyms of protagonists in the *Bhagavad Gītā*, such as "Arjuna" and "Bhima," also examined communication through mediums and similar themes as Kardec. Additionally, Madero founded the Center of Psychological Studies of San Pedro, Coahuila in which, as Chaves notes, he held spiritist meetings and experimented with electricity and photography.[46] Madero also presented himself as a heroic leader of the Mexican nation, positioning himself as similar to Arjuna being guided by Krishna in the *Bhagavad Gītā*.[47] Thus, Madero's writings come to embody the struggle for democracy and the principles of the revolution via this reference to the heroic narrative of the *Bhagavad Gītā*. His readers such as Vasconcelos would also come to refer to him as the "Arjuna of Mexico."[48]

Caso and his fellow *Ateneístas* were thus familiar with these writings by Madero and his interest in *el espíritismo*. Vasconcelos's writings and those of Madero, as Torres-Rodríguez has argued, serve to "Orientalize the Mexican Revolution" by using the *Bhagavad Gītā* as a means by which to reconfigure the political and educational stakes of the nation.[49] Furthermore, she states that Vasconcelos projects "his intellectual program for Mexico onto India's history" and in his romanticization of that history, he essentializes Dravidic peoples by casting them as a dominated population that nonetheless contributed "intuitive" and spiritual knowledge to "Hindustani society."[50] Comparing Mexico to India, Vasconcelos celebrates what he describes as the cultural and biological *mestizaje* [mixing] between "the white-skinned Aryan invaders" and "the mysterious and subtle Dravidians of dark skin."[51] On this point, Torres-Rodríguez writes, "Curiously, Vasconcelos postulates India—a country whose social organization is based on a prohibition of mixing instituted by an ancient caste system—as an example that demonstrates the positive qualities of mestizaje."[52] Similar to the *indigenismo* policies that would become instituted during the post-revolutionary period of the nation, Vasconcelos's odalisque-mania would also include studying the works of the Bengali poet Rabindranath Tagore and the Hindu monk Swami Vivekananda.[53]

Unlike Vasconcelos's writings in *Estudios indostánicos* from 1919, some of Caso's writings on "el Oriente," which appeared over two decades later, became situated in the context of twenty years of national transformation since the end of the revolution, and arose in the context of World War II. Moreover, during the 1920s and 1930s, Mexico had witnessed significant socio-political events, including the Cristero Rebellion (1926–1929) wherein the anticlerical law known as the *Ley Calles* sparked conflict between the Catholic Church and the Mexican state. This period of Mexican history also included a series of legislative reforms impacting indigenous populations in the nation. Under Lázaro Cárdenas's presidency (1934–1940), state efforts became focused on "Mexicanizing the Indian," including assimilationist policies and agrarian reforms that negatively impacted the consolidation of indigenous political demands against the state.[54] Cárdenas's economic plan was to revitalize the internal economy of the nation state by redistributing millions of hectares of farmland to peasant farmers in an effort to stimulate domestic food production.[55] However, during the 1920s there were significant regional differences impacting indigenous populations across the country, with some groups in the coffee-rich area of Soconusco being offered land reform and labor policies that sought to improve the conditions of the populations in the region. In the highlands of Chiapas, indigenous laborers drew up petitions for labor redistribution, but the state paid little interest to their concerns.[56] While some strides were taken to end debt servitude in the highland areas, politicians interested in gaining support during the Obregón administration overlooked the communities in these areas.[57] It was not until the Cárdenas administration and the political interests of the Partido Revolucionario Mexicano that these populations began to experience state-sponsored land and labor reform.[58]

Lastly, as I will defend in the final section of this chapter, it is important to note that in 1941 Caso was writing in the midst of the Second World War and witnessing the spread of National Socialism across Europe. In *La persona humana*, Caso warns of the spread of fascism, totalitarianism, and "mystical" invocations of nationalism, noting the political efforts of Stalin, Hitler, and Mussolini as examples.[59] Unlike Vasconcelos, Caso's later reflections on the "Occidental" fascination with "Oriental" religions is couched in what he describes as an ongoing crisis regarding the relationship between the individual and the state. As Torres-Rodríguez aptly notes for Vasconcelos's use of Hindu sources, the author "uses stereotypes of India found in European and North American Orientalism to construct forms of cultural self-representation for Mexico."[60] However, as Torres-Rodríguez argues, Vasconcelos was also closely attending to the work of Indian writers who were themselves developing "nationalist discourses of spiritual and racial exceptionalism . . . to construct a modernizing cultural program" in India.[61] The conclusion here is that Vasconcelos work, while engaging directly with European and North American sources also sought resources from "subjectivities and traditions mediated by the impact of colonialism."[62] This difference, then, gives us resources by which we can examine Caso's writings on the West's fascination with the East. However, as we will see, Caso's invocation of Hinduism and Buddhism in his later work does not draw on the nationalist writings of authors such as Tagore or other nationalist figures. Instead, his works further entrench a conception of primitivism and a depoliticization of the cultural impact of Hinduism and Buddhism.

Caso's subsection in *La persona humana* "El Oriente en la mentalidad occidental" begins by analyzing Europe's fascination, post-World War I, with Hinduism and "Chinese philosophy." Citing the conservative French theorist Henri Massis's 1927 *Defense de l'Occident* (*Defense of the West*), Caso endorses a growing concern with Europe's investment in Confucianism, Buddhism, and "Hindustani philosophy."[63] Massis's own writings depict Europe as a region in decline, and the fashionable trends that brought the French, German, and British to texts and lectures by "Eastern sages promoting the purported 'wisdom of the East'" as a sign of Europe's decline.[64] A commentator on Massis's *Defense de l'Occident*, Paul Mazgaj writes:

> At the most fundamental conceptual level there existed a curious identity among Orientalism, Germanism, and Slavism: a common rejection of the Western insistence on form, finitude, and the authority of reason while, at the same time, an unhealthy fascination with the fluid, the infinite, and the individual imagination unfettered by the constraints of reason. Nowhere were the pitfalls of this mind-set more apparent than in questions of religion. Oriental religious imagination, according to Massis, was nothing more than an "immense ocean of speculation, a vast dream into which everything penetrates, embraces and mingles, until it falls into the gulf of the indeterminate. . . ." Its polar opposite, Latin Christianity, possessed a solid core of doctrine, tempered by centuries of debate and the reasoned refutation of heresy.[65]

Similar to this form of othering and fearful warning, we find a concerted effort to understand the relationship between Christianity and "Eastern" religions in Caso's text. Along with Massis, Caso cites Oswald Spengler's *Der Untergang des Abendlandes* (*The Decline of the West*), and German writer Hermann von Keyserling as an example of the fascination of *el Occidente* with *el Oriente*.[66]

For instance, focusing on Buddhism, Caso contrasts "the abandonment of desire, the negation of personality, the mystical contentment of renunciation" with Europe's post-war search for "peace, abandonment, [and] rest."[67] He writes: "As life has become poor, through the work of war, as social and political theories preach 'class struggle' within each nation and the struggle of nationalisms in humanity, the troubled consciences of Europe ask the East for a medical herb that predisposes them to the obscurity and the Nirvana of birth and death ....."[68] Caso then interprets this longing as "a mistake," because within the Christian and rationalist principles of the West there is an irreducible conception of the person and the self; he then reads against this view an impersonal quest to abolish these elements in "the East."[69] He cites Socrates, St. Augustine, Descartes, and Husserl among the West's philosophical defenders of a strong conception of personalism and selfhood. He states that "Occidental personalism cannot become Oriental impersonalism" and that all the values of the West are centralized around its sense of self.[70] Thus, he claims that to abolish the individual "is beyond the limits of Western thought."[71]

He continues with a prescriptive claim that "Hopefully our civilization rejects the attacks of the East, [and] enriches itself with a contingent that enlists the great thinkers of China and Hindustan."[72] He concludes that "India was never a nation; it was never a fatherland" and contrasts this claim with the view that Israel was a people with "tight traditional ties."[73] Caso appears to claim in the defense of this distinction that monotheism affirms the power of the individual, as a necessary element of civilization and nationhood. Pantheism, he claims, leads to "the dissolution of the personal and spiritual into the vicissitudes of the fauna and flora."[74] The concluding part of this subsection of *La persona humana* turns to the work of European philosophers who "introduced and affirmed *el Oriente* in the Occident," such as Baruch Spinoza and Arthur Schopenhauer. For example, *Die Welt als Wille und Vorstellung* (*The World as Will and Representation*) constitutes the West's ability to inscribe the "asceticism and moral aspirations to Nirvana" through "the genius" of Schopenhauer, who Caso describes as "the Buddha of the West."[75] Following Schopenhauer, Nietzsche's analysis of the problem of the value of existence is read as an affirmation of the West's rightful investment in the human person as well.[76]

In another subsection of "El Oriente y el Occidente" titled "El personalismo y el panteísmo" ("Personalism and Pantheism"), Caso discusses the *Bhagavad Gītā* explicitly. He quotes several phrases from the text about Krishna and the abolition of desire, such as "full devotion [to Krishna] renounces good and evil."[77] Caso reads such passages as a renunciation of action and a form of motionlessness, stating "The Orient is motionlessness, the Occident, action: behold here the unmistakable difference."[78] Further cleaving apart these differences, Caso states "there are two souls, two great distinct and distant souls," the former he describes as "blissful ecstasy ... ten thousand years old ... [and] a priestly initiation ... [that] lives galvanized, like the Pharaohs in their ancient bones in white shrouds of centuries."[79] The latter is "subtle dialectics ... of yesterday ... of secular science in Berlin and Paris ... [and] is almost dying of feverish activity."[80] The remaining subsection of "El Oriente y el Occidente" analyzes the works of Nikolai Berdyaev, the significance of German Idealism, and the naturalism and axiological concerns of Rousseau and Nietzsche, defending in each case the development of an emphasis on the creative powers of the human person and the moral necessity of the will of the person.

In Caso's writings, we can certainly note temporal distinctions and descriptions of action and inaction that are characteristic of a great deal of British, German, and French Orientalist writings. Caso appears also to be debating within a specific strand of what Suzanne Marchard calls German "vitalist Orientalism" that emerged during the early twentieth century.[81] Unlike the nineteenth-century conceptions of stagnation that were projected onto Asian cultures and religions, the twentieth century, including figures that Caso read such as Hermann von Keyserling, were praising the resilience of "the East" in withstanding the moral and political decline that many Germans felt during the interwar years. Keyserling's work, in particular, "sought to reconstruct Western self-formation not by reviving Greek and Christian norms, but by juxtaposing German and oriental Geist."[82] In this sense, Marchard claims that had the German Empire expanded its colonial efforts past 1914, it likely would have created an Orientalist archive comparable to the French or the British.[83] Yet, due to the events of World War I, the "utilitarian" functions for creating an Orientalist archive waned given the loss of German colonies to Belgium, the UK, France, and Japan.[84]

Caso's writings are clearly in dialogue to some extent with this recent history, and his defense of personalism, and his trenchant critique of "the perils of man" and the decline of the human person respond to European trends circulating at the time. However, unlike Keyserling's romanticization of Indian and Chinese cultures and religions, Caso's defense of Christianity as a core component of personalism distinguishes his interest in comparative assessments of "el Oriente y el Occidente." As I describe in the final section, while such patterns of Mexican Orientalism appear in dialogue with other notable European variants of Orientalism, the form of Other- and self-reconstruction produced in Caso's work demonstrates Mexico's precarious placement in the global politics of the period.

3. Revisiting Mexican Orientalism

Commentators have noted the self- and Other-making Orientalist practices of Mexican literary authors such as Octavio Paz, José Juan Tablada, and Amado Nervo; however, less emphasis has been placed on the Orientalist archives of

Mexican philosophers. As we have outlined above, significant authors of the *Ateneo de la Juventud* drew resources from Indian and Chinese texts to comment on the philosophical efforts taking place during and after the revolution. While we can note the nation-building project in early Orientalist writings like those of Madero and Vasconcelos, Caso's later 1940s work appears to have been directly opposed to the idea of adopting spiritual and philosophical teachings from Asian authors and cultural traditions. In this vein, for example, note that Caso refers to Mexico, by the 1940s as firmly within "el Occidente." Madero's appropriation of the title of "Arjuna" sought to justify the Mexican Revolution as a mythic and divine struggle, and Vasconcelos' aesthetics heralded racial mixing and incipient *indigenista* beliefs about indigenous populations in Mexico. Caso's work, however, presupposes "two souls" between "el Oriente y el Occidente" that are divided firmly on metaphysical principles regarding the nature of the self and the state.

This last point regarding the "two souls" view in Caso points his readers to the changing terms of Mexican Orientalism in the 1940s. By the 1940s, the relationship between global views regarding communism and capitalism, as well as views regarding the function of the state with respect to differing economic and anti-imperialist aims have become quite pronounced. Caso's writings reject capitalism, communism, and imperialism, and his stances on these political issues become interwoven with his lifelong philosophical writings on the relationship between the natural and moral attributes of the human being. These latter themes bore their primary significance in response to the trenchant positivism of the Porfiriato, and thus gained philosophical momentum as a response to the materialist and secular philosophical period that preceded the revolution. Caso's *La existencia como economía, como desinterés y como caridad* (*Existence as Economy, Disinterest and Charity*) was a lifelong philosophical project that he revised twice throughout his life. The first edition was published in 1916, the second in 1919, and the last edition in 1943. Accordingly, by the end of his life, this masterwork proved itself adaptable to the shifting socio-political terms that impacted his thinking.

One such significant shift that helps explain Caso's "two souls" view was the influence of communism in Mexico. In 1919, a Bengali nationalist living in Mexico City, M.N. Roy, founded the Mexican Communist Party. Several years later he would become the Mexican delegate chosen to attend the second congress of Communist International. At that meeting, Roy offered a series of criticisms of an early draft of Vladimir Lenin's writings on nationalism and colonialism. The two initially disagreed on the role of bourgeois-democratic nationalism within revolutionary struggle. Roy expressed distrust for the national bourgeoisie in India, whereas Lenin expressed optimism in support of such groups to further the goals of anti-imperialism, and hence anti-capitalist struggle.[85] In Mexico City, as Tenorio-Trillo proposes, Roy would become a central figure linking Orientalist mysticism to Marxism. Tenorio-Trillo writes: "Indeed Theosophy, New Thought, and Hinduism were never far away from Mexican Marxism—as filtered through Roy, and their Mexican affiliates—represented a long-developing and powerful amalgam of Tolstoy plus Tagore; spirituality, sensuality, and the ecstasy of faraway wisdom; and the promises of eternal peace through divine violence."[86] Thus, while the combination of Christian and Hindu unification was a concerted project for Theosophy and for Vasconcelos in the 1920s, by the 1940s, Caso is embroiled in debates regarding what he sees as totalitarian tendencies of communism and the Aryan mysticism of National Socialism. Christianity now becomes a pronounced "soul" that must be distinguished from Hinduism, Confucianism, and Buddhism.

Also, in light of the complicated relationship between imperialism and capitalism evidenced through Roy's debates with Lenin, Caso's writings support a strong preference for what he identifies as a "Western" form of state-making. Alongside the primitivization of Indian and Chinese cultures, Caso's writings also evince a view regarding "Asiatic despotism" that harkens back to tropes found in theorists such as Johann Gottfried von Herder, G.W. F. Hegel, and Karl Marx in the nineteenth century. In Herder, for example, was a "non-developmental political form, which did not permit the restless pursuit of knowledge which was the driving force of Western nations."[87] Hegel writes that "Oriental despotism" deprives the state of rights for the individual.[88] Both Herder and Marx also describe the Chinese Empire as "a mummy" that has been embalmed or carefully preserved, and as stagnant and ancient. Such nineteenth-century invocations can be easily seen in Caso's "two souls" passage mentioned above. However, the placement of Mexico in the context of thriving Western nation states appears to be a consistent thread in his writings as well. In this sense, in an effort to respond to the national identity that Mexico built for itself following the revolution, Caso navigates the tropes of Mexican Orientalism alongside those of the German. In addition, this conception of "el Oriente" would also serve to further undermine the needs of indigenous groups in Mexico. While during the 1910s and 1920s Mexico's indigenous populations were viewed as crucial to the revolution and as part of a mythically united civilization with "el Oriente," by the 1940s, Caso appears to consider indigenous populations as somewhat irrelevant to the political stakes of the nation state.

German philosophy also begins to take a very prominent role during the 1920s and 1930s in Mexico with the publication of José Ortega y Gasset's *Revista de Occidente* (*Journal of the West*), a text that circulated throughout Latin America.[89] Moreover, Caso's students such as Samuel Ramos and Adalberto García de Mendoza were reading Husserl, and Ramos even criticizes Caso for his "ignorance of all philosophy after Croce, Bergson, Boutroux and James."[90] Caso appears, then, to begin to examine Husserl and German phenomenology in the early 1930s and publishes several books in the 1930s and 1940s dedicated to phenomenology. As Antonio Zirión has argued, in 1941 Caso interprets phenomenology and Husserl's conception of the transcendental ego as an important critical tool against positivism.[91] Zirión writes: "Caso summarizes his opposition to positivism old and new with the help of Husserl's weapons: the revindication of universal objects and an ideal world, the independence of logic from psychology, the possibility of an essential intuition, the widening of the positivistic principle of experience into a 'positivism of essences.'"[92] Thus, we can note here that Caso's turn toward German philosophical writings, including the political works of Spengler and Keyserling, constitute a long-standing effort to situate Mexican philosophy and the Mexican nation state in the context of the "el Occidente" and against "el Oriente."

While there are many other important avenues to explore regarding these links between Mexican and German Orientalisms, or between Mexican Marxism and mysticism, one facet that this analysis of Caso brings to the fore is the set of differential modes by which Caso and other Mexican intellectuals are vying for a conception of modern nationhood and futurity at the expense of an understanding of colonialism and anti-colonial struggle. What Mignolo calls the "colonial matrix of power" is an understanding of the constitution of modernity via colonialism and its replicants. Thus, as an analytical tool, the colonial matrix of power highlights epistemic currents, and socio-economic modes of labor and racialization that constitute modern nation states. As we can see through Caso's work, the othering of Asian cultures, politics, and religion denies the laboral, racial, and epistemic products of decolonial struggle taking place globally. Moreover, we see a conservatism in Caso's writings about "el Oriente y el Occidente" that further neglects the relationships between capitalism, Christianity, and imperial domination. Latin American decolonial authors of the twentieth century, such as Aníbal Quijano and Enrique Dussel note such connections and point to the continued need to understand the vast epistemic mechanisms by which coloniality becomes reinforced and recirculated across Latin America and the Global South. As we have seen in Caso's writings, the "two souls" hypothesis and his defense of Christian personalism demonstrate a further obstacle to unpack, understand, and overturn.

Notes

1 Kushington, *Orientalism in the Hispanic Literary Tradition*; Taboada, "Oriente y mundo clásico en José Vasconcelos"; Torres-Rodríguez, "Orientalizing Mexico."

2 Kushington, *Orientalism in the Hispanic Literary Tradition*; Chaves, "La Bhagavad Gita según San Madero"; Torres-Rodríguez, "Orientalizing Mexico."

3 Kushington, *Orientalism in the Hispanic Literary Tradition*, 1 (citing Said, *Orientalism*, 3).

4 Kushington, *Orientalism in the Hispanic Literary Tradition*, 1–2.

5 Nagy-Zekmi, *Moros en la costa*, 15–16.

6 Kushington, *Orientalism in the Hispanic Literary Tradition*, 3.

7 Torres-Rodríguez, "Orientalizing Mexico," 80–81.

8 Mignolo, "Global Coloniality and the World Disorder," 2016.

9 Said, *Orientalism*, 5.

10 Kushington, *Orientalism in the Hispanic Literary Tradition*, 2.

11 Torres-Rodríguez, "Orientalizing Mexico," 80.

12 Ibid.

13 Tenorio-Trillo, *I Speak of the City*.

14 Mendieta, "The Death of Positivism and the Birth of Mexican Phenomenology," 3.

15 Ibid., 4.

16 Ibid.

17 Ibid.

18 Ibid., 2.

19 Ibid.

20 Joseph and Buchenau, *Mexico's Once and Future Revolution*, 20–21.

21 Ibid., 21.

22 Tenorio-Trillo, *I Speak of the City*, 147.

23 Ibid., 162.

24 Joseph and Buchenau, *Mexico's Once and Future Revolution*, 25.

25 Mendieta, "The Death of Positivism and the Birth of Mexican Phenomenology," 6.

26 Stehn, "From Positivism to Anti-Positivism," 59.

27 Ibid., 60.

28 Ibid., 66–67.

29 Ibid., 68.

30 Caso, *Obras completas*, vol. VII, vii.

31 Haddox, "Latin American Personalist: Antonio Caso," 115.

32 Ibid., 114.

33 Caso, *Obras completas*, vol. VII, 43.

34 Ibid.

35 Ibid., 44.

36 Ibid., 118.

37 Ibid.

38 Ibid. 119.

39 Ibid. Caso's conception of "spirituality" is based in a Christian ethics of love and charity. For more on this, see Haddox, "Life as Love," in *Antonio Caso: Philosophy of Mexico.*

40 Caso, *La persona humana,* 93.

41 Chaves, "La Bhagavad Gita según San Madero," 75.

42 Ibid., 74.

43 Ibid.

44 Ibid.

45 Hess, Spirits and Scientists, 2–3.

46 Chaves, "La Bhagavad Gita según San Madero," 75.

47 Ibid., 76.

48 Ibid., 73.

49 Torres-Rodríguez, "Orientalizing Mexico," 79.

50 Ibid., 81.

51 Ibid., 82.

52 Ibid.

53 Tenorio-Trillo, *I Speak of the City,* 261–262.

54 Joseph and Buchenau, *Mexico's Once and Future Revolution,* 189.

55 Collier, "Peasant Politics and the Mexican State," 74.

56 Ibid., 77

57 Ibid.

58 Ibid., 78.

59 Caso, *La persona humana,* 76–81.

60 Torres-Rodríguez, "Orientalizing Mexico," 89.

61 Ibid.

62 Ibid., 90.

63 Caso, *La persona humana,* 91.

64 Mazgaj, "Defending the West," 113.

65 Ibid., 114–115.

66 Caso, *La persona humana,* 91.

67 Ibid.

68 Ibid., 92.

69 Ibid.

70 Ibid.

71 Ibid.

72 Ibid.

73 Ibid., 93.

74 Ibid.

75 Ibid., 96.

76 Ibid.

77 Ibid., 98.

78 Ibid.

79 Ibid., 100.

80 Ibid.

81 Marchard, "German Orientalism and the Decline of the West," 471.

82 Ibid., 471–471.

83 Ibid., 471.

84 Ibid.

85 Haithcox, *Communism and Nationalism in India*, 13.

86 Tenorio-Trillo, *I Speak of the City*, 277.

87 Sawer, *Marxism and the Question of the Asiatic Mode of Production*, 26.

88 Ibid., 27.

89 Zirión, "Phenomenology in Mexico," 76.

90 Ibid.

91 Ibid., 78.

92 Ibid.

References

Caso, Antonio. *Obras completas*, volume VII. Mexico City: UNAM, 1975.

Chaves, José Ricardo. "La Bhagavad Gita según San Madero." *Literatura Mexicana* 23, no. 1 (2012): 69–81.

Collier, George A. "Peasant Politics and the Mexican State: Indigenous Compliance in Highland Chiapas." *Mexican Studies/Estudios Mexicanos* 3, no. 1 (1987): 71–98.

Haddox, John. *Antonio Caso: Philosopher of Mexico*. Austin: University of Texas Press, 1971.

Haddox, John. "Latin American Personalist: Antonio Caso." *The Personalist Forum* 8, no. 1 (1992): 109–118.

Haithcox, John Patrick. *Communism and Nationalism in India: M. N. Roy and Comintern Policy, 1920–1939*. Princeton: Princeton University Press, 2015.

Hess, David J. *Spirits and Scientists: Ideology, Spiritism, and Brazilian Culture*. University Park: Penn State University Press, 1991.

Joseph, Gilbert M. and Jürgen Buchenau. *Mexico's Once and Future Revolution: Social Upheaval and the Challenge of Rule since the Latin Nineteenth Century*. Durham: Duke University Press, 2013.

Kushington, Julia A. *Orientalism in the Hispanic Literary Tradition: In Dialogue with Borges, Paz, and Sarduy*. Albuquerque: University of New Mexico Press, 1991.

Marchand, Suzanne. "German Orientalism and the Decline of the West." *Proceedings of the American Philosophical Society* 145, no. 4 (2001): 465–473.

Mazgaj, Paul. "Defending the West: The Cultural and Generational Politics of Henri Massis." *Historical Reflections / Réflexions Historiques* 17, no. 2 (1991): 103–23.

Mendieta, Eduardo. "The Death of Positivisms and the Birth of Mexican Phenomenology." In *Latin American Positivism: New Historical and Philosophic Essays*, edited by Gregory D. Gilson and Irving W. Levinson. Lanham: Lexington Books, 2013.

Mignolo, Walter. "Global Coloniality and the World Disorder: Decoloniality after Decolonization and Dewesternization after the Cold War." *World Public Forum: Dialogue of Civilizations* (2016). http://wpfdc.org/images/2016_blog/W.Mignolo_Decoloniality_after_Decolonization_Dewesternization_after_the_Cold_War.pdf.

Nagy-Zekmi, Silvia. *Moros en la costa: Orientalismo en Latinoamérica*. Iberoamericana/Vervuert: Madrid, 2008.

Said, Edward W. *Orientalism*, 25th Anniversary Edition. New York: Vintage Books, 1979.

Sawer, Marian. *Marxism and the Question of the Asiatic Mode of Production*. The Hague: Martinus Nijhoff, 1977.

Stehn, Alexander. "From Positivism to Anti-Positivism: Some Notable Continuities." In *Latin American Positivism: New Historical and Philosophic Essays*, edited by Gregory D. Gilson and Irving W. Levinson. Lanham: Lexington Books, 2013.

Taboada, Hernán G. H. "Oriente y mundo clásico en José Vasconcelos." *Cuyo: Anuario de filosofía argentina y americana* 24 (2007): 103–119.

Tenorio-Trillo, Mauricio. *I Speak of the City: Mexico City at the Turn of the Twentieth Century*. Chicago: University of Chicago Press, 2012.

Torres-Rodríguez, Laura J. "Orientalizing Mexico: *Estudios indostánicos* and the Place of Indian in José Vasconcelos's *La raza cósmica*." *Revista hispánica moderna* 68, no. 1 (2015): 77–91.

Zirión, Antonio Q. "Phenomenology in Mexico: A Historical Profile." *Continental Philosophy Review* 33, no. 1 (2000): 75–92.

3

The Indian Veil: The Metaphysics of Racial Origins in the Americas

Adriana Novoa

The cultural connections between India and the Americas were developed over the nineteenth century and became extremely important by the first quarter of the twentieth century. These links have been explored in history and literature, but less from the philosophical context that framed the popularity that Orientalism had during the first quarter of the twentieth century. In this essay, I will explain how the importance that India acquired in the Americas should be related to the philosophical debates between materialism and spiritualism, and how these debates were not a local expression, but a problem that was simultaneously addressed in the Americas and Europe.

This essay is organized around the analysis of Indian philosophical ideas as an indispensable part of the development of post-Enlightenment culture and their re-emergence at different periods of philosophical renewal, addressing the possibility of national and universal identities. The re-contextualization of philosophical thought will help explain the relevance that Indian philosophy acquired in the Americas. Starting by the mid-nineteenth century we can observe that references to India were used for two reasons: first, to create a unified narrative about the origins of humanity; second, to provide a philosophical foundation to the debates between spiritualists and materialists, particularly after the dominance that Darwinian science had by the last quarter of the century. It is in the context of the debates about science and metaphysics that we can understand the shift toward a new understanding of spiritualism with roots in India's philosophical ideas, which incorporated the different intellectual traditions that existed in Europe and the Americas. Finally, the previous analysis contextualizes one of the most well-known books written in Latin America: José Vasconcelos's *The Cosmic Race*, a text that has not been appreciated for its role in synthesizing the narratives of oriental origins and scientific evolutionism that developed over the nineteenth century.

1. Oriental origins

European philosophers and thinkers developed a new relationship with the Orient during the beginning of the Enlightenment. Dorothy M. Figueira has explained how Orientalist and postcolonial criticisms have ignored "the fundamental texts" beginning with those written in the late-eighteenth century."[1] She demonstrates that the Enlightenment employment of the Orient indicates "a subtle rhetorical strategy: Asia is portrayed as the victim of prejudice and superstition as well as the domain of reason and virtue."[2] As victim, Asia "engendered political discussions and emphasized secularized history"; while as domain of reason, "the Enlightenment depiction of Asia helped define the disciplinary parameters of the History of religions."[3] In France, interest in the Orient was closely related to such Enlightenment thinkers as Montesquieu and Voltaire.

Voltaire, for example, thought that "Asia was the ideal."[4] After concentrating on China and Egypt, he became interested in India, and the Aryans, describing the latter as "chaste, temperate, and law-abiding." Figueira describes Voltaire's appraisal as follows: "Paragons of morality and specimens of physical perfection, the Aryans embodied prelapsarian innocence and sobriety. Their gentleness, respect for animal life, and deep religiosity incarnated the virtues of 'Christianity' far more than anything found in the civilized West."[5] Aryans also "found nourishment" in a religion based on universal reason.[6] Voltaire's appropriation of the data gathered by Jesuits who had traveled through Asia helped him to argue that "Vedism comprised the oldest religion known to man and represented a pure form of worship whose lofty metaphysics formed the basis of Christianity."[7] The origin of spiritual practice itself was very much at the center of this interpretation.

The theme of origins produced different historical narratives during the Enlightenment, the one about Atlantis being one of the most popular throughout the nineteenth century. For example, Plato's mythological Atlantis became "a national substitute" through the work of Olof Rudbeck (1630–1702), the rector of Uppsala University, whose *Atlantica (Atland eller Manheim)* "set out to show that Atlantis, the cradle of human civilization, was no other than Sweden."[8] In German-speaking regions, the idea that European man originated in India triggered an interest in Sanskrit language and poetry among intellectuals like Johann Gottfried Herder (1744–1803). The early romantic writers "called for a 'new mythology,' which would supplant both the biblical and classical mythologies and transform a fragmented modern society into a unified whole."[9] By the 1830s this search for origins made it "widely accepted that the ancient Aryans had spoken the root language of the Indo-Germanic peoples."[10] There followed an interest in philology, a field that was small and marginal at the time, but produced pioneering work on the origins of the German people and in general the roots of European civilization.

Eventually, the American continent was also included in the narratives of origins that connected India with Western culture. In the United States, Asahel Davis (1774–1850), a proponent of the Viking "discovery" of America, wrote in 1840 a book that "presumed" that this continent's population had come "from the old world."[11] In support of this fact, he asserted in 1849 that the land that united Africa and America "was the Atlantis, spoken of by Plato, Homer, and Hesiod. Plato saw an account of this land which disappeared, in the hieroglyphs of Egypt."[12] This connection placed America's developments along those of Egypt and India. This kind of interpretation made Mayans and Aztecs a source of information regarding early civilizations, and in the process of explaining these civilizations some scholars Orientalized them.

R. Spence Hardy's book *Eastern Monarchism*, published in London in 1850, for example, affirmed that "the ancient edifices of Chichen in Central America bear a striking resemblance to the topes of India."[13] Abbot Charles E. Brasseur de Bourbourg (1814–1874) proposed in 1858 that the New World was the source of world civilization, an idea that became popular and ignited the imagination of many intellectuals. In an article published in *The Edinburgh Review* in 1867, for example, the authors "hope[d] to establish the general fact of mankind in the New World" where the "civilisation which they had inherited from their progenitors" came "from the northern regions of India, that 'real primordial land' (as Schlegel emphatically calls it), where everything combines to point out a common origin of our faith, our knowledge and our history."[14] This merger of India and America's antiquity would continue throughout the century.

In addition to this information circulating about human origins, the Darwinian revolution that started in 1859 provided a new way to understand the evolution of humans, one that slowly coalesced into a biological and mechanistic explanation. In time, the emphasis on materialism by the natural sciences came to question the relevance of metaphysics and any other explanation for the evolution of human societies, and human origins, not based on the transformation of matter. This literature focused on the link that humans had with apes, and the future formation of other races from human bodies that were constantly adapting and transforming. In turn, the preoccupation about origins was not only in terms of culture, but mostly about race. Imagining possible future evolutionary outcomes gave rise to stories that addressed racial uncertainty, and in this context many literary works attempted to bridge pre-Darwinian myths of origins with the new science, including the narratives about the Aryans and Atlantis.

The assimilation of mythical narratives and science became over time very popular, and in them we can see an attempt to reconcile ideas about the meaning of Western civilization that were quite contradictory. At a time in which Darwin's theory pointed to a future of continuous diversity, where forms such as race were not fixed, racial ideas started to point toward exactly the opposite. Metaphysical notions of race started to suggest the mythical origins of the Aryans, their historical relevance, and their eventual return to glory. The most relevant and influential book of this kind was *The Coming Race*, published in England in 1871 by Edward Bulwer-Lytton (1803–1873), an aristocrat in close contact with the ideas circulating at the time. He was also well versed in Orientalism, as shown by the fact that the book was dedicated to Max Müller, the well-known philologist. In Lytton's words, the "only important point" his fictional story had was "the Darwinian proposition that a coming race is destined to supplant our races, that such race would be very gradually formed, and be indeed a new species developing itself out of our old one, that this process would be invisible to our eyes, and therefore in some region unknown to us."[15] This race also acquired through the narrative "some peculiarities so distinct from our ways, that it could not be fused with us, and certain destructive powers which our science could not enable us to attain to, or cope with."[16] The permanent evolution of the matter contained in the human body became a post-Darwinian cultural obsession.

As we will see, the metaphysical interpretations of race were influential and would eventually tie the narratives of Atlantis into the formation of old and new races. They also promoted archaeological expeditions that attempted to find evidence for the different arguments about origins circulating at the time. For example, an admirer of Brasseur's book organized an expedition to Mexico to find evidence of his understanding of civilization's origins, which were by then contradicted by evolutionary science. In 1873 Augustus Le Plongeon (1826–1908), a Franco-American amateur archaeologist and photographer, began his travels through the Yucatán peninsula searching for Mayan monuments with his wife, Alice, a search that they continued until 1884. He was a Freemason, with ties to Theosophy, interested in demonstrating that the symbolism of the masons originated in that of ancient civilizations. In his book, he compared Egyptian mysteries to those he had discovered in "the mausoleum of high pontiff Cay, in the city of Chichen-Itza, in Yucatán."[17] Le Plongeon placed the origin of sacred mysteries in America, where "Maya colonists transported their ancient religious rites and ceremonies, not only to the banks of the Nile, but to those of the

Euphrates, and the shores of the Indian Ocean less than 11,500 years ago."[18] While this went against existing evidence, he did not change his theories, which led to them being ignored by academics, though they aroused interest among occultists, particularly theosophists.

It is in this context that the argumentation about the origins of humans began to be defined around materialist and spiritualist positions and the role of metaphysics. These two positions also addressed the disturbances of the self that were connected with the inability to provide a unified answer to the questions of origins and future development, which was strictly connected to the emergence of human races and their meaning. This partly explains the reappearance of India in the 1870s as a source of knowledge and intellectual renewal in the work of philosophers and intellectuals. As Figueiras has explained, the texts of early Orientalism were quintessentially political "in the sense that [they] articulated the Western writers' political reaction to their own society: their vision of themselves as individuals within that society and their sense of entitlement."[19] The interaction with India, then, was not so much about battling others, but the battles of these writers "with their own culture."[20] In the next section we will analyze how Figueiras's characterization also fits the role that India had acquired by the end of the nineteenth century in the Americas.

2. Philosophical origins

The connection between the Americas and India was linked to the spreading of spiritualist ideas to support anti-materialist positions, and to the discussion of humanity's origins; both coming from philosophical and esoteric sources. The early spiritualist movement in the Americas was not connected to India, since it was mainly a defense of the ability that some had to communicate with the spirits of the dead that became popular in the United States by the 1840s. This reaction was connected with how the "changing economy seemed to some to have fostered materialism and sapped Americans' commitment to things spiritual."[21] Spiritualism defended the existence of the afterlife and the possibility of communicating with the dead, sustaining a hermetic perspective that asserted that "both the visible and invisible worlds are different manifestations of an infinite or cosmic Mind; nature blends seamlessly with the supernatural, while the ultimate destiny of every sentient being is to realize its unity and connection with the conscious whole."[22] This perspective also opened a renewal of esoteric practices used to reach the dead.

The same happened in Latin America, where popular religious forms started to emerge as a reaction to modernization and secularization. In Mexico, for example, there was in 1866 a movement led by Roque Rojas (1812–1879), the father of the "espiritualismo trinitario mariano." This type of religiosity was the result of the liberal reforms that Mexico was undergoing and that favored a religious decentering of the Catholic Church's power. Rojas organized a movement that was messianic and syncretic through his claim that he descended from Jews on his father's side and indigenous (Otomí) on his mother's. His basic belief defended the existence of "el Gran Jehová" and a divine trilogy of Moses, Jesus and the prophet Elias that had ruled the Earth at three different moments. The movement's practices included contacts with the spirits, with trance and possession.[23] Since Rojas's followers traveled to the United States, his popular religiosity entered in contact with forms that existed in both countries, and these expressions of esoteric beliefs were soon discussed in France.[24]

Allan Kardec (1804–1869), whose real name was Hippolyte Léon Denizard Rivail, developed a popular brand of French spiritualism, following the interest in the world of the spirit of the dead that had emerged in the United States. In addition, he also added Indian and ancient texts that by this time had become well known. In the 1850s he created a movement that he called spiritism, in order to distinguish it from philosophical spiritualism. It was described as based on ancient knowledge, so Pythagoras and his followers were identified as precursors of this movement, in part because of the importance that numerological symbolism had for occult lodges and associations. In 1858 Kardec founded the Société Parisienne des Études Spirites, which started to publish *La Revue Spirite* (*The Spiritist Magazine*) the same year. Kardec, a mathematician who defended the supremacy of reason, classified his contribution as philosophical, and in his view by the mid-nineteenth-century progress and rationality dominated life, which "had led spirits to reveal new teachings more in keeping with the times, such as the principles of progressive reincarnations," which linked India as a source of spiritual development.[25]

Kardec assimilated the belief in the spirits with Orientalist literature. According to him, ancient Indians and Egyptians had believed in metempsychosis: that souls could be reincarnated, something that he interpreted at the time as always happening "in a progressive direction." This allowed him to combine his spiritism with the material ideas then developing in science and philosophy. "As such, spiritism embodied progress, the ultimate goal for humans, realized in a series of reincarnations, each one allowing for the expiation of past faults and leading humans toward improvement."[26] Kardec understood the philosophy of his spiritism as aiding the understanding of morals, since it provided those who believed it with a sense of justice and purpose.[27]

Philosophical ideas that linked Indian and Western thought arrived in America from France and Germany. German Romanticism placed India in the imagination of those intellectuals who followed this movement. As Azade Seyhan has explained, among the romantics "India emerged as one of the historically suitable sites" for their project. The Orient, "as an uncharted domain of the poetic, as the topos of unified consciousness, and as the site of humanity's encounter with its mythical heritage and lost language, became the metaphor of transcendental freedom."[28] It is for this reason that German romantic authors were and remained very influential among those who fought for independence and the establishment of early Republicanism in the Americas. India appeared in the imagination of the New England Trasncendentalists and Latin American followers of romanticism by the 1830s. More importantly, this connection will remain active throughout the nineteenth century, influencing aesthetic ideas and the philosophical renewal of racial ideals of the end of the century.

The ideology of the Americas' early republicanism was a mixture of English, German, and French philosophies. The French philosopher Victor Cousin (1792–1867) was very important politically because his eclecticism allowed the rejection of extreme materialism through a philosophical mixture similar to the one that already existed in the Americas. Reacting against the materialism of the Idéologues, *Cours de philosophie* (*Introduction to the History of Philosophy*), included an analysis of *Bhagavad Gītā* based on the 1785's translation by Charles Wilkins that had introduced many intellectuals to ideas coming from India. In the United States, by the 1830s, Cousin started to influence the Transcendentalist philosophers, and Ralph W. Emerson (1803–1882) became the most interested in exploring Indian philosophy. According to Daniel Riepe, he was the "leading exponent of Indian thought among the Transcendentalists, many of whom saw it as not only curious and interesting but also as an antidote to the rising American materialism."[29] In Spanish America, Cousin also became a leading thinker, and his ideas appeared in the works of readers such as the Argentina writer Domingo F. Sarmiento (1811–1888).

In 1877 a famous French psychologist, Théodule-Armand Ribot (1839–1916), complained of the hold Eclectic philosophy still retained in France, writing that this approach "had unvarying solutions for all the problems, a fixed number of proofs of the existence of God and the immortality of the soul."[30] Those who now promulgated Cousin's philosophical tenants, according to Ribot, had renovated some of this system, but their representatives continued attacking "evolutionist and experientialist theories," or attempted to assimilate them "as far as possible." Ribot, who defended evolutionary ideas, reduced spiritualism, as this philosophy was known, to a "collection of opinions founded on common sense, and adapted to the religious beliefs of the majority. If we extract from the different religions subsisting in Europe the common basis that is called deism or natural religion, and deduce from this deism the theology, the morals, and the psychology which it involves, we shall have Spiritualism."[31] Unlike the more innovative work produced by the sciences, it was "the philosophy of men of the world."[32]

One of the adaptations Ribot disliked, Félix Ravaisson's "Spiritualistic Realism," was called the philosophy of "*Pure Love*," but Ribot concluded his negative assessment of it affirming that "his obscure and mystical metaphysic seems little suited to the precise and rather skeptical character of the French," and even when many of the younger men were "fascinated by it, its triumph is uncertain and its duration doubtful."[33] Ravaisson (1813–1900) incorporated Christian theology into his philosophy to articulate a new spiritual understanding of religion in which love, generosity, and charity were the basis of a good life.[34] For those who were interested in renewing Catholicism to address the philosophical problems of the time, Ravaisson was an important source, and his work started to be spread in Latin America by the 1870s.

By the end of the nineteenth century, spiritism (*espíritismo*) and spiritualism (*espiritualismo*) became popular throughout the Americas because there was a need to contain the supremacy of a materialist science linked to racial ideas that eliminated a metaphysical meaning for the nation.[35] In Mexico, for example, the growth of anti-materialism was in part explained because the strong moral foundation and political reformism provided by thinkers like Kardec. While those that followed scientific materialism slowly moved to negate metaphysical assumptions related to morality, defending a determinism that made social progress contingent to material changes, spiritualism and spiritism did the opposite. As happened elsewhere, Masonic lodges started to blend into secret societies that represented anti-materialist ideas, helping simultaneously the process of secularization and the growth of a political movement that had spiritual and transcendental beliefs. This movement was scientific, but it was against the interpretation of science as purely related to a materialist philosophy.

The translation of several books by Kardec and his disciples by Mexican intellectuals during the 1870s popularized some of the ideas of the movement through publications that addressed the same issues discussed in France. In 1872 they began the publication of the journal *Ilustración Espírita*, which was inspired in the *Revue Sprite* founded by Kardec.[36] The latter's Mexican followers also created an association the same year to spread his teachings. This organizational growth was reflected in the debates that begun among the spiritualists, positivists, strict materialists, and Catholics, which ended up in the debates that took place in 1875. The Cuban revolutionary José Martí (1853–1895), at the time living in exile in Mexico, was one of the speakers in one of the sessions, where he promoted a position that reconciled materialism and spiritualism.

In this same year, Helene Blavatsky (1831–1891) and Henry Steel Olcott (1832–1907) founded in New York the Theosophical Society. Olcott was an American author who, before meeting Blavatsky, was devoted to the spiritualism developed in the 1840s. He had written books that incorporated scientific ideas into religious categories, similarly to what was happening in Latin America and Europe. He opposed slavery and proposed social reforms fostering a more democratic system, though this did not mean that he did not defend a distinction between superior and inferior individuals. Notwithstanding her partner's interest in radical democracy, Blavatsky had different goals. She was an aristocrat born in Ukraine of Jewish parents, self-educated, and knowledgeable in the spiritualism that had developed in Europe. In Egypt she had first tried to create an esoteric secret society but had failed, which led to her moving to New York in 1873, where she met Olcott.

Theosophy's founders brought the popular and philosophical spiritualism that circulated in Europe and the United States together; more importantly, Blavatsky's ideology renewed an interest in India, Aryanism, and the Vedic texts. Steven Prothero has described the Theosophical Society as "an elite attempt to reform spiritualism from above." Blavatsky and Olcott wanted to uplift the masses "out of their supposed philosophical and moral vulgarities—to transform the masses of prurient ghost-seeking spiritualists into ethically exemplary theorists of the astral planes."[37] In 1879 Blavatsky and Olcott traveled to India and moved the society with them. It is at this point that their work became oriented to a more international philosophical movement that attempted to integrate Indian religious practices into a new philosophical system.

Blavatsky described the expansion of Theosophy in an article published in 1890, reminding her critics that whatever "else may be thought of Theosophy and its movement, time has at least proved that it is not the ephemeron which the American and foreign press called it upon its first appearance."[38] At the time, the society had seven centers of publication: Madras, Bombay, Colombo, Stockholm, London, Paris, and New York. In 1889, in Paris, Blavatsky edited the *Revue Théosophique* and *Le Lotus Bleu*. In New York, W.Q. Judge edited *The Path*. The same happened in Latin America, where the first society was founded in Buenos Aires in 1893, under the authorization of Olcott after Blavatsky's death.[39]

3. India and the metaphysics of race

As was the case with Kantec, Blavatsky and Olcott framed their contribution as philosophical. Its novelty was that this was a philosophy built around their "theory regarding the origins of spiritual phenomena."[40] Philosophically, this meant a war against modern science, which was viewed as "arrogant, materialist, and atheistic."[41] In terms of religion, Theosophists were critics of certain aspects of Christianity, and fought against slavery and in favor of a religion that aided social reform. This explains the multiple philosophical interests of Theosophy and the plasticity that allowed it to be applied to different cultures and countries around the world. In *Isis Unveiled*, published in 1877, Blavatsky framed her historical narrative by reference to the occult tradition of Atlantis as the place where the chosen people, or the gods, lived, returning to a common thread that placed India as the origin of civilization. She used a citation of Bresseur de Bourbourg to affirm that the words Atlas and Atlantic were not of European origin: "But in the Nahuatl (or Toltec) language we find immediately the radical *a*, *atl*, which signifies water, war, and at the top of the head."[42] In the same way, the name America was not derived from that of Americo Vespucci, "whose real name was Alberico," but to "Meru, the sacred mount in the centre of the *seven* continents, according to the Hindu tradition."[43] In Blavatsky, continental America is completely integrated in a dialogue of correspondences that broke traditional regional barriers.

Blavatsky's historical narrative incorporated the evolution of America's ancient civilizations, and in 1890 Blavatsky invited Alice Le Plongeon (1851–1910) to deliver "a lecture titled 'The Mayans' to her lodge of the society."[44] This was related to the proposal to "form a nucleus of a Universal Brotherhood of Humanity," renewing old Enlightenment ideas that had been challenged by materialism and science. The brotherhood was created "without distinction of race, creed, sex, caste, or colour" to promote the study "of Aryan and other Eastern literatures, religions, philosophies and sciences, and to demonstrate its importance; and to investigate unexplained laws of nature, and psychic powers latent to man."[45] It was from this new humanism and its revitalization of a universal narrative of origins that India was introduced in the Americas with much success.

Blavatsky wanted to establish a balance between spirituality and materialism based on Platonic philosophy; in her words, "the most elaborate compend [sic] of the abstruse systems of old India, that can alone afford us this middle ground." Plato was the "world's interpreter," mirroring "faithfully in his works the spiritualism of the Vedic philosophers" and "its metaphysical expression."[46] Vyasa,

Djeminy, Kapila, Vrihaspati, Sumati, and so many others, will be found to have transmitted their indelible imprint through the intervening centuries upon Plato and his school."[47] Blavatsky claimed that her work was scientific at the same time that she disregarded two darker assumptions associated with evolutionary science: (1) the reduction of humanity to the material body, and (2) the determinism derived from the idea that humans descended from apes and were constantly evolving and differentiating among themselves. Following this logic, as we have seen, some groups, races, would not exist in the future. Blavatsky's view of the body was completely different.

> The basis of this assimilation is always asserted to be the preexistence of the spirit or nous . . . . The present earth-life is a fall and punishment. The soul dwells in "the grave which we call the body," and in its incorporate state, and previous to the discipline of education, the noetic or spiritual element is "asleep." Life is thus a dream, rather than a reality. Like the captives in the subterranean cave, described in The Republic, the back is turned to the light, we perceive only the shadows of objects, and think them the actual realities.[48]

The body, the center of the post-Darwinian political system, is here identified with the grave; matter that regardless of its superiority or inferiority had to be left behind. Evolutionary theory was wrong because it was searching "that link which unites man with his real ancestry" in the "material world for forms," when it in fact originated "in Spirit—evolution having originally begun from above and proceeded downward, instead of the reverse, as taught in the Darwinian theory."[49] This explains why the formation of the modern human's body is not a process of perfecting race, but of reacquiring what was needed to restore its spiritual perfection. According to her, "Occult Sciences claim less and give more, at all events, than either Darwinian Anthropology or Biblical Theology."[50] Toward this end she provided an evolutionary history of man that mixed Indian texts, Western esotericism, and Darwinian ideas. A good example of this synthesis is how she took the paleographic record of Lemuria, a lost continent, and turned it into the home of the "Third Root-Race" that preceded mankind. In *Isis Unveiled* Blavatsky explained her plan to restore all the myths and legends from everywhere using the ancient knowledge that was "far better acquainted with the fact of evolution itself" than the authorities of her time.[51] She also used literary ideas to explain the formation of future races. *The Coming Race* (1871), for example, was one of her inspirations.

In Theosophy, race becomes a narrative of quasi-evolutionary stages, although in this case the path of transformation is not vertical but circular and mythical.

According to Blavatsky, original perfection was followed by a degeneration that led to humans, and the future would see the emergence of the body equipped to allow perfection to return. Blavatsky's "Story of Man" developed in "seven clearly marked stages called Root-Races. The first three were occupied in the work of building a serviceable physical body and developing the senses of hearing, touch, and sight."[52] The first two races were made "of such fine matter that no fossils could be left, and they did not build cities or temples." The third was closer to modern humans. It inhabited the continent of Lemuria and was "therefore a contemporary of the gigantic saurians." The fourth root race lived in Atlantis and had originated modern humans. The fifth root race was the present one, and the sixth would emerge in the future from sunken Lemuria, which would arise "from its age-long sleep, and lie again beneath the sun rays of our earthly day."[53] The seventh root race would appear in Atlantis.

Blavatsky's universalism did not prevent her from echoing the racism of her time; she promoted a metaphysical understanding of the different races related to historical missions with messianic aims, potentially amplifying the superiority of certain groups over others. Sumathi Ramaswany has explained that Theosophy generated "a complex geography of human races in which all the black peoples of the world are either Lemurians or their degenerate descendants, while the most advanced peoples of today—white Caucasians—are members of the Fifth Root-Race, far removed from them."[54] While the Spirit was manifested "in the form of the various Root-Races and sub-races," those who were black "are deemed to be descendants of a 'root-race' that was ultimately transcended by other, superior, forms" (i.e., the fifth root race, or Caucasians).[55] Those who were considered degraded specimens were consigned to another place and time "to isolate them further from the more evolved races by tracing their origins to a totally different continental configuration."[56] In proposing such isolation, Blavatsky was naturalizing the process of racial exclusion to preserve purity and superiority, an idea that other followers would develop, further betraying the very universality that she proposed.

Blavatsky was right in depicting the last decades of the nineteenth century as a period in which hopes had sunk among those who believed in the universalism of the early Enlightenment and its metaphysical concerns; something which was also evident in France. Kandec died in 1869 and, according to Sophie Lachapelle, while his work had carefully separated "his doctrine from esotericism," the next important leader of spiritism after him, León Denis (1846–1927), began by the 1880s to bring "spiritism closer to occultism, ancient revelations, and esotericism." For Denis, "the ancients had possessed great wisdom on matters of life and death.

In the lost worlds of India, Egypt, and Gaul, sacred knowledge treasured and controlled by an elite priesthood had been divulged to the population and presented as magical religions."[57] French spiritism spread in the Americas at the same time as Theosophy, and many found it superior to Blavatsky's esotericism, which led to several mixes that blended concepts coming from different traditions.

The last two decades of the nineteenth century saw in the United States the reaffirmation of the "foundational premise of Americans as a chosen people living out their lives in their promised land that extended from sea to shining sea." This process coincided with a "flourishing occult revival, a virtual 'esoteric boom'" that was not different from the ones taking place in Europe or, as we will see, in other parts of the American continent, though expressed differently according to local circumstances.[58] In this climate the work of Blavatsky and the Theosophical Society became very popular throughout the continent. By the 1900s Theosophists' networks included many prominent intellectuals from the Americas. This movement was not interested in India itself, but in the thought that had emerged from the association of Indian ideas with narratives of origin or with anti-materialist philosophical positions that had been developed over the nineteenth century, as discussed above.

By the 1900s Theosophy became more philosophically interesting because of the work of Blavatsky's follower Annie Besant (1847–1933). She expanded the philosophical premises of the society in a way that facilitated the internationalization of the movement, which made the connections with India more important than certain practices of the occult. Besant was born in London to Anglo-Irish parents in 1847 as Annie Wood. She was an active member of the National Secular Society, a socialist, and a member of the Fabian Society until she converted to Theosophy in 1889. Unlike Blavatsky she was more formally educated, and had earned respect in academic circles before converting to Theosophy. She lived mostly in India beginning in 1893, and traveled all over the world delivering lectures that promoted Theosophy, including in Mexico. Theosophy's popularity grew because it was simultaneously religion, science, and a program for social reform; all qualities that attracted thinkers in the Americas. Martí, who heard Besant talk in New York, liked her very much and saw in her views the beginning of a new religion.[59]

According to Besant, Theosophy had come to the world "as at once an adequate philosophy and an all-embracing religion and ethic."[60] It also offered an arc of knowledge that could satisfy anyone from the simplest person to the most devoted intellectual. In Blavatsky and Besant the Pythagorean, Platonic, and Neo-Platonic schools are linked to Hindu and Buddhist thought. Besant also described these philosophical correspondences as a new synthesis that closely aligned Western philosophy with the Orient. Pythagoras becomes an important figure, because his philosophy is the result, according to Theosophy, of his traveling to India, where he had learned philosophy, which explains how his thought linked ideas from Sanskrit texts. She also mentioned how Buddhist ideas played a prominent role in Gnosticism, how Sāṃkhya thought was "very plainly evident in the Neo-Platonic writers"; indeed, the very basis of Christianity could be traced to the conception of Logos in India.[61]

Blavatsky and Besant drew a new map to understand the development of Western philosophy. Not only was Pythagoras trained in India, but Plato had studied in Egypt, which pointed "to a single source, and that is the Brotherhood of the White Lodge, the Hierarchy of the Adepts who watch over and guide the evolution of humanity, and who have preserved these truths unimpaired; from time to time, as necessity aroused, reasserting them in the years of men."[62] The pillars of this lodge were "Love and Wisdom," and through "its straight portal" only those who had abandoned desire and selfishness could pass.[63] As Besant explained, Theosophy offered the reconciliation of spirit and matter in a way that was harmonic, echoing the ideas of the early Enlightenment. As a philosophy, Theosophy could be held intellectually apart from Hinduism, since atheists, Christians, or Muslims could all become theosophists. But, as Besant made clear, for those who entered Theosophy as she did, "from Materialism," the satisfaction could be dual: on one side the philosophical satisfaction introduced by the new ideas; on the other, the satisfaction of religious devotion that had found "in Hindûism its most ancient and most natural expression."[64] Spirit was linked to matter because it infused everything with life.

Together with French spiritism, Theosophy became very influential in the Americas because both reconciled science with a philosophy that sustained metaphysics; they both contained a scientific and historical narrative of origins that was not confined to biological evolution: antiquity. Greece, Egypt, America and India became sources of philosophical thought among devotees. But the attempt to reconcile religion with science, and materialism with spiritualism, created a contradiction; while there was a claim that the materiality of the body (race) was not important, the mythical narration of human origins was connected to India and the Aryan, a group that was understood also as the most advanced in the racialized discourse of the nineteenth century. This led to a spiritualized notion of Aryanism that presented them as a pure population that would return to save humanity. In this sense, India was simultaneously a place of philosophical reconciliation and racial separation.

4. The Indian Veil: The oriental origins of Vasconcelos's racial ideas

Following Figueiras, we can understand the expansion of Orientalism in the Americas by the end of the nineteenth century as a symptom of the disturbances of the self. At a time in which philosophical debates were being articulated around materialism and racial determinism, which negated the possibility of ideological unity, or consensus on the meaning of the Enlightenment, India appeared as a source of unity, both in terms of racial unity and philosophical knowledge. It is for this reason that in Latin America the last decade of the nineteenth century and the first quarter of the next saw experimentation with different philosophical approaches, sometimes synthetized in different combinations. Theosophical and spiritualist readings happened at the same time that the vitalist ideas of figures like Nietzsche and Bergson were becoming popular, along with a revival of Greek philosophy, and the emergence of neo-Idealism and neo-Kantianism. Orientalism was also renewed through the work of Schopenhauer. By the 1900s, the interest in Theosophical ideas continued in the Americas, reinforcing the existent networks and the collaboration among intellectuals. For example, in 1901, Olcott traveled to Buenos Aires, invited by the local Theosophical Society. An article covering this event in the most popular magazine of the day made clear that unlike other more esoteric associations, Theosophy was "a high philosophy" that attempted to "create harmony between religion and science."[65] In Argentina there were four branches of the Theosophical Society, with more than seventy members and a monthly journal, *Philadelphia*. The interest in this type of thinking grew into diverse groups, one of them founded in 1911 by the Spaniard Joaquín Trincado (1866–1935). The "Escuela Magnético-Espiritual" (Magnetic-Spiritual School) which quickly expanded to other countries, including Mexico.[66]

Amid all this diversity, the common thread was an anti-materialist proposition that challenged both the role of positivism as the official philosophy of the Americas and the emergence of U.S. imperialism based on the supremacy of the Anglo-Saxon race. The resulting synthesis implied breaking the association between modernity and Europe, providing a new origin for Western thought by forging a new historical account of evolution, and a new understanding of race. In Mexico, the implicit presence of India was very important, and part of the same Orientalism that was described in the previous sections. India became part of the discussions of secularized history and the problems of constituting a national self, which was indispensable after the Mexican Revolution of 1910. The problem of defining the nature of modern Mexico, its origins, and its racial diversity facilitated the appropriation of Indian ideas, and Theosophy and its derivatives were important to address the two issues that were always connected with India: the search for origins and the return to a philosophy that supported metaphysics.

This popularity of Indian texts by the 1890s was not constrained by literacy in English or French. In 1896, José Roviralta Borrell, a theosophist from Spain, translated *Bhagavad Gītā* to Spanish from a French translation of the original Sanskrit.[67] The revolutionary leader Francisco Madero, a spiritist, based his commentaries on this text. He also authored the most popular spiritualist manual that circulated in Mexico, and before dying he argued that Kardec and the original Buddhism and Hinduism were superior to what Blavatsky had to offer. The end of the nineteenth century saw the inauguration of several journals devoted to spiritualism, among them *Helios, La Cruz Astral*, and *Siglo Espírita*. In addition, in the work of followers like Madero, the interpretations of the *Bhagavad Gītā* were also useful in designing a political plan of action and social reforms.[68] José Ricardo Chaves has shown how the battle announced when Krishna convinces Arjuna to take up arms is associated by Madero with his own battle against the old political system. This text offered him an "ethical and philosophical compass" to provide his political action with spiritual direction.[69]

Chaves correctly points out the mistakes made by Madero in his interpretation, or what he called his "historic and philological ingenuity," but this criticism seems to disregard the international origins of this form of spiritualism. Madero was not unaware that he was decontextualizing the text; indeed he understood that Orientalism was precisely about *re-creating* a text, after all this has been the way India had entered the Western philosophical world since the time of the Enlightenment. It was not about understanding the Indian context in which the texts were composed, but contextualizing a self that could challenge problematic ideas with the aid of Indian thought. In this sense, Madero does what everybody else was doing in bringing local context to the Indian texts. His interpretation should be viewed as another branch of the spiritualism that was popular at the time in the United States and Europe.

The second moment of spiritualist renewal in Mexico had roots in the late-nineteenth century, but it was fully developed in the first quarter of the twentieth, particularly through the creation of the *Ateneo de la Juventud* in 1909. By then the interest in comparative treatments of ancient Meso-American civilizations had increased, and with it the idea that they were an originary part of human development. Turning back to indigenous civilizations was by now no cause for shame, as it had been in the past, since India and Egypt might well be the mirror of ancient Mexico. This is one explanation for the references to Indian sacred texts that began to be popular among modernist writers like Amado Nervo (1870–1919) and the members of the *Ateneo de la Juventud*, including José Vasconcelos (1882–1959). Vasconcelos explained in *Estudios indostánicos*, published in 1920, that he used to meet with Antonio Caso, Pedro Henríquez Ureña, and Alfonso Reyes to discuss "all the issues that directly affected the spirit," but none of their readings satisfied them. In these meetings they commented on texts drawn from the positivism that dominated Mexico, and from Europe.[70] The former lacked any metaphysical project; in the latter, philosophy was in such state of disarray, undergoing a period of "materialist corruption", that left them "disappointed." Confronted with this lack of answers they "delighted" themselves with readings from India, one of their sources being the comments that Francisco Madero had made on the Spanish translation of the *Bhagavad Gītā*.[71]

The revolution that started in 1910, with Madero as one of its leaders, transformed Mexico, since it forced its intellectuals to renew the philosophical ideas in an effort to contextualize past and the future. Vasconcelos noted in 1919 that the rebuilding of philosophy required sources that were not complicit in the failed politics that had led Europe to a war of extermination from 1914 to 1918. Metaphysical speculation was tied to the constitution of new foundations for the nation, and it is here that India was useful. *Estudios Indostánicos* was a manual of Indian thought that Vasconcelos put together using the reading notes he had made over the past years. He identified this book as a "synthetic exposition" that could aid Mexicans in the process of developing a new system of thought.[72] In the introduction, Vasconcelos himself explained his motivations, citing two as most important: first, the possible relationship between Buddhism and the gnostic theories emanating from Alexandria's Neo–Platonism; second, the study he made of Buddha as a prophet of the coming of Jesus. In this chapter he developed his "aesthetic monism" explaining that Jesus was the supreme Buddha, "the Maitreya Buddha, or the merciful one that Sakya Muni had announced as the one that would renew and found the definitive truth."[73] This thesis reflected an interest in "all the races, at all times, and to all people", which revealed an understanding of Indian thought as universal.[74]

Vasconcelos's interest in a Monist aesthetic was not a novelty at a time in which philosophical debate was structured around materialist and spiritualist positions. The German naturalist Ernst Haeckel (1834–1919), a supporter of Darwinian evolutionism, had also developed it in the last decades of the nineteenth century. He reproduced "perfect geometrical shapes, *evolutionary* archetypes," that were "the first organisms on earth, from which all others forms of life gradually emerged." According to the theory of archetypes, "those morphological forms that came closest to the basic geometrical form of the sphere were considered 'pure and perfect.'" Haeckel "believe[d] in the existence of morphological universals," and their empirical counterparts proved the "natural law of harmonic form and order."[75] Blavatsky had taken some of these ideas in her development of the concept of root race, though she despised Haeckelian materialism.

This materialist monism was contradicted by the philosophy of Blavatsky and Besant. According to Gauri Viswanathan, Besant, for example, amplified her mentor's understanding "of the pull towards unity" to develop "the concept of progressive messianism—the illumination of absolute reality as unity of the mind and matter, alongside the ferment of evolutionary change—as Theosophy's attempt to resolve the debates about monism and dualism."[76] In his own monism, Vasconcelos synthesized these ideas together with other sources that emphasized the supremacy of the aesthetic in the development of morality. Against Kant's distinction between the creation and enjoyment of beauty, Vasconcelos proposed the existence of an innate desire for the beautiful, deeply connected with self-improvement and morality. Human nature could not be divorced from the aesthetic sense. The psyche was organized around the sense of what was beautiful.

Vasconcelos called modern philosophical Brahmanism a "Vedic Renaissance" because in it all the religious theories conceived by humanity had a place, which indicated its synthetic power. Hindustani thought was relevant for him because it was not "contained by form and was impregnated by Infinitude."[77] Hindustani metaphysics inspired Vasconcelos because it had a "conviction of eternity" that did not exist in any other philosophy. By contrast, his generation lived in perpetual movement, trapped by representation, and lost in mere details. The example of India showed him the possibility of a new path.

> La idea de que una cosa perezca, es una idea absurda, y si los sentidos constantemente nos están demostrando el perecer, eso no es sino una mala interpretación de los sentidos. El entendimiento, en cambió, concibe que hay un plano y una manera en que todo es perpetuo, desde que nace; "ab eternam." *Lo que es no puede dejar de ser.*[78]

> (The idea that a thing can perish is an absurd idea, and if the senses are constantly showing us perishment it is due to their bad interpretation. On the contrary, our understanding conceives that there is a level and way in which everything is perpetual from birth; "ab eternam." *Whatever is cannot stop being.*) [Chapter author's translation]

At a time when those like himself were considered less important and prone to extinction, Vasconcelos found in India a reaffirmation of the eternal continuity of life. "India is a country of Ideas," said Vasconcelos, and this meant that while in Greece objects were conceived in a precise and defined way, in India the same objects were "symbols and signs of the world that transcended what was sensible."[79] This removal from "material values" had produced a "constant benevolent idealism" that never had been "stained by the cruelties of fanaticism."[80] The Hindustani mystics had always understood, according to Vasconcelos, that ideas are "a divine miracle" unaffected by external action and spread by "inspiration, persuasion, and sympathy."[81] In opposition to the examples of Muslim and Christian religions, this mysticism was more "noble" because it was not based in securing the enjoyment of paradise—what remains and what is finite seemed to Indian mystics unworthy of the sublime greatness of the spirit.[82]

Philosophically, Vasconcelos's understanding of India contextualizes his own project for Mexico. It is for this reason that after praising Indian thought he clarifies that Hindu speculation was not a model to follow step by step, since it was not geared toward the specific problems faced by his generation. "True philosophy is not a thing of the past or present, it is not owned by a certain age, nor does it belong to a certain race", Vasconcelos affirmed.[83]

Nuestra especulación metafísica hállase fatigada y necesita el renuevo de las ideas hindúes; cierto que muchas de ellas se han filtrado desde hace siglos en el alma europea; mas ahora comienzan a llegarnos en su imponente totalidad, y es indudable que el vasto aporte ha de producir un renacimiento de todas las cuestiones del espíritu. Y en ninguna parte ese renacimiento será más fecundo que en la América Latina [. . .] Todo el pensamiento contemporáneo ha de ir a la India en busca de las ideas esenciales que allí han elaborado grandes espíritus.[84]

(Our metaphysical speculation [. . .] needs to be renewed by the ideas from India. It is true that for centuries many of the latter have been filtered through the European soul, but now they are starting to arrive in their imposing totality, and it is without a doubt a vast contribution that will produce a renewal of all the spiritual issues. In Latin America, this renewal will be more productive than in any other place [. . .] All contemporary thought will go to India in search of the essential ideas that were elaborated there by great spirits.)

The inspiration provided by Indian thought was the starting point to develop "the philosophy that we all desire: a philosophy that it is not the expression of only one race, or only one historical epoch. This philosophy will be the synthesis and triumph of all human experience: a world philosophy."[85] Curiously, just as Spain and Spanish America were moving toward a philosophy of circumstance, or of local context, Vasconcelos interprets India as the source of a universal community of purpose and meaning. It is here that we see the impact that spiritualist and Theosophical ideas had on him.

For example, for him the world we see "is not real, *it is not what it is.*"[86] The world described in the book was concealed, and had to be revealed through the removal of the veil, which was the convention imposed on our senses by the forms of our intelligence, space, time, causality, etc. It was "the illusion of the phenomenal world."[87] As was the case in France among those who opposed materialism, the phenomenal world depended on moral necessity, and the importance of morality is one of the crucial elements for Vasconcelos in containing materialism.

> El Uno aspira a ser Todo, sin dejar de ser Uno, y sin dejar de abarcar Todo. Este anhelo irrefrenable del ser, que la razón y la experiencia contradicen, pero que el corazón y la voluntad imponen, eso es lo que late en toda filosofía profunda, en toda religión verdadera; esa es la tesis de los Upanishads esa es la tesis vedántica, esa es la tesis neoplatónica, esa es la tesis cristiana, eso es lo que preocupaba a San Agustín, y eso es lo que no pudo demostrar Kant, y eso es lo que quiere la más humilde de las conciencias que medita el Universo. Desde Yajnavalkia, desde Parménides, hasta nuestros días, esa es la tesis eterna, el enigma insoluble, el misterio fecundo, la esencia de nuestra vida, vida absurda, pero redimible, y capaz de servir de tránsito para otras vidas más altas. En realidad, la India y el Occidente coinciden en la apreciación de este problema: del yo como Todo, y el yo como Uno. [...]La comunión con Brahma no es el aniquilamiento: es como si poco a poco fuéramos ensanchando nuestra conciencia individual, hasta hacerla total, hasta refundirla en el poder y la infinitud de Brahma.[88]

(One aspires to be a totality, but without ceasing to be One, and without ceasing to encompass the totality. This is an irrepressible desire of one's being [ser] that is contradicted by reason and experience, but imposed by heart and will. This is what beats in all deep philosophies, in all true religions; this is the thesis of the Upanishads, of the Vedic thesis, of the Neo-Platonic thesis, of the Christian thesis. This is what worried Saint Augustine, and this is what Kant was not able was not able to demonstrate. And this is what the humblest consciousness that thinks about the Universe wants. From Yajnavalkia and Parmenides to our present time, this is the eternal thesis, the unsolved enigma, the fecund mystery, the essence of our life; a life that is absurd but redeemable, and able to serve as the path to other, and higher, lives. In reality, India and the West coincide in the appreciation of this problem: The Ego as a totality, and the Ego as One. [...] The communion with Brahma is not annihilation: it is like if we were widening our individual consciousness bit by bit, until making it whole, until melting it down in the power and infinitude of Brahma.)

Philosophy needed religion, and in this Vasconcelos showed his agreement with German Romanticism, French eclecticism and Theosophy. He recognized that in a country that was rebuilding amid the threat of the materialism imposed by United States imperialism, the realm of the spiritual needed to become part of the nation. The nation should be metaphysical and not based exclusively on the materiality of its bodies. In his analysis, the culture of the Orient and the culture of the West were now united and would remain inseparable in the future, because "now the whole world is an Alexandria, where all doctrines get compared, studied, and elaborated in a synthesis."[89] What Vasconcelos called "Our Christianity" was the only certainty on which the metaphysical basis of the nation could be built, synthetizing French ideas on the subject.

> Nuestro cristianismo supo resistir triunfante el enriquecimiento y la crítica de que fué objeto en Alejandría, y ahora, también, no le esperan sino frutos copiosos de su nueva inmersión, en las ideas ancestrales de esa rama vigorosa del pensamiento humano, la raza de los indo–arios. Porque el cristianismo es verdad, y nada tiene que temer de la verdad; por eso no debemos los cristianos acercarnos con temor a los preceptos extraños, sino con ese espíritu de conciliación y de ese eclecticismo que caracterizó a los Padres de la Iglesia, a los obispos platonistas, que gracias a su elevación mental, supieron depurar el cristianismo, apartándolo de la teología bíblica, para ennoblecerlo, como la doctrina de Cristo lo merece, en las claridades transparentes de la filosofía griega.[90]

> (Our Christian thought knew how to triumphantly resist the enrichment and criticism that underwent in Alexandria, and now, too, will also obtain copious fruits from this new immersion on the ancestral ideas of that branch of the human thought that comes from the Indo-Arians. Since Christianity is the truth it has nothing to fear from true ideas; and for this reason, Christians should not approach with fear foreign ideas, but with the spirit of conciliation and eclecticism that characterized the Fathers of the Church, the Platonic bishops that thanks to their mental elevation were able to purify Christian thought to make it more noble through the transparent clarity of the Greek philosophy, as the doctrine of Jesus deserved.)

Alexandria, and the Fathers of the Church and their struggles, are themes that appeared in Theosophical literature. In Besant's *Esoteric Christianity*, published in

1902, there were similar affirmations. She also viewed Christian religion as a later branch of a religious stem that reaffirmed "ancient traditions" placing "in the grasp of western races the full treasure of the ancient teaching."[91] This aspect of Besant is also clearly present in Vasconcelos's understanding of Christianity, together with the view of Alexandria as the place in which Plato's philosophy and the concept of gnosis were synthetized by early Christians. In his historical narrative the present was the time for a second synthesis, this time taking place all over the world.

Vasconcelos was living in exile while writing *Estudios Indostánicos*, which made the book a political project for a nation that was being consumed in the civil war that had revealed the urgent need for a common project. He also recognized that the metaphysics of the nation could not be divorced from the metaphysics of race if Mexico was to be brought together, and the interpretations of India inherited from Theosophy became very helpful in making this connection. In his view, Theosophy had been rescued, and achieved a degree of respectability, because it had recruited Annie Besant, "a noble and powerful soul" who had popularized the ideas of the "charlatan" Blavatsky.[92] He forgave Besant because she had written a book "as intelligent" as *Esoteric Christianity*, but still he resented her lack of seriousness in failing to cite her sources with the excuse that they were obtained through esoteric and secret methods.[93] He probably had in mind all the charges against Blavatsky that had circulated while she was alive, including her plagiarism of several books. But regardless, Vasconcelos consulted Besant's work in developing many of his ideas, from those related to race and philosophy to his explanation of how yoga worked.[94]

A few years later, in 1925, Vasconcelos wrote his best-known book, *The Cosmic Race*, a synthesis of all his spiritualist readings. In it there is a new understanding of race and its mission in Latin America. The timing was right for this kind of project, according to its author, because important changes had taken place. Individual life was before deprived of a metaphysical finality and providential plan, but now the scientific changes sparked by Einstein's physics, chemistry's interpretation of atoms, and a renewed biology that admitted some degree of plan and design through Mendelianism, had provoked a new scientific revolution. These new sources contradicted "Darwinism, at least in the sense of the Darwinist interpretation that denied that Nature followed a plan."[95] The combination of all these scientific developments had undermined, in the words of Vasconcelos, "the theoretical structure that supported the domination of only one race."[96] Based on this, the "material power" of those who had created a false science to favor conquest had also ended.

In 1948, Vasconcelos clarified that this book had been written "when the Darwinist doctrine of natural selection, which preserves the fittest and dooms the weak, was still prevalent in the scientific world;" and this was the doctrine which, "applied to the sociological field by Gobineau, gave origin to the pure Aryan theory, supported by the English and carried to aberrant imposition by Nazism."[97] It is interesting to note that this explanation included facts that Vasconcelos for sure knew were incorrect. First, Gabineau had not applied Darwinian ideas to his views. He described the Aryan race as the superior one, though it had declined over time because of its mixing with inferior groups with darker skin, indicating a transition toward understanding India's heritage in racialized terms, but this happened before the publication of Darwin's writings. In fact he died in 1855, before evolutionary theory existed.[98] Second, the emergence of Nazi racism was not the result of scientific thought, but of the spiritualism that contradicted it. Theosophical sources had brought together, as we saw, evolutionary science and mythical origins, and the German Theosophical movement blended neo-romanticism and Theosophy becoming one of the roots of Nazi racial ideology, whose swastika symbol is the most well-known evidence of this connection. Obviously, after the end of the Second World War it was in the interests of Vasconcelos to separate his book from the racist ideas of Aryanism that were behind it. But he had written this interpretation of racial spiritualism synthetizing the narratives of Aryan superiority and in the process he had kept some of its basic assumptions, such as the inferiority of the population of African origin, or the messianic nature of a given race.

Vasconcelos's synthesis is obvious when we compare his book to Guido List's racial narrative of the Aryans; another synthetic interpretation of racial development. It is difficult to tell if he knew about this book, and certainly the latter's racial ideas were not uncommon among theosophists, but the tone of the narrative is so similar that it helps us to contextualize the role of India in the metaphysics of race of the first quarter of the twentieth century. The Austrian Guido List (1848–1919), a leading theosophist for those who read German, published in 1910 *Die Bilderschrift der Ario-Germanen* (The Picture-Writing of the Ario-Germans), in which he interpreted Blavatsky's seven root races by asserting "that the Ario-Germans represented the fifth and current race in the present round, while ascribing the names of mythical Teutonic giants to the four preceding races."[99] In 1914 his last report on the formation of the Aryan-German race was published, and in it the "root races of the Lemurians and Atlanteans" are assigned "homelands on sunken continents" and an Atlantean 'island' survived "within the modern European continent."[100] He also created a history centered on the struggle "between master-races (the Ario-Germans) and the slave races (non-Aryans) and a theory about the original homeland of the Aryans, a vanished polar continent called Arktogäa."[101] The Aryans were from the North Pole, but they had moved south due to the Ice Age. It was at this time that they had "brought culture to all mankind," paying a price for their generosity in their "mixing" with the "southern races" and had decreased their purity. This meant that in the process of sharing their culture with others, they had compromised their racial superiority. Only in the North could the Aryans remain pure.[102]

List explained that the pure Aryan master race "should be regained by 'demixing' and strict segregation from the mixed peoples". The latter should be given the position of "servants."[103] In his study of these texts, Nicholas Goodrick-Clarke has explained that Theosophy, and by extension the fusion with India present in the texts, offered to people like List "an integrated view of the world, in which the present was understood in terms of a remote past." This imaginary past legitimated "a variety of social, political, and cultural ideals such as racism, magic, and hierophantic elitism, which were all negations of the modern world." This mythological legitimation included "the apparent scientific findings of the present, a sense of meaning in society and history, and supernatural references. This perspective was likely to appeal to people for whom a variety of contemporary developments were disturbing."[104] List's interpretations have close similarities with *The Cosmic Race* in its links to India, its connection with a new era of racial restoration while, at the same time, supporting the idea that the future would be a return to racial purity.

If List created a Germanization of racial metaphysics, Vasconcelos made it Latin American, contradicting the main claims made by a racial theory that turned Latins into inferior servants. This may also explain his worries about Theosophy, from which this version of Aryanism derived, and his careful separation of India from this ideology. His solution implied the negation of a future that was only a restoration of the past: to replace it by a fifth race that was in the process of formation through mixing, eliminating any possibility of purity. There was no return to purity, but rather the attainment of a final embodied synthesis. *The Cosmic Race* is a liberating work for Vasconcelos, since in writing it he was able to analyze the different interpretations of India developed before, including the placing of Mayan culture on a map that included "the Orient and Europe."[105] Basically, he was free to attempt a new theory of history to reaffirm a vision for his country and himself based on the synthesis of past Orientalist depictions of India. As a result, Atlantis, "the cradle of a civilization" that had flourished thousands of years ago, was located in a disappeared continent and "in part of what is today America."[106] While it is true that, as mentioned, there was an abundant literature about Atlantis, Vasconcelos's treatment closely followed Blavatsky's own interpretation, using Atlantis as a place of origin and return.

> El continente hiperbóreo desaparecido, sin dejar más huellas que los rastros de vida y de cultura que a veces se descubren bajo las nieves de Groenlandia; los lemurianos o raza negra del sur; la civilización Atlántida de los hombres rojos; enseguida la aparición de los amarillos y por último la civilización de los blancos. Explica mejor el proceso de los pueblos esta profunda teoría ocultista que las elucubraciones de geólogos, como Ameghino, que ponen el origen del hombre en la Patagonia, una tierra que desde luego se sabe es de formación geológica reciente.[107]

> (The disappeared hyperborean continent, which did not leave more traces of life and culture than the ones sometimes found in the snow of Greenland; the Lemurians or black race of the south; the Atlantis civilization of the red men followed immediately by the emergence of the yellow men, and, lastly, the civilization of the white men. This profound theory of the Occult explains better the creation of the different peoples than the elucubrations of geologists like [Florentino] Ameghino, who placed the origin of man in Patagonia, a land that is well known by its recent geological formation.)

Empirical history had only provided general conclusions and some relevant details without "a vast and comprehensive theory."[108] In search of this theory, Vasconcelos proposed a new historical narrative based on "a leap of the spirit" ["un salto del espíritu"] that could provide the ability to analyze, synthetize and create. His historical narrative was grounded in an "intuition based on historical and scientific data."[109] This narration seems inspired by a spiritual invocation of Theosophy straight out Blavatsky's writings. Clearly, Vasconcelos had an ambiguous attitude toward esotericism, which was revealed in a story that appears in *Estudios Indostánicos*. At a party in California he struck up a conversation with a woman who had met Henri Bergson (1859–1841), one of the philosophers he admired the most. Vasconcelos anxiously asked her what his French counterpart was like in person, to which the woman replied that he had said something "very amusing"— muy divertido— Bergson had assured her that he believed in the existence of "evil spirits". At hearing this Vasconcelos could not "repress" his emotion and "made her repeat" the information again, which she did—confirming that Bergson had some esoteric beliefs.[110] Vasconcelos's excitement at learning of Bergson's approval of the occult was probably due to his own philosophical dilemmas, since those recognized as "Latins" could only access modernity through beliefs related to transcendental truths related to the spiritual. Bergson himself had struggled with similar problems. His philosophy made some scholars claim that he was a supporter of Theosophy, like his sister, Mina Bergson, who was married to MacGregor Mathers, a leading British occultist, and was known as the "Great-Priestess Anari."[111] An article about Bergson published in *The Theosophist* in 1908, offers us an illustration of this situation:

> [Bergson remarks that] consciousness can only be compared to the totality of the universe. Ceaselessly creative, ceaselessly our consciousness evolves, just as the universe ever evolving is eternally transformed. It will be evident how closely these ideas approach those of Theosophy. This "other thing" than intelligence M. Bergson names instinct or intuition. Is this not the reflection of Buddhi in Manas? and is it not by a withdrawal into the Self by meditation that a man may attain knowledge of himself and his "Dharma?"[112]

The article ends by noting that this similarity may have not been a coincidence, since when Bergson was a professor of the University of Clermont "he was brought into touch with George Robert Stowe Mead," a well-known academic, expert in antiquity, who was a member of the Theosophical Society.[113] This short digression serves the purpose of making clear that Vasconcelos's confusing philosophical path was also walked by some of his contemporary philosophers at the time. They saw the need to restore metaphysics into philosophy at a time in which there was no need for it. Vasconcelos's close relationship with contemporary philosophers is apparent in *The Cosmic Race* when he proposed a historical narrative based on intuition that is simultaneously similar to interpretations of Indian's texts he knew and Bergson's and William James's (1842–1910) philosophies. But this does not indicate that these intellectuals were copying each other's ideas, only that there were a limited number of alternatives for those seeking to develop a metaphysical account in the philosophy of the time and they were using similar ideas. The Theosophical intuitionism that Vasconcelos uses to explain the cosmic race makes its appearance in the preface of the book:

> Laraza que hemos convenido en llamar atlántida prosperó y decayó en América. Después de un extraordinario florecimiento, tras de cumplir su ciclo, terminada su misión particular, entró en silencio y fué decayendo hasta quedar reducida a los menguados Imperios azteca e Inca, indignos totalmente de la antigua y superior cultura. Al decaer los atlantes la civilización intensa sé trasladó a otros sitios y cambió de estirpes; deslumbró en Egipto; se ensanchó en la India y en Grecia injertando en razas nuevas. El ario, mezclándose con los dravidios, produjo el Indostán, y a la vez, mediante otras mezclas, creó la cultura helénica.

En Grecia se funda el desarrollo de la civilización occidental o europea, la civilización blanca, que al expandirse llegó hasta las playas olvidadas del continente americano para consumar una obra de recivilización y repoblación.[114]

(The race that prospered and decayed in America is the one that we agreed in calling Atlantean. After its extraordinary prosperity, after fulfilling its existential cycle, it finished its particular mission, entering a time of silence and decadence until it was reduced to the diminished Aztec and Inca empires, totally unworthy of the old and superior culture. The intense civilization moved to other places and changed lineages because of the decline of the Atlanteans. It dazzled in Egypt; it expanded in India and in Greece through the grafting of new races. The mixing of the Aryan with the Dravidians created the Hellenic culture. In Greece, Western civilization was founded, the white civilization that in its expansion arrived to the forgotten beaches of the American continent to consummate a work of recivilization and repopulation.)

Atlantis is now located in America, and Meso-America ends up becoming the link to India in the process of racial formation that gave rise to Western civilization. Obviously, Vasconcelos was very aware of the lack of evidence for this claim, but just as their vision allowed theosophists to achieve a notion of wholeness and totality, "intuition" is here a way out to explain the metaphysics of race, lending each race a mission, a purpose that gives it historical meaning. In Blavatsky and Besant, the spirit of each race needed to be embodied to fulfill the evolutionary cycle culminating in the final stage. Similarly, in Vasconcelos, the "transcendental mission" belonged to the most "audacious, strongest and most different" branches of the European family: the Spanish and the English.[115] The struggle between Latinism and Anglo–Saxonism was the most important struggle of modern times, and it represented different institutions, goals and ideals. As was the case in Theosophy, the body was only the location of the spirit, and it would have to be discarded once it had completed its mission, which explains the famous sentence "por mi raza hablará mi espíritu" ("my race will speak through my spirit"), which turned race into a spiritual and metaphysical notion.

The goal of Latin America was, then, to accomplish its evolutionary mission: to complete the assimilation of all bodies; in fact the destruction of their own embodied form in order to allow the new body to emerge. In turn, this new embodiment, the *mestizo*, would signal the beginning of the new aesthetic stage. This was the cycle of full realization, as explained by theosophists, but changing the historical role of the Aryans and removing the esoterism. For Vasconcelos the final destination is the Earth, an Earth populated by equals who housed the same spirit.

Meanwhile, in the present, and until the realization of the final body and destination, "the weak nations" needed to defend their "material and moral interests", while seeking "vast and transcendental goals", all pointing to the final objective, which was the return to the "universal historical destiny" of humankind.[116]

The body acquired in this narration has a metaphysical significance, because its form corresponded to the spirit. Each race fulfilled its historical and evolutionary mission and once that this was done, they all ceased to exist. "Ninguna raza vuelve" ("no race returns"), proclaimed Vasconcelos, because each one was an expression of a transient stage in spiritual evolution.[117] But, while this *mestizaje* seems at first a synthesis that sanctions the elimination of difference, the fulfillment of the ancestral desire for wholeness and final unity, it was extremely violent to the indigenous population of Mexico, who only had one door, that of modern culture, by which to enter. As with Blavatsky, the end is synthetic and universal. Since the members of the Latin race were more aware of their "divine mission" they had already begun the work that would end "the dispersion" and would consummate "unity through the triumph of fecund love and the overcoming of all the genealogies."[118] Furthermore, and again as with Blavatsky, this universality did not mean the races of modern humans were all equally valuable.

Vasconcelos tried to resolve the philosophical dilemma of its time: the debates about matter and spirit, by reviving a metaphysics that came from spiritual sources. This also included a detailed account of how the new embodiment, the new race, would come about. The first piece of evidence presented is the very body of Latin Americans, "a conglomerate of types and races that persist in avoiding taking into account ethnicity in their sexual relationships."[119] The fact that they did not have "a form" to protect meant that they did not feel imprisoned by it, unlike the Anglo–Saxons. For the latter, the protection of a homogenous form led to the "last empire of one race: the final empire of the white power." Like that of the Brahman caste, the white race's destiny was decadence, while the Latins were inspired by a force that came from a "remote" and "mysterious" place in the "distance" whence "came the premonition of the future" (presagio del porvenir).[120] This last description is an obvious reference to Theosophy, from the intimation of mysteries to the remote vision of the final totality. Here the final product was not the result of mechanistic natural selection, but of spiritual design that guided nature through aesthetic taste. Appropriating Blavatsky's concept of root race, Vasconcelos explained that a "raza matriz" [root race] would be the origin of the new civilization. This would be the fifth race, with its origins in the Latin American portion of the American continent.

Tenemos, pues, en el continente todos los elementos de la nueva Humanidad; una ley que irá seleccionando factores para la creación de tipos predominantes, ley que operará no conforme a criterio nacional, como tendría que hacerlo una sola raza conquistadora, sino con criterio de universalidad y belleza; y tenemos también el territorio y los recuerdos naturales. [...]Reunidos están ya en abundancia los materiales biológicos, las predisposiciones, los caracteres, las genas de que hablan los mendelistas, y sólo ha estado faltando el impulso organizador, el plan de formación de la especie nueva.[121]

(We have, then, all the elements of the new Humanity in the continent; a law will select factors to create the predominant types; a law that will not operate according to the national criteria, as it should be done by a conquering race, but by criteria of universality and beauty; [...] The biological materials have been already gathered in abundance: the predispositions, the characters, the genes mentioned by the Mendelians. Only the organizing impulse has been missing, the plan to form a new species.)

Vasconcelos also introduced a material argument together with the spiritual one. He explained the actual biological formation of the cosmic race through the rediscovered Mendelian laws that had been formulated in the 1860s. In the 1890s, through the study of hybridization, biologists had begun to "look for changes in varietal characters, and test whether new species could be evolved by subsequent crosses."[122] In the 1900s these experiments led to renewed interest in Mendel's work and its application; if before, the interest was in the replacement of one race by another, hybridization allowed for the introduction of human design in both the alteration and retention of traits in a stable human population. In this sense, Vasconcelos had resources that those who had written about race during the nineteenth century had lacked. Mendelian laws confirmed for Vasconcelos "the intervention of vital factors in the physical and chemical exchanges" and for this reason Mendelian law "must take its place in our new patriotism."[123] Hybridization allowed experimentation and the use of human design in achieving the desired modification of a group, which opened the possibility of modifying human embodiment—of racial improvement.

For Vasconcelos the new law supported the establishment of an aesthetic principle, based on taste and not on violence.[124] In the third period in which the last race would be formed, Vasconcelos defined the dominant force as follows: "[the law is made] by the emotion of beauty and a love so powerful that it is confused with divine revelation."[125] Continuing with the combination of esoteric sources with evolutionary science, Vasconcelos explained that there would be five races and three stages, yielding the number eight, which according to

Pythagorean gnosis was a sign of equality among all men. This esoteric revelation, presented as a "coincidence," shows Vasconcelos's ambiguity toward esotericism, which he both followed and rejected according to his need to explain racial evolution.

Vasconcelos's plan also coincided with spiritualists' interest in social reform. It was for this reason that when he was in charge of the educational system of Mexico, he added "signs" to the Education Palace in each corner of the interior patio, containing allegories of Spain, Mexico, Greece, and India, "the four particular civilizations that have most contributed to the formation of Latin America."[126] Under these signs four stone statues were to have been placed, each of them indicating the four great contemporary races: white, red, black and yellow. The purpose was to indicate that America was the home of all and needed all of them.[127] The location of the final race would be in the tropics, after a new technology helped to eliminate the hostile aspects of heat for humans, while preserving the life-giving benefits of warmth.

The "conquest of the tropics" would create a new promised land, this time comprising Brazil, Colombia, Venezuela, Ecuador, part of Peru and Bolivia, and northern Argentina. Near the Amazon, *Universalópolis* would rise and become the main city from which planes and armies would embark to educate all humanity. Life founded on love would express itself in all forms of beauty, showing the connection with the French literature that linked love and beauty in its spiritualism. Even the whites, "unhappy with materialism and social injustice into which this race would fall," would come to Latin America to help to achieve freedom.[128] This vision of the tropics as the place of the final race may also be partially related to a reading of Blavatsky's *Isis Unveiled*, and a footnote that quoted a selection from Louis Jacolliot's twenty-one volumes about India. The latter was a reference that indicated that the "Indo-Hellenic tradition, preserved by the most intelligent population which emigrated from the plains of India, equally related the existence of a continent and a people to which it gives the name of Atlantis and Atlantides, and which it locates in the Atlantic in the northern portion of the Tropics."[129] Vasconcelos's book was not the first one implying the development of humankind in a tropical area.

Vasconcelos's racial narrative is what allows him to justify his political project of assimilation and justification of a future of unity among the racialized international politics of the time. He also acknowledged that in order to believe in his historical vision a metaphysical project needed to be behind it, a side that connected him to the signs of the future referred to by theosophists. It is no coincidence, then, that the narration of the cosmic race ends with a description of a dream he had had while exiled in California, in which he had "fallen from a very high destiny," or his future place in history. He explains how he had forgotten about this dream until "violent changes happened in Mexico and there were rumors" about the creation of a diplomatic mission. Even when his own name was not associated with this plan, Vasconcelos "felt" that he "would be going because [he] remembered [his] dream. . . ."[130] The dream became a vision that predicted his return to power, a very concrete evidence of the esoteric mark that spiritualism had left on him.

5. Conclusion

This essay contextualized the role of India in the Americas within the philosophical debate between materialists and spiritualists that took place among the followers of the Enlightenment. As we have seen, a tension between materialism and spiritualism was present throughout the nineteenth century, but it was with the emergence of Darwinism that it became a critical issue for the continuity of metaphysical ideas, particularly in what was related to race. In this context India reappeared as the source of universal ideas about origins and philosophy. This was a common philosophical issue for Europe and the Americas, and it was addressed simultaneously in both regions, a point which is contrary to a top-down model that assumes that everything written in the Americas was derivative.

In addition, we also saw how India became in the eighteenth century an "alibi" that allowed those who were against some of the effects of the transformations produced by the Enlightenment to talk about themselves; something that continued in the following centuries. While the European chapter of this story is well known, the same cannot be said of its American counterpart. In this essay I showed how India played an important role in the renewal of a metaphysical project of human and national origins in the case of Mexico. Vasconcelos's ideas on race need to be situated within the international revival of spiritualism and its incorporation of Indian sources that led to messianic and metaphysical conceptions of race. He created his own synthesis in order to articulate his political answer to the problems of his own country and, in general, of Western thought. His metaphysical account of race made possible the restoration of universal history and a common evolutionary future for humankind. Curiously, through India he opened the path to incorporate Meso-American thought about nature and life in the discussion of modernity in Mexico, something that would be finally done in the 1950s by Samuel Ramos (1897–1959) and Octavio Paz (1914–1998). At this point, though, India became in Vasconcelos a mirror to reflect Mexican thought in Western philosophy. His *Cosmic Race* was in the 1920s a narrative of origins that made Mexico an essential part of modern civilization.

Finally, this essay analyzed the influence that Theosophy, spiritism, and spiritualism had on Vasconcelos, even when he rejected the esotericism that was part of this movement as mere superstition devoid of philosophical interest. But his historical narration in *The Cosmic Race* is not that different from Blavatsky's: from his appropriation of India to the placing of antiquity in Mexican territory as another of the regions that, together with India, Egypt, and Greece, gave rise to civilization. The main difference is that he carefully dissected the Aryanism promulgated by the new theosophist interpretations coming mostly from Germany to propose a "Latinism" instead. While it is true that Vasconcelos was well informed about Indian culture, practicing yoga and adopting some of its spiritual ideas, his Latinism continued the tradition of talking about self through others, as he himself explained in *Estudios Indostánicos*. His take on India followed the traditional Enlightenment pattern that had been established since the eighteenth century, which explains why he completely avoided any reflection on Mayan or Aztec thought, science, or origin myths. The Indian Veil obscured the reality of a part of the self that needed to be assimilated prior to the arrival of modernity: the indigenous bodies that *The Cosmic Race* made invisible. In doing so, he made the spiritual more powerful than material forms, destroying the association between matter and form.

Notes

1   Dorothy M. Figueira, *Aryans, Jews, Brahmins*, 8.
2   Ibid.
3   Ibid.
4   Ibid., 10.
5   Ibid.
6   Ibid.
7   Ibid., 11.
8   Pierre Vidal-Naquet, and Janet Lloyd, "Atlantis and the Nations."
9   George S. Williamson, *The Longing for Myth in Germany*, 2.
10 Ibid., 213.
11 Asahel Davis, *A Lecture on the Discovery of America*, 10.
12 Ibid., 11.

13 Robert Spence Hardy, *Eastern Monachism*, 262–263.

14 "Archeology of North America," 339.

15 Victor Alexander George Robert Bulwer, *The Life of Edward Bulwer*, 465.

16 Ibid., 465.

17 Augustus Le Plongeon, *Sacred Mysteries Among the Mayas and the Quiches.*

18 Ibid., 3.

19 Dorothy M. Figueira, *Translating the Orient*, 5.

20 Ibid.

21 Bret E. Carroll, *Spiritualism in Antebellum America*, 3.

22 Darryl Caterine, "The Haunted Grid," 5.

23 Isabel Lagarriga Attias, "Reelaboración Sincrética," 90.

24 The term "spiritualism" is used at the same time in France and the United States to identify anti-materialist ideological and religious movements, but this does not indicate that the two were related, or acted in a coordinated way.

25 Sofie Lachapelle, *Investigating the Supernatural*, 21. Also, see Joseph Bizouard, *Des rapports de l'homme avec le démon: essai historique et philosophique.*

26 Sofie Lachapelle, *Investigating the Supernatural*, 21.

27 Ibid.

28 Azade Seyhan, *Representation and its Discontent*, 78.

29 Dale Riepe, "Emerson and Indian philosophy," 115.

30 Théodule-Armand Ribot, "Philosophy in France," 384.

31 Ibid., 385.

32 Ibid.

33 Ibid., 386. Emphasis in the original.

34 Clare Carlisle, "The Self and the Good Life," 19.

35 "Spiritism" was used in relationship to societies that were interested in esoteric practices and believed in the communication with the dead. "Spiritualism" was more associated with philosophical ideas that contradicted materialist philosophy; typically these were different versions of idealist and neo-platonic views.

36 Yolia Tortolero Cervantes, "El Espiritismo Seduce," 781.

37 Stephen Prothero, "From Spiritualism to Theosophy," 198.

38 Helena P. Blavatsky, "Recent Progress in Theosophy," 173.

39 See Soledad Quereilhac, *Cuando la Ciencia Despertaba Fantasías. Prensa, Literatura y Ocultismo en la Argentina de Entresiglos.*

40 Stephen Prothero, "From Spiritualism to Theosophy," 203.

41 Ibid., 206.

42 Helena P. Blavatsky, *Isis Unveiled*, 591.

43 Ibid., 591.

44 L. C. Desmond, "Of Facts and Hearsay," 139.

45 Ibid., 24.

46 Helena P. Blavatsky, *Isis Unveiled*, xi.

47 Ibid.

48 Ibid., xiii.

49 Ibid., 154.

50 Qtd. In Sumathi Ramaswamy, *The Lost Land of Lemuria*, 58.

51 Helena P. Blavatsky, *Isis Unveiled*, 591.

52 Sumathi Ramaswamy, *The Lost Land of Lemuria*, 55.

53 Ibid.

54 Ibid., 58.

55 Ibid.

56 Ibid., 68.

57 Sophie Lachapelle, *Investigating the Supernatural*, 47.

58 Sumathi Ramaswamy, *The Lost Land of Lemuria*, 72.

59 José Martí, "Carta de Martí, December 7th, 1891," 504.

60 Annie Besant, *The ancient wisdom*, 1.

61 Ibid., 34.

62 Ibid., 47.

63 Ibid.

64 Annie Besant, *The Building of the Kosmos*, 6.

65 "La Teosofía en Buenos Aires," 18.

66 Eduardo Devés Valdés and Ricardo Melgar Bao, "Redes Teosóficas y Pensadores (Políticos) Latinoámericanos," 83.

67 See José Ricardo Chaves, "La vida de Buda en lengua castellana (1890–1920)."

68 See Marco Mancera's review in "José Ricardo Chaves. *México heterodoxo: Diversidad religiosa de las letras del siglo XIX y comienzos del XX.*"

69 José Ricardo Chaves, "La Bhagavad Gita según San Madero," 76.

70 José Vasconcelos, *Estudios Indostánicos*, 9.

71 Ibid., 10.

72 Ibid., 14.

73 Ibid., 13.

74 Ibid., 14.

75 Bernhard Kleeberg, "God-Nature Progressing," 549. Emphasis on the original.

76 Gauri Viswanathan, "Monism and Suffering," 105.

77 Ibid. Vasconcelos used the term "Indostánicos," which I translated by the word "Hindustani."

78 José Vasconcelos, *Estudios Indostánicos*, 15.

79 Ibid., 16.

80 Ibid.

81 Ibid.

82 Ibid., 17.

83 Ibid., 18.

84 Ibid.

85 Ibid., 19.

86 Ibid., 262. Emphasis in the original.

87 Ibid., 250.

88 Ibid., 281.

89 Ibid., 289.

90 Ibid., 290.

91 Ibid., 43.

92 Ibid.

93 Ibid., 69.

94 Ibid.,151.

95 José Vasconcelos, *La Raza Cósmica*, 36.

96 Ibid., 18.

97 José Vasconcelos, "Prologue to the 1948 Edition," 3.

98 See Arthur de Gobineau, *Essai sur l'inégalité des races humaines*; also Ernest Antoine Aimé Léon Seillière, *La philosophie de l'impérialisme: Le comte de Gobineau et l'arayanisme historique*.

99 Nicholas Goodrick-Clarke, *The Occult Roots of Nazism*, 53.

100 Ibid., 54.

101 Ibid., 55.

102 Brigitte Hamann, *Hitler's Vienna*, 207.

103 Ibid., 207.

104 Nicholas Goodrick-Clarke, *The Occult Roots of Nazism*, 55.

105 José Vasconcelos, *La Raza Cósmica*, 1.

106 Ibid.

107 Ibid., 1–2.

108 Ibid., 3.

109 Ibid., 3.

110 José Vasconcelos, *Estudios Indostánicos*, 302.

111 See René Guénon and Alvin Moore Jr. *Theosophy: History of a Pseudo-Religion*, 29

112 "France," 379.

113 Ibid., 379–380.

114 José Vasconcelos, *La Raza Cósmica*, 4.

115 Ibid.

116 Ibid., 8.

117 Ibid., 13.

118 Ibid., 15.

119 Ibid., 16.

120 Ibid., 18.

121 Ibid., 37.

122 Daniel J. Kevles, *In the Name of Eugenics*, 43.

123 José Vasconcelos, *La Raza Cósmica*, 36.

124 Ibid., 37.

125 Ibid., 38. Original text: "... la verdadera potencia creadora de júbilo está contenida en la ley del tercer período, que es emoción de belleza y un amor tan acendrado que se confunde con la revelación divina."

126 Ibid., 40.

127 Ibid.

128 Ibid., 23.

129 Helena Blavatsky, *Isis Unveiled*, 594.

130 José Vasconcelos, *La Raza Cósmica*, 42.

References

"Archaeology of North America." *Edinburgh Review* Vol. 125 (January 1867–April 1867): 339–345.

Besant, Annie. *The Building of the Kosmos and Other Lectures*. London: Theosophical Publishing Society, 1894.

Besant, Annie. *The Ancient Wisdom: An Outline of Theosophical Teachings*. London: Theosophical Publishing Society, 1899.

Besant, Annie. *Esoteric Christianity: Or, The Lesser Mysteries*. London: Theosophical Publishing Society, 1912.

Bizouard, Joseph. *Des rapports de l'homme avec le démon: essai historique et philosophique*. Vol. 2. Gaume frères et J. Duprey, 1863.

Blavatsky, Helena Petrovna. *Isis Unveiled: A Master-Key to the Mysteries of Ancient and Modern Science and Theology*. Vol. 1. New York: J. W. Bouton, 1877.

Blavatsky, Helena Petrovna. "Recent Progress in Theosophy." *The North American Review* 151, no. 405 (1890): 173–186.

Bourbourg, Charles–Etienne Brasseur de. *Quatre lettres sur le Mexique, exposition absolue du systeme hieroglyphique Mexicain, la fin de l'age de pierre* (etc.). Vol. 4. Auguste Durand, 1868.

Carlisle, Clare. "Between Freedom and Necessity: Félix Ravaisson on Habit and the Moral Life." *Inquiry* 53, no. 2 (2010): 123–145.

Carlisle, Clare. "The Self and the Good Life." In *The Oxford Handbook of Theology and Modern European Thought*, edited by Nicholas Adams, George Pattison, and Graham Ward. Oxford: Oxford University Press, 2013.

Carroll, Bret E. *Spiritualism in Antebellum America*. Bloomington: Indiana University Press, 1997.

Caterine, Darryl. "The Haunted Grid: Nature, Electricity, and Indian Spirits in the American Metaphysical Tradition." *Journal of the American Academy of Religion* 82, no. 2 (2014): 371–397.

Chaves, José Ricardo. "La Bhagavad Gita según San Madero." *Literatura mexicana* 23, no. 1 (2012): 69–81.

Chaves, José Ricardo. "La vida de Buda en lengua castellana (1890–1920)." *Acta poética* 33, no. 2 (2012): 77–94.

Cousin, Victor. *Introduction to the History of Philosophy*. Boston: Hilliard, Gray, Little, and Wilkins, 1832.

Davis, Asahel. *A Lecture on the Discovery of America by the Northmen, Five Hundred Years Before Columbus: Delivered in New York, and in Other Cities, Also in Some of the First Literary Institutions of the Union*. New York: Bartlett, 1840.

Desmond, L. C. "Of Facts and Hearsay: Bringing Augustus Le Plongeon into Focus." *Tracing Archaeology's Past: The Historiography of Archaeology* (1989): 139–150.

Devés Valdés, Eduardo and Ricardo Melgar Bao, "Redes Teosóficas y Pensadores (Políticos) Latinoámericanos." In *"Redes intelectuales en América latina." Hacia la construcción de una comunidad intelectual*. Eduardo Devés Valdés, ed. Santiago, Colección IDEA-USACH 30 (2007): 75–92.

Figueira, Dorothy M. *Translating the Orient: The Reception of Sakuntala in Nineteenth-Century Europe*. Albany: SUNY Press, 1991.

Figueira, Dorothy M. *Aryans, Jews, Brahmins: Theorizing Authority through Myths of Identity*. Albany: SUNY Press, 2002.

"France." *The Theosophist* 29 (1908): 379–380.

Gobineau, Arthur de. *Essai sur l'inégalité des races humaines*. Firmin-Didot, 1855.

Goodrick-Clarke, Nicholas. *The Occult Roots of Nazism: Secret Aryan Cults and Their Influence on Nazi Ideology*. New York City: NYU Press, 1993.

Guénon, René, and Alvin Moore Jr. *Theosophy: History of a Pseudo-Religion*. Hillsdale, NY: Sophia Perennis, 2004.

Hamann, Brigitte. *Hitler's Vienna: A Portrait of the Tyrant as a Young Man*. London: Tauris Parke Paperbacks, 2010.

Hardy, Robert Spence. *Eastern Monachism*. London: Williams and Norgate, 1860.

Kevles, Daniel J. *In the Name of Eugenics: Genetics and the Uses of Human Heredity*. Cambridge: Harvard University Press, 1985.

Kleeberg, Bernhard. "God-Nature Progressing: Natural Theology in German Monism." *Science in Context* 20, no. 03 (2007): 537–569.

Lachapelle, Sofie. *Investigating the Supernatural: From Spiritism and Occultism to Psychical Research and Metapsychics in France, 1853–1931*. Baltimore: Johns Hopkins University Press, 2011.

Lagarrita Attias, Isabel. "Reelaboración sincrética en el espiritualismo trinitario mariano." *La Palabra y el Hombre* (January–March 1996), no. 97: 87–97.

Lagarrita Attias, Isabel. "Lenguaje y ritual terapéutico en el Espiritualismo Trinitario Mariano." *Antropología. Boletín Oficial del INAH* 68 (2002): 2–10.

"La Teosofía en Buenos Aires." *Caras y Caretas* 4 no. 157 (October 5, 1901): 18.

Le Plongeon, Augustus. *Sacred Mysteries Among the Mayas and the Quiches, 11,500 Years Ago: Their Relation to the Sacred Mysteries of Egypt, Greece, Chaldea and India*. London: Theosophical Publishing Company, 1909.

Lytton, Edward Bulwer-Lytton Baron. *The Coming Race*. New York: Lovell Brothers, 1882.

Lytton, Victor Alexander George Robert Bulwer, and Victor Alexander George Robert Bulwer-Lytton. *The Life of Edward Bulwer: First Lord Lytton.* Vol. 2. London: Macmillan and Company, 1913.

Mancera, Marco. "José Ricardo Chaves. *México heterodoxo: Diversidad religiosa de las letras del siglo XIX y comienzos del XX*" (review). *Acta Poética* 36, no. 1 (2015).

Martí, José. "Carta de Martí, December 7th, 1891." *Obras Completas* 12. Editorial de Ciencias Sociales, 1992.

Mitzman, Arthur. "Michelet and Social Romanticism: Religion, Revolution, Nature." *Journal of the History of Ideas* 57, no. 4 (1996): 659–682.

Prothero, Stephen. "From Spiritualism to Theosophy: 'Uplifting' a Democratic Tradition." *Religion and American Culture: A Journal of Interpretation* 3, no. 2 (1993): 197–216.

Quereilhac, Soledad. *Cuando la Ciencia Despertaba Fantasías. Prensa, Literatura y Ocultismo en la Argentina de Entresiglos.* Siglo XXI, 2016.

Ramaswamy, Sumathi. *The Lost Land of Lemuria: Fabulous Geographies, Catastrophic Histories.* Berkeley, CA: University of California Press, 2004.

Ribot, Théodule-Armand. "Philosophy in France." *Mind* (1877): 366–386.

Riepe, Dale. "Emerson and Indian Philosophy." *Journal of the History of Ideas* 28, no. 1 (1967): 115–122.

Seillière, Ernest Antoine Aimé Léon. *La philosophie de l'impérialisme: Le comte de Gobineau et l'arayanisme historique.* Plon–Nouritt, 1903.

Seyhan, Azade. *Representation and Its Discontents: The Critical Legacy of German Romanticism.* Berkeley, CA: University of California Press, 1992.

Tortolero Cervantes, Yolia. *El espíritismo seduce a Francisco Madero.* México: CONACULTA/FONCA, 2003.

Trompf, Garry W. "Imagining Macrohistory? Madame Blavatsky from Isis Unveiled (1877) to The Secret Doctrine (1888)." *Literature and Aesthetics* 21, no. 1 (2011).

Vasconcelos, José. *Estudios Indostánicos.* Ediciones Mexico Moderno, 1920.

Vasconcelos, José. *La raza cósmica, misión de la raza iberoamericana.* Agencia Mundial de Librería, 1925.

Vasconcelos, José. "Prologue to the 1948 Edition." In *The Cosmic Race/La raza cósmica,* by José Vasconcelos, translated and annotated by Didier T. Jaén. Baltimore: Johns Hopkins University Press, 1979.

Vidal-Naquet, Pierre, and Janet Lloyd. "Atlantis and the Nations." *Critical Inquiry* 18, no. 2 (1992): 300–326.

Viswanathan, Gauri. "Monism and Suffering: A Theosophical Perspective." In *Monism,* edited by Todd S. Weir, 91–106. Palgrave Macmillan, 2012.

Williamson, George S. *The longing for myth in Germany: Religion and aesthetic culture from romanticism to Nietzsche.* Chicago: University of Chicago Press, 2004.

4

The Search for the Orient in Creole America: The Nineteenth Century and its Paths

Hernán G. H. Taboada

Translated by Alba Lara Granero and Maria C. Vera[1]

Whether explicitly or not, the question of Latin America's belonging in so-called "Western civilization" remains pertinent. In other words, the question constitutes an important part of the ideological debates that take place in front of us, as much in quotidian conversations, television shows, and student discussions as in works that have enjoyed an unprecedented level of circulation in our times, reverberating in great social movements both popular and indigenous. Given this context, it can be deduced that the relationship between Latin America and belonging to "Western civilization" is part of wider ideological discrepancies.

I am under the impression, after historicizing the discrepancies, that they did not manifest themselves until the 1980s. Up until that time, the Western character of Latin America was accepted by all sectors of the political spectrum. This widespread agreement was a result of the supremacy of Creole groups, who, since the nineteenth century, had substituted their traditional alliance with the Spanish monarchy for a more informal alliance with the powers of the North Atlantic world.

As has been widely recognized for several decades, the Orient constitutes an essential piece of that paradigm. Edward Said's classic description communicated the image of the Arabic and Islamic neighbor created by the colonialist countries as an unreal subject: stereotyped, apprehended from a textual obsession, an inverted reflection of the virtuous West, an artifact designed for domination. While not completely accepting Said's premises, I do believe that the Orient, here understood better as a subject undifferentiated in its extension from the Balkans to Japan, is one of otherness fundamental to the self-construction of the concept of the West, whose name surged belatedly and precisely as an antithesis to the Orient.

Following the vicissitudes of the reception of ideas about the Orient, and implicitly about the West, can tell us much about the paths of modernity in the periphery, specifically in economic and culturally dependent countries, such as those in Our America.

1. A legacy

During colonial times, a solid academic system was forged in Spanish and Portuguese-American territories, which produced works of merit. While it is true that Orientalist topics were scarce, anecdotal evidence shows occasional individuals with knowledge of languages such as Hebrew and Arabic, and libraries with titles related to China, India, and the Ottoman Empire. Among these, the works of the Jesuit Athanasius Kircher stand out. For instance, *Oedypus Aegyptiacus* (1652) and *China Ilustrata* (1667) were widespread in the colonies, as demonstrated by catalogs and references, including some by Sor Juana Inés de la Cruz. Kircher corresponded with individuals like Joseph Anchieta in Brazil, Moscardo in Chile, Juan Ramón Conink(a Belgian living in Peru) and especially with *novohispanos* like Carlos de Sigüenza y Góngora.[2] Such readers applied Kircher's interpretations of China and its evangelization to the American context. Sigüenza even dared to publicly argue against Kircher's deciphering of Aztec signs, which were undervalued by the German Jesuit in comparison to the scriptures of China and pharaonic Egypt.[3]

However, as is evidenced by the publication of *Historia de las cosas más notables, ritos y costumbres del gran reyno de la China* (*History of the Great and Mighty Kingdom of China*, 1585) by Juan González de Mendoza, European scholarship was not accepted without question. González de Mendoza was an Augustinian priest who arrived in Mexico at a young age. He documented oral traditions on handwritten and printed notes from the many individuals who arrived from China. González himself never visited China, but he learned the rudiments of its language. The book he assembled, although not the first European history of China, was certainly the most prominent for a long time and referenced, among other things, for containing the first sample of its written language. González's achievement is better appreciated when compared to the level of knowledge in metropolitan Spain, where in 1544 Sebastián Caboto cites Marco Polo as the authority on the Mongolian Empire.[4] Such knowledge would likely be reflected in other countries at the time, thus González de Mendoza's book became a success in Europe, with multiple editions and translations into Italian, English, French, Dutch, and Latin. The author died in Popayán in 1617.

González's book is not an isolated case, but rather a link within a certain tradition of Chinese and Japanese studies in colonial America exemplified by pious reports and writings by clergymen (Alonso Sánchez, Antonio de Morga, especially Bishop Juan de Palafox, Juan Torrubia) for visitors, or by those who compiled abundant information that arrived through the Pacific route that on occasion were locally printed and used by González de Mendoza. There are also references to Asia in poetic and even theological works that are not a result of the echoes of European information, but rather of direct contact with Asia. Of particular significance is the description in Nahuatl by the Chalcah chronicler San Antón Muñoz Chimalpáhin regarding the Japanese embassy from Hasekura to New Spain (1614). Further, the martyrdom of Francisco Javier and his companions in Japan was the object of sermons, reports, and even a series of paintings in the cathedral of Cuernavaca.

Contact with Asia was the result of Spanish and Portuguese colonial ties developed through the Brazilian Nao da India and the *novohispano* Galeón de Manila; the latter was the center of a broad network spanning the Pacific Coast from California to Chile. It has been said that this was the only sector belonging to the modern world system that was not controlled by Europeans.[5] The existence of routes to the Orient restulted in Spanish America to Asian merchandise, migrations, and technological and artistic influences, as well as a curiosity about the Orient as noted earlier. Therefore, we can talk about an "intellectual history of the Galeón de Manila,"[6] to which I would add chapters beyond New Spain, in Peru, and even in the faraway Río de la Plata.[7] The Creole Enlightenment captured this tradition.

The movement to explore the Orient had European representatives (Voltaire is a well-known case) who had a certain breadth in terms of their field of vision: without denying their centrism toward Europe, the curiosity of Enlightenment thinkers spread toward China, India, and the Islamic world as they were territories deemed worthy of discovering sources of aesthetic, moral and political learning, in contrast to the provincialism of previous authors. Aspects of this attitude included Sinophilia; the zeal for the study of India and its languages; the discovery of the Old Orient beyond biblical and classical sources; and the cultural relativism that "provincialized Europe." Even in Spain and Portugal, signs of Enlightened Orientalist interest emerged through the efforts to rekindle the academic study of Arabic, which had been lost.

In the American colonies, these facets had their equivalents, but it is possible to find others that corroborate how the Creole Enlightenment had particular characteristics, whose originality must be highlighted. A notable particularity is found in the effort to interpret and exalt America, which resulted in a series of investigations into local nature and indigenous antiquities that coincides with a rich moment in history of population growth, and the self-confidence of dominant groups. In order to understand the latter, appeals were made among the first chroniclers, through comparisons with Old World civilization, biblical history, Greece and Rome, barbarian Europe, and increasingly with the Orient, which appears more and more in Enlightenment writings.

The previous paragraphs, more than summarizing knowledge of the Orient during colonial times, point out that the reproduction of the echoes of the European construction of the Orient in modernity occurred in its own register. I believe it happened because the scholarly intellectual production was responding to different motivations from those in the metropolis. As scholarly production increased and became more refined and varied, the differences acquired new dimensions. The established elaboration of a Creole argumentation and symbolism relied on a progressively more complex image of others. In the first place, these were the Spaniards and Portuguese, but they came to also include the Trans-Pyrenean Europeans and all the inhabitants of the Old World, including those who dwelled in the Orient. These came to constitute the embryo of a particular Orientalist construction that took up European elements, but contained peculiarities of its own.

In this context, Sinophilia disappeared from Europe in the nineteenth century, but remained in America for some decades in authors from Peru and Río de la Plata. It is prominent in the late edition of the novel *El Periquillo Sarniento* (*The Mangy Parrot*) by José Joaquín Fernández de Lizardi, which started to gain fame in 1816, but was not completely published, including its Filipino and Chinese scenes, until 1831.[8] In other authors, references persisted to China as the wealthiest and most flourishing empire as well as the one best populated and ruled. We know that some of Confucius's writings had been translated and published in a collection of philosophers and moralists in Madrid in 1802. They sometimes appear quoted by Creole authors. The instructions given to the Central American representative Antonio Larrazábal in 1811 reminded that: "Confucius said that the art of ruling men is in essence the same as the art of sustaining them."[9] Amid the controversy over the freedom of religious belief in Venezuela, the conservative patriot Antonio Gómez, a priest and enemy of such freedom, known for quoting Enlightenment authors, defended his contention using a series of examples from universal history. Confucius was among these. He stated: "Confucius has darkened the fugitive merit of the modern publicists and the Chinese are a great nation, manufacturing and populated."[10] There are more examples.

It is worth questioning whether other territories in the Orient evoked the same American curiosity and incited the study of languages. For instance, among the books that Simón Bolívar received in his inheritance from his parents there featured an Arabic grammar.[11] The New Grenadian poet Luis Vargas Tejada (1802–1809) had some knowledge of Greek, Hebrew and Arabic. Vicente López (1785–1856), author of the Argentinian anthem, knew some Hebrew, and the canonical Chilean Manuel Lacunza (1731–1801) had an even greater knowledge. He was also author of a Millenarian work, published in 1816 under the pseudonym of Josafat Ben-Ezra. Evidence of this sort could also be found in Spain and Portugal during the Enlightenment, but these examples serve as signs of the limits of comprehension of European Orientalist science at the end of colonial times.

2. Independence

It has been previously argued, today I believe confusedly so, that Orientalist images played a certain role in the ideological disputes of independence and further demonstrated how they were present in Simón Bolívar's ideology.[12] I would now add that such uses emanated from a growing intimacy with the wider world: the reproaches that were then often directed to Spain for isolating their territories from other nations were at the very least exaggerated. In fact, many Creole references, as well as reports of visitors, reveal knowledge of international affairs at the end of colonial times, as well as interest in the political institutions and systems of various peoples and, as a derivation, their history and culture. This point is reflected by the nascent patriot press at the outbreak of the independence movements, which informed people as soon as it could about the state of Europe but also of Russia, the Ottoman Empire, India, the Southern Seas, and other remote places. The press encouraged people to listen to what Simón Bolívar called "the lessons of history, the examples of the old and the new world."[13]

The Orient also offered lessons, which probably led some of the protagonists of independence to accumulate in their private libraries titles of subjects foreign to the needs of the moment. For instance, the Argentinian José de San Martín carried with him books about the Turkish wars, Turkish customs, Christian Turkey, Indian issues, and a trip to Morea, Turkey, and China, all written in French.[14] Further, a detailed investigation of Simón Bolívar's books reveals the existence of, besides the aforementioned Arabic grammar, certain trips to Africa, certain *Béautés de l'histoire de Turquie*, a copy of *Descripción de China y Tartaria*

(*Description of China-Tartary*) by Father Du Halde (1735), and mentions of Volney in his writings.[15] The library of Francisco de Paula Santander included a "Viaje a África," ("Travel to Africa") possibly the one authored by Domingo Baldía, and a "Viaje pintoresco a las orillas del Ganges" ("Picturesque Travel at the Edge of the Ganges"), a book about the African military campaigns of Bonaparte, and again several by Volney.[16] Even in the remote library of the Paraguayan dictator Gaspar Rodríguez de Francia (1766–1840) it was possible to find, along with the not-to-be-missed *Las ruinas de Palmira* (*Ruins of Palmyra*) de Volney, the book *Los beduinos o árabes del desierto* (*The Beduins, or the Arabs of the Desert*).[17]

A focus on the history of Arabs in Spain was made possible by the Spanish liberal Antonio Conde in 1820, and attracted attention because of the connections it suggested. Conde noted that the Ecuadorian Vicente Rocafuerte funded the publication of *Cuadros de la historia de los árabes: desde Mahoma hasta la conquista de Granada* (*A Collection of Arab History: From Mahoma to the Conquest of Granada*) in London in 1826, written by another Spanish liberal, José Joaquín de Mora,[18] who resided in America. He pointed out how we were descendants of former peoples, "for the same reason the peoples who speak the Spanish language cannot look indifferently or oddly at that big and brave nation, which, propelled by religious zeal and the thirst of conquests, surpassed its natural limits, started its Empire, and funded a powerful state in the Peninsula.... we should at least consider them as part of our family, and, in many aspects, as our masters and reformers," and Mora compared this relationship with the one that they maintained with Spain "the republics of Mexico and Peru."[19]

The use of books of exotic themes is demonstrated by the sheer amount of annotations, such as the one made by the Peruvian Enlightenment thinker Manuel Lorenzo de Vidaurre (1773–1841). He writes:

> I have scrupulously examined the government of Constantinople and compared it with the one in Peru; the former is less barbarous, perverse and unjust. Sultans have no limits to their power, but they continually descend from the throne to prison and from prison to death.... the laws are few but always obeyed and faithfully executed; not so in America, where the viceroys lived without fear of punishment and were not fair with the people nor with individuals.

The same Vidaurre would complain about the deformed vision that prevailed: "Who has made a deep study of all the religions? We read the Koran disfigured. If we find in it species that seem ridiculous to us, do we not have the same in the Gospel?"[20]

The function of the Orient is a source of sobering examples that shows the persistence of ecumenical curiosity. Further, the new states, although wrapped up in problems of all kinds, found time to acquire objects of oriental art destined for their new museums. In 1824, the government of Buenos Aires bought a collection of 1,600 medallions, a unique treasure in America and uncommon in Europe, from a "medalist of the Vatican," many of which were Greek, Sicilian, Egyptian, and Gallic.[21] The acquisition was not an isolated operation. The Italian Nicola Fiengo, had obtained a collection of Egyptian antiques from the explorer Giovanni Battista Belzoni, and also thought to sell them to Buenos Aires, although political problems led him to sell them to the empire of Brazil (1825).[22]

Certainly these episodes were part of a Eurocentric tradition dominated by the negative imagery of the Orient, but the heritage of the Enlightenment and the political and diplomatic developments allowed the patriots a certain critical attitude toward Europe. An article in the newspaper *El Sol de Cuzco* reveals a healthy distance from Europe and a sincere approach when reflecting on the relationship between population abundance and respect for individual guarantees:

> a single people is on the land where, according to many writers, there is an immense population under a despotic government; moreover, we do not yet know whether this opinion is a revenge of the outrages suffered by that nation at the hands of the Europeans who maintain their trade, or whether it, as a paternal government like that of Abbas in Persia or that of the Incas of Peru, by a sum of political acts anticipates the needs of the governed, that are totally unknown.

The argument is framed by a quote from Filangieri.[23] China is once again under consideration, offered to demonstrate that the author knew the European political economy but contended that America should develop a different science once necessary knowledge had been gathered.

Behind these constructions was an optimist vision of America. America was the final destination of a journey of civilization that began in the Orient, continued in Greece and passed through Europe, where the Restoration began to divert its course toward that future site to the West: "all of the nations of the Old World have shined before us, and the time for the New World to shine is coming soon"; "it will in turn conquer the Old World without inundating it, enslaving it, or stupefying it."[24] In the case of Río de la Plata, it has been said that, within the birth of "a new American identity articulated around a progressive conception of history," "Europe is helpful, so to speak, as a textbook. . . . we are attending a simultaneous appropriation and instrumentalization of European history on the part of Americans."[25] However, in these constructions of America I also see a utilization of the Orient.

The role of the Orient is demonstrated in certain expressions, where humanity appears "greeting this venturous asylum / from Asia and Europe, where it weeps / among the peace of the sepulchers."[26] The public announcement of Bolívar to the peoples of the world, in 1814, involves an idea that was later developed by Guatemalan José Cecilio del Valle (1821): with American independence, "the Asian, the African, both subjugated like the American, will begin to feel their rights: they will at last proclaim their independence during the course of time and American freedom will finally make the whole Earth free."[27] A monument erected in Buenos Aires in 1815 reflects a similar Creole fantasy, which displayed a freed America admired by Europe for its liberty; Asia chained, and Africa rescued by the freedom of its American sons.[28]

Visions of the blissful future of America depended on its establishment as an emporium between Europe and Asia, and on the strengthening of the new governments "with arms, opinions, foreign relations, and immigration coming from Europe and Asia that will necessarily increase the population";[29] which would be "a people of brothers / a brotherhood of men / that makes no difference / with tender love / between the Persian and the Breton."[30] Immigration projects in the first years of independence mentioned the arrival of the Chinese, and Asians in general. Asian immigration of this sort was unlike the subsequent years of the nineteenth century, when immigration preferences would be almost exclusively for European migration. Necessity forced the admission of East Asian migrants, who received the worst treatment upon arrival. Located between Asia, Africa, and Europe, "in the center of the globe,"[31] a bright future awaited the liberated territories: Colombia, like Tyre or Alexandria, "can incorporate the perfumes of Asia, ivory of Africa, products of Europe, leather of the North, and whales of the South. It can enjoy the commerce of China, Greenland and Kamchatka without confronting the dangers of the Cape of Horn and the Cape of Good Hope [sic]."[32] The states of the Isthmus of Panama are located in magnificent position and, like Byzantium, "will strengthen the bonds of Europe, America, and Asia."[33] They dreamed of the Panama Canal, and in the midst of battles and problems, Bolívar found the time to order the initial cut; a fantasy that obviously did not last much longer.

The optimistic position of the Americans is reflected in the reception of Volney. His name has already been mentioned, but continues to reappear as he was easy to locate in the writing of the decades between the eighteenth and nineteenth centuries. He was among the authors prohibited by the Spanish

Inquisition, and further requested in already independent Peru.[34] Once the censorship was abolished, his travels to Syria and Egypt and, above all, *Les ruines de Palmyre* (1791) were often quoted, glossed, and even translated. Among these translations, was one by the Argentinian Mariano Moreno, now recently published. A French copy of *Las ruinas* had been given to the Paraguayan García Francia by the Spaniard Félix de Azara, who passed it down to his son, Gaspar Rodríguez de Francia (1766–1840) who eventually became the dictator of Paraguay. The Englishman Robertson saw the copy on his table next to other books by Voltaire and Rousseau: "this one is the most impressive," commented Francia.[35] In *Discourse of Angostura* (1819); Simón Bolívar mentioned (the only citation of a book in his speeches) the copy of the translation he owned, which included, by Volney himself, a dedication "to the rising peoples of the Castilian Indies."[36]

These examples reflect Volney's ubiquitous presence. His influence on thinkers like José María Heredia, Domingo Faustino Sarmiento or José María Alberdi has been worthy of specialized studies. The question that remains involves linking Volney's thought to Orientalist thought. He was one of the first traveler-spies; he knew spoken and literary Arabic, and filled his work with data on social and economic conditions that were not just archaeological, from the regions that he visited in Egypt and Syria. He judged these conditions severely in his book on travels and more severely in *Les ruines*. His judgments were supported by an exact and true knowledge of the traditions of the Orient, which was often missing in the other works by Enlightenment figures, who, in criticizing religion, were limited to Christianity. More than just the text, the footnotes of *Les ruines* are also full of references, names of peoples, works, languages, exotic traditions, cultural comparisons, and erudite hypotheses. Yet, the facets of hostile Orientalism are framed in a general condemnation of all traditions,[37] including that of Christian peoples, and colonial conquests in America and Africa, as well as condemnation of the colonial conquest of Egypt by Napoleon. *Les ruines* was the ecumenical moment of the French Revolution.

There were reasons why *Les ruines* was frowned upon by the Catholic sectors and condemned by the Inquisition. A series of lectures attributed to Volney was given in 1795 on the study of history, which among other things warned of reigning Eurocentrism.[38] The lectures were later translated by Lorenzo de Zavala, who presented them as his own work in Mexico (1824) and Venezuela (1831). The translation that was not identified as Volney's read as follows:

> We have, indeed, many books with the title of Universal Histories. But in addition
> to the declamatory style of the school (which is noted in the most famous), it
> also has the fault of not writing but partial histories of small towns and family

panegyrics. Our classical historians of Europe have spoken only of Greeks, Romans, and Jews, because we, if not the descendants, are at least their heirs.... so far history has not been approached with the universality it should be.[39]

3. Three thinkers and the Orient

If Lorenzo de Zavala could reproduce a critique of Volney in 1824 on the Eurocentrism of universal history, it was because Creole culture had in an Americanist sense assumed and extended the ecumenical aspects of the Enlightenment, but also, embryonically, the understanding of other cultures, including those from the Orient. The legacy that was reached during the first years of independence was one of optimism about the future, during which young America would complete a civilizing work that had been started in Asia and Europe. The belief of young America's civilizing mission assumed the form of a widespread philosophy of history. Three examples situated between the Enlightenment and independence demonstrate Orientalist dimensions.

The case of the Venezuelan Francisco de Miranda (1750–1816) is one where Orientalist dimensions can be most observed. Miranda spent a few months in the Ottoman Empire, Greece, and Anatolia, continuing on to Russia, whose southern regions had recently been incorporated by the czars. The region still retained an abundant Islamic population and culture. Some writing has been done on Miranda in Turkey and a little about his time in Russia.[40] Unlike other travelers after him, he wanted to understand the terrain he was walking through, and did so by reading books on the specialized literature of his time, which is still widely quoted today: Lady Montagu, Richard Pococke, the Baron de Tott, Mouradgea d'Ohsson, Hill. These authors are mentioned with comments that reveal at least a partial reading, which allowed him to write the chronological picture of the Ottoman history that appears among his papers.

Miranda obtained political teachings from his experiences in conjunction with his search for exoticism, which allowed him to modify the image of "despotism" that denounced his European readings. About the Baron de Tott, he comments: "he has presented us only the picture of defects, without any mention of virtues"; he senses that this is the result of a lack of information and notes that if we had better translations of their books, "we would have a better and more true opinion of them than what generally reigned in Europe at the time," since knowledge exists "that no one expected to find in the body of despotism." He questions further: "a people that dethrones three sovereigns in less than sixty years is not a dead body, and much less a passive nation that does not think." An *obiter dictum* reveals that upon finding some Chinese books in Russia they seemed to him a more solid and lasting production than "ours in Europe, when we think we know all."[41]

Miranda's opinions were based on his experiences, but also on an extensive library in several languages where there were books about the Orient; a hundred works in addition to those he cited as he traveled the Ottoman Empire. Among these travel stories, those from various eras and of different value were predominantly featured (for example, Chardin, Thevenot, along with other less famous ones). There are also history books (Jones, *Life of Nader Sha*, 1773), studies on the political situation, but also some that denote a bigger curiosity: an edition of the Koran (*L'Alcoran de Mahomet*, translated by Galland, 1783), a Persian and Chinese anthology, the life of Confucius and a collection of his works, and a book on Turkish grammar.[42] The readings of the Koran by Thomas Jefferson had a correlate in Miranda's Spanish-American readings.

Miranda is among the protagonists of independence. Lesser known is the Chilean Juan Egaña (1768–1836), an enlightened Catholic and conservative, who was interested in philosophy and morals, for which he did not confine himself to European authors. When his son Mariano moved to Europe to buy books, he asked him to include works by Confucius and the Chinese moralists. His library included biographies and anthologies of Confucius, as well as translations of his writings; one in French and one in Spanish. On the topic of China, he had travel books and stories, one of them translated from a Chinese historian, and descriptions or memoirs of the contemporary state of China. He was not a passive presence. On the contrary, Egaña considered China a prosperous and industrious country and was influenced by some ideas of Confucianism: specifically, the ideas also expressed by Montesquieu on the influence of the geographical environment on social morality; the importance of customs and family for the state; the priority that should be given to agriculture; the possibility of eliminating trade; and the choice of the best persons for public positions. He argued by using Confucian ideas in his proposed constitution of 1811. He relied on the authority of "Likoangti, a Chinese doctor," in order to promote altruism and popular education through meticulously regulated parties featuring music and dance.[43]

Finally, the Venezuelan Andrés Bello (1781–1865) best exemplifies the ways that newborn states could have adopted Orientalist science. Andrés Bello was educated under the Old Regime, and also resided in London, which at the time was a center of confirmation that modernity was giving way to the past and otherness. When he went to Chile, where he died, he worked to establish the new country's basic institutions of high culture, notably the University of Chile. Unlike other Creole authors, Andrés Bello was a serious and conscientious scholar who took an interest in a wide range of subjects, including Islam, for a better understanding of Spanish medieval literature and of the *Poema del Cid (Poem of the Cid)*, which occupied him for many years. Some knowledge of Sanskrit became necessary given his linguistic studies. He also knew of pharaonic Egypt as he found the deciphering of the writing novel and caught his attention during his European stage.

On all of these subjects, his readings were broad, partly specialized,[44] with variable results: a rather informative writing on the pharaonic language and a series of subterranean inspirations in his texts on grammar and on the contributions of al-Andalus, which are still valued in the study of the medieval Spanish epic. Bello's perspective distanced him from a positive understanding of the Orient: in studying medieval Spain, his sympathies were on the Christian side. He rejected Sismonde of Sismondi's suggestion (1813) that the *Poem of the Cid* had been written in an Islamic court. He privileged the Greek and Roman inheritance in the conformation of the Creole culture. Islam was an otherness in the same way as were the Araucanians of the Chilean South.

All this, however, matters less here than the Americanist dimension of Bello's ideology. He thought the new countries had to be developed by incorporating European science, a classical education, and from this a new culture of its own should emerge, which included the Spanish tradition and the other remote heritage that filtered through due to its ideas about the past. This was a heritage that went back to Asia, the master of Greece and Europe, just as Europe was by then the master of America, which in the future would surpass Europe as it had surpassed Asia. Orientalist knowledge was important in the birth of America, and for that reason Andrés Bello's courses included the literatures of the Orient based on what he could know about them from the southern corner where he lived and where he died: Santiago.[45]

4. The reaction against the Orient

Andrés Bello's proposals found an echo in Chile as well as the rest of Ibero-America. During subsequent decades, his followers included in their conferences or writings some views about classical antiquity, the medieval world, and the

Orient. Nevertheless, the times were not favorable for continued reflection on these types of interests, given the social and political chaos that followed independence, academia's fall into disorder, the disappearance of idle time, the scarcity of resources, and the pressures to dedicate efforts to more urgent matters.

The new generation was influenced by what I have termed the "Europeanization" of America. Against the dominant narrative, which points to an early incorporation of America into European culture after its "discovery" in the sixteenth century, I maintain that, during the colonial period, American regions received low European migration. By all measures European migration was inferior to the human trade of Africans that was accompanied by the arrival of Asians. The economic and cultural bonds with Europe were scant and encouraged the creation of a series of closed cultural archipelagos. This began to change with the European expansion of the nineteenth century. It was the start of a strong European migration, paradoxically superior to the one during the colonial centuries, and, by the end of the second half of the century, the importation of Africans stopped. At the same time, the Creole states imposed a politics of European cultural assimilation.

For dominant classes, European cultural assimilation became the focus of their concerns as a model to achieve. If the Enlightenment had reinforced the conviction of a distinctive American character, the nineteenth century spread the idea of creoles being "Europeans born in America" (Juan Bautista Alberdi). A study of Mexico shows how the press was dominated by illustrations depicting European nature, history, and culture; meanwhile other areas, including America,[46] were less prominent. Any history of thought, any search through preferred authors, confirms this preponderance. Our countries were invaded by a flood of printed materials and theories coming from Europe that brought readings about other humanities, more or less distant in time and space. These included readings about Antiquity, the Middle Ages, savage people, marginal European countries like Russia and Spain, about America itself, and, of course, readings about the Orient.

The readings presented a variety of nuances that have been grouped into two basic interpretations. One (championed by Raymond Schwab) has been seen since the end of the eighteenth century as a second Renaissance—scientific, philosophical, literary—caused by the discovery of other traditions, especially those of India, analogous to the one that provoked the discovery of classic antiquity in the fifteenth century. The other (championed by Edward Said) has emphasized the apparition or the reinforcement of a series of stereotypes about the Islamic world, a product and impulse of the colonialist domination that was in progress. Both interpretations have received criticism, and debates and investigations of the case have served to show the complex interrelation of points of view that the European intelligentsia experienced before the phenomenon of the Orient. In any event, neither denied the presence of the Orient.

During the first decades of independence, the Orient's influence over America can be seen in poems, narratives, theater, journalistic works, and even plastic arts, translations of European authors, or writings discussed here. In Mexico, which continued to be an important cultural center with printing houses, libraries, scholars, publications, and academic institutions, there was a continued presence of both Enlightenment Orientalism and romanticism in magazines. The influence that Italian and French opera pieces set in the Islamic world (*Maometto II*, *L'italiana in Algeri* (*The Italian in Algiers*) by Rossini, and others) has been studied while the Spanish tradition of admiration for the Moors fell into disgrace.[47] Similar works in other countries are missing, but this lack reveals that Creole Orientalism did not provoke any local renaissance nor did it encourage the construction of the Orient as a mirror of the self. A rather passive derivation of a coherent discourse that did not transcend superficial and contradictory notes occurred and was reiterative and fairly marginal in production, reflected in small annotations to historic and sociological treatises that had different focal points.

Due to its relevance, there was an exception with a series of writings that had become the subject of investigation. It was a discourse born in Buenos Aires, a city that started to become the most dynamic spot in terms of economic and population growth linked to the North Atlantic, with a rich intellectual movement that impressed its neighbors even as it developed in the midst of political chaos (with a permanent Argentinian characteristics). Buenos Aires was a city open to the European way of thinking, "that receives, it can be said, the first reflections that reached the continent of the productions of the wise men that consecrated themselves to the enlightenment and venture of humanity; and it gathers them, nurtures them, and makes them reverberate in the other nations of young America."[48]

Among this abundant enlightenment and venture, the new European Orientalist message arrived, which has been studied diligently by Axel Gasquet. Thanks to Gasquet, vast themes are revealed among local writers. However, at the same time Gasquet also discovers that in Esteban Echeverría, the man that introduced romanticism, the orientalistic subject, "is enunciated diagonally, deviating from the original model" and enclosed in an intertextual system, in the epigraphs and themes that refer in a cryptic way to the Orients of Lord Byron,

Victor Hugo, Lamartine, and other authors.[49] Such caution in presenting an Orient that was nevertheless enthusiastically offered in his European readings, and corresponds to a similar caution in the treatment of the American topic, one that, if we were to be guided by the frequent declarations of this intellectual group, would constitute the core of its preoccupations.

In the mentality of traditional creoles, especially during this period, we find a permanent tension between the value of the America they inhabit and the value of the Europe in which their personal mythology locates their familial origins. There is a historic swinging in the emphasis from one pole to another—about the exuberant nature, the great Meso-American civilizations, the good savage in the forests, and the nice Creole, where each side alternately proclaims telluric or foreign symbols. The Enlightenment and independence had emphasized America, and the following generation saw its evils, the failed promises of the revolution, the opposition, the fanaticism, and the colonial past still current, and compared itself with a Europe that was growing at a fast pace. When it tackled American evils, it found useful terminology tied to feudalism and the Orient. It was said that the American world was feudal, falling back into a new conceptualization. In a parallel fashion it was said that the American world was oriental.

It should also be noted that Spain was also being Orientalized by those who emphasized Andalusian ascendance. The Orientalization of America was not an absolute novelty and had remote precedents in the collective imagination of the conquest, but it had been renovated during the battles for independence and, mainly, in the following decades by the work of European travelers. It has been shown that Humboldt had used Orientalist comparisons of America in his portrait of the continent.[50] This topic was gathered by authors who followed his steps in the descriptions of the Venezuelan plains and its nomadic inhabitants, using his text as a guide and going deeper in the comparisons: the llaneros became Bedouins or Tatars, and their leader, José Antonio Páez, a khan or an Arab sheik. This explanatory machinery moved to other American plains, the pampas, by the works of other travelers who picked up where those who described the plains left off and, at the same time, had an influence in the configuration of the national image by works of the first Argentinean authors.[51]

The Venezuelan llanero continued to be explained, with some frequency, through the Bedouin comparison. Rafael María Baralt believed that it was necessary to vindicate it when he warned that, besides having other qualities, the llanero was indeed "astute and cautious, but unfairly compared in all aspects with the Bedouins. The llanero never betrays those who trust him, neither is faithless nor honorless like those desert bandits." However, almost a century later, Laureno Vallenilla Lanz supported the comparison with a conceptual apparatus that he said to be of solid sociological science.[52] On occasion, just like other American settlements, Latin American populations were described as Oriental hordes, and described with Orientalist models. Any dictator was called a sultan and any village provoked Moorish reminiscences. Nevertheless, in no place did this comparison have as much diffusion as in Argentina.

Examples of the subject are many and take the following forms: to denigrate the gaucho at the start, to acclaim him later, dozens of sociologists, in the style of Vallenilla and other aficionados, stressed the resemblance the gaucho had to Arabs. In this long comparative history, which continues today, a mandatory reference is Domingo Faustino Sarmiento (1811–1888), who is often quoted as the origin. However, it has been recently shown that Sarmiento "gathers, synthesizes, and spreads a vision that was already available in a good measure in the Orientalist representations of Río de la Plata, at least in the years that followed the Revolución de Mayo."[53] This tradition was collected in the notes of travelers like Arsène Isabelle, in the pictures of the European artists who visited the continent, like Raymond Monvoisin and Moritz Rugendas, and in the essays of interpretation of native nature and society made by the Argentinean scholars.

On a similar yet related note, was a massive uncritical reception that served as more than a comparative adornment, which the aforementioned journal described as "the sparkle of the productions of the wise men consecrated to the enlightenment and venture of humanity." Today we see these as the fundamentals of the sociological paradigm of European modernity, the new story of the universal history, developed with the fervor of the new events and the advancement of European hegemony toward the world. We associate the said story with the name of Hegel, but during this time they referred to the universal stories written by authors unknown today, which branched out into adaptations, extracts, vernacularizations, and copies. All this material was read and from it Creole scholars derived notebooks, books, translations, and adaptations.

These materials reflected the expansion of the historical horizon thanks to new discoveries in the philology, epigraphy, and archaeology of Sanskrit, Chinese, Persian, and Arab literature, and the ancient languages of Egypt, Syria, and Mesopotamia. However, they also recycled modernity's heritage at the service of the new "regime of historicity." The past was no longer a source of examples, but rather a process that led to the future,[54] and was represented in the Eurocentric scheme that still rules our idea of the world. An ancient history dominated by the Orient and a modern one in which the protagonist is Europe. In that Orient, stopped in time, the vast despotic empires and the nomadic hordes of the desert had a place. Following his teacher Bossuet, while considering new historians, the Mexican José Lacunza advised his readers not to tire themselves over the study of nations that "had been erased from the face of the Earth by the finger of God," like those of the Orient and pre-Columbian America, even though he noted ancient Germans should be studied.[55]

The Argentinian Vicente F. López, while in exile in Chile, published some journalistic pieces in 1845 that expressed the same feeling of those years. Based on French authors, he discussed the subject under the ambitious title of *Memoria sobre los resultados generales con que los pueblos antiguos han contribuido a la civilización de la humanidad (Memory over the general results of ancient people and their contributions to the civilization of humanity)*. The South American rival of Hegel tried to establish the role that the Egyptians, Chaldeans, Chinese, Indians, or Phoenicians had in the progress of civilization before the Greek flourishing. He established his creations only to see them later come to a halt, much like Greece and Rome. He wrote: "the most modern among the ancient nations . . . are today the oldest of the modern nations . . . later you will find, in a more finished fashion, that in the true ancient peoples, the Asians, the Arabs, the Jewish, the Africans . . . there are venerable traces of the antiquity that move and live in the midst of our young world." The Western world (in his terminology) was pushed by its youth to destroy the oriental past: "The English in Asia and the French in Africa fight with this purpose, but it should be said that they still have work for many more centuries."[56]

The philosophy of history that was being spread took these kinds of considerations as part of its background; the most studied example of the Latin American Orientalism of that time is the previously mentioned Domingo Faustino Sarmiento (1811–1888), another Argentinian exiled in Chile.[57] Those who have studied this author have pointed out that the Orient is the model that he used to understand America, and, in an interesting way, it takes the first known term to explain the second, which was unknown. Often it has been proven that both terms are targets of disdain, except for some occasional passages, and it has been noted that Sarmiento aimed with this to insert himself into European culture.

It is also necessary to add that more profound analyses show, against schemas that are too absolute, "the permeability of the borders in between the representations of civilization and barbarity, of Orient and Occident, of the literate and the oral-popular," and together with the instability of Sarmiento,[58] it must be noted that he was not much interested in the Oriente, and criticized civilized Europe for allowing itself to be charmed by Orientalist illusion. "The antiques and traditions of the Orient, full of prestige to the European, are death letters for the American, the youngest son of a Christian family. Our Orient is Europe, and we are not prepared to receive any light that shines past it unless it is through the European prism."[59]

It is clear in the quoted text that Sarmiento is not only telling us that Europe is the only guiding lighthouse, but also that the study of the Orient is useless, as we can only know it through what the Europeans wrote of it. He writes: "from a distance, what happened in Europe, where the Orient could have been an early reason of pure aesthetic evocation compared to the adverse aspects of modernization, the Orientalist outpouring by Sarmiento and other Argentinian romantics was generally subordinated to the subsequent political aims or to the social knowledge valuable to the civilizing paradigms that they pretended to encourage."[60]

There was a parallel estrangement from the classical world, which had been omnipresent for the enlightened. According to the new political thinking of Latin America, the models of Greece and Rome had nothing to teach. The *magistra vitae* history was losing its appeal, and between mockery and truths, Sarmiento denounced those who were dedicated to these exotic worlds:

> If the law of ostracism were in use in our democracy, in time we would have requested the exile of a great scholar living among us, one who has no other reason than being too much of a scholar and for delving into the mysteries of the language more than our rising civilization demands. He made our youth enjoy the study of the exterior of thought and the forms in which our mother tongue unfolds, with a diminishment of ideas and true enlightenment.[61]

The ostracism he demanded was for Andrés Bello, from whose erudition Sarmiento was very far. "The sources that feed his orientalism are not always of the first order"; "there is evidence of highly diverse discourses . . . an astonishing heterogeneity of languages."[62] His sources came from a dedicated reading of *Revue de Deux Mondes*, which had some Orientalist paintings by the European painters Monvoisin and Rugendas, who lived in America. Worse yet, a pamphlet about Ali Bajá de Janina written by Vicente Fidel López, who was a contributor in the newspaper he managed, and a source for a historical novel by Alexandre Dumas, also provided facts for the posterior Orientalist portrait of the Argentinian leader Facundo.[63] When Sarmiento was ready to visit Algeria he consulted material about the country, as was frequently done by other travelers like Miranda who read previous stories of trips, travel guides, books about customs, history, literature. On the contrary Sarmiento limited himself to the press and the political authors of the time.[64] Moreover, when he was there he only saw what he wanted to: "Has Sarmiento seen Algeria? Because in some way, as M. de Maistre, who never left his room, Sarmiento's circumnavigation trip is an extended allegory to a center (the North's civilization and industry) and its borders (the literal or metaphoric desserts of the South) and his search for means to integrate them."[65] His travel diary is no more than political propaganda, saturated with fiction, and disguised as a moralizing tale where he pretends to see the surroundings.[66]

5. Ebb and flow

Returning to the general context, it is widely known that Sarmiento and his generation wanted to transform our countries based on a model that today termed the North Atlantic world. At the time some called it Europe, others called it Europe, or the Christian countries, and a few began calling it the Western world. The reference encompassed the vast paradigm of civilization and barbarism that was naturally interwoven with changes in the world system and by the superiority of certain social groups in our countries. They identified themselves with liberalism, or, more extensively, with the bourgeois culture, and the benefits of their political rise meant extension of liberties and political participation. However, on the loser's side, it has also been brought to light that this control meant exclusion of the indigenous or popular groups. For women, it represented restrictions on sexual and familial morality. A rampant racism was introduced in the official culture, a situation worse than the previous one. All these are fragments of a "counter history" of Latin American liberalism that paralleled the one that Domenico Losurdo found for the Euro-North American.[67]

I postulate in a pendulum-like movement that liberalism made Creole thinking oscillate toward the side of European symbols. Every study of the history of ideas shows that in the most isolated places the "Sarmientian" paradigm of civilization and barbarism, named after his main exponent, prevailed and was marked by Leopoldo Zea, in his outline of the "dialectic of the American conscience," as an emblem of this time. The subordinated groups received little attention. The indigenous languages that the University studied during colonial times, and the indigenous cultures that were the reason for famous works like Francisco Javier Clavijero's *Historia de México* (1780–1781) were neglected. The more well-meaning hoped to convert through education the indigenous peoples, mestizos, Afro-Americans, and others groups. The less merciful planned to submerge them in waves of European migration or thought that the feebleness of their race would carry them to extinction. No inspiration could come from them.[68]

No inspiration could come from the Orient either, which, in a mysterious way, resembled these marginal groups. There was not, I repeat, a coherent Orientalist discourse in nineteenth-century Ibero-America, but with the spread of the civilizing paradigm, the antipathy of the liberal sectors toward the Orient became constant. The mentions that were reserved for it were those of disdain, lack of awareness, and disinterest. When remembered, the Orient was a metaphor for oppression, fanaticism, and ignorance. Moreover, as a correlative, the same incomprehension found in Sarmiento about finding in the Orient some instruction for the efforts made in Europe, the Mexican positivist Telésforo Gacía asked in 1880,[69] "can the servile nations that inhabit the banks of the Ganges be a model?" The colonizing campaigns of France and England in Asia and Africa were seen with indifference or with sympathy, because of the civilizing effects they were deemed to produce.

Although further nuances should be introduced, conservative thinking (once more the defeated are those that look with more diligence upon history) showed itself open to the Spanish and Creole legacy, and, maybe, it had some curiosity for that of the indigenous. Conservative thinking possibly directed some attention toward the Orient: some linguists went deeper in the study of Sanskrit and Arabic. Ezequiel Uriccoechea (1834–1880), a Colombian Arabist, stands out. In 1878, he won a position to teach Arabic in Brussels by public examination, and then died in Beirut during a study trip. Catholic and conservative, he showed appreciation for the cultural expression of the locals and feared the invasion of strange fashions. This subject deserves broader study, but I close here concluding that the decadence of the "Sarmientian" paradigm also had a side story related to Orientalism.

Such decadence has been studied by those who analyze the history of Latin American ideas as the nineteenth century ended. I also see its causes in the transformation of the world system: due to modifications in it, the new century brought to our countries the end of demographic and cultural Europeanization. The new stage had its losers, and with them the rivalries inside the Creole elites pushed some sectors to search for allies with groups that until then were held in disdain. New projects of nationhood had to be outlined. There were political disorders and significant social movements. In the Mexican Revolution (1910–1917), and in the cultural field, we find a brilliant renovating movement, which gave birth to modernism, the criticism of positivism and of philosophical normalization giving way to different variants of the modern narrative.

A new national-popular paradigm also appeared, and it would mark the totality of the Latin American nineteenth century. The groups excluded as useless—indigenous, mestizos, and popular sectors—that before had to be eliminated or at least transformed, became protagonists and the representative characters of the nation and its culture (a term that by then started to acquire the meaning that we predominantly give it today). It is true that these conceptions were still born from the elite, but both the indigenous and popular studies started to fog the European focus, especially after the Great War when the symbols of America received a new shine among scholars.

In the midst of the mutation of Creole reflection, we also find the subject, subordinate but lasting, of the Orient. A series of annotations that increased during the transition to the 20th century reveals the growing attention given to this subject: modernist literature and even plastic movements held it as an aesthetic referent. The thought, immersed in the fight against positivism, discovered the wisdom of India in Madame Blavatsky's writings. One could say it was a simple imitation of European fashions but there was also an idea that started to open its own path: the identity of destinies in the nations of the Orient and of Latin America, and the consequent attention to their political mutations, to the Japanese Meiji period, to the Turkish Revolution of 1908, to the Chinese Revolution of 1911, to the Abd el-Krim's Republic of the Rif (1923–1926).

Anyone will recognize in this the precedents of Third-Worldism, whose definition has continued to grow into our time. Early manifestations have been traced once again to Argentina, maybe because it was still the most innovating cultural center for the reception and re-elaboration of European themes. However, its presence has also been found in the works of the Peruvians José Carlos Mariátegui (1894–1930) and Raúl Haya de la Torre (1895–1979), imposed as the principal idea of the mid-twentieth century. With an increasing rhythm, the political thinking of Latin America referred to Asia and Africa, and their cultures received careful attention.

Unlike the predecessors of the Enlightenment, the authors of the twentieth century that turned around to face the Orient had broader resources, with established cultural and academic institutions. They had more abundance of books, local translations, the migration of erudite persons, local training of scholars, the possibility of traveling, and, finally, the Internet. This allowed direct access to the sources of these faraway worlds that until then were only known through the mediation of Europe. The idea that our countries belong to the so-called West slowed down until it took a shelter, non-exclusive, in the traditional sectors.

It is a process in which we are still immersed; one I cannot stop thinking about it as I write this.

Tlalpan, October 2016.

Notes

1   The translation was supported through funding by Drake University's Center for the Humanities and William Paterson University.

2   Ignacio Osorio Romero, *La luz imaginaria: epistolario de Atanasio Kircher con los novohispanos*; Rafael Sánchez Concha, "Athanasius Kircher: los caminos del saber erudito."

3   Paula Findlen, "De Asia a las Américas: las visiones enciclopédicas de Athanasius Kircher y su recepción," 105–140.

4   Juan Gil, "Libros, descubridores y sabios en la Sevilla del quinientos," lxiii.

5   Mariano Ardash Bonialian, *El Pacífico hispanoamericano: política y comercio en el imperio español (1680–1784), la centralidad de lo marginal.*

6   On this quote and all the paragraph, see Rubén Carrillo Martín, *La génesis de Sacheofú: Asia en las letras novohispanas de González de Mendoza a Fernández Lizardi (1585–1831).*

7   José M. Mariluz Urquijo, "La China, utopía rioplatense del siglo xviii," 7–31.

8   Carrillo Martín, *La génesis de Sacheofú*; Hernán G. H. Taboada, "La Gran China en el horizonte de la independencia," 375–384.

9   Adolfo Bonilla Bonilla, *Ideas económicas en la Centroamérica ilustrada 1793–1838*, 301.

10 Antonio Gómez, "Ensayo político contra las 'Reflexiones' de William Burke," 267.

11 Manuel Pérez Vila, *La biblioteca del Libertador*, 16.

12 Taboada, "La sombra del Oriente en la Independencia," 75–97; and "De la España africana a la América despótica: notas sobre el ideario de Simón Bolívar," 35–59.

13 Simón Bolívar, *Bolívar al Congreso de Colombia*, 20-i-1830, 812.

14 Catalogue of the Library of San Martín, in *Obra gubernativa y epistolario de San Martín*, 440 and following.

15 Pérez Vila, *La biblioteca del Libertador*, 18.

16 Eduardo Ruiz Martínez, "Catálogo de libros de la biblioteca de Santander," 107–273, records 82, 91, 98, 414, etc.

17 José Antonio Vázquez, *El doctor Francia visto y oído por sus contemporáneos*, 362; see below with regard to Volney.

18 Jaime E. Rodríguez O., *El nacimiento de Hispanoamérica: Vicente Rocafuerte y el hispanoamericanismo 1808–1832*, 238.

19 José Joaquín de Mora, *Cuadros de la historia de los árabes: desde Mahoma hasta la conquista de Granada*, vi–vii.

20 Manuel Lorenzo de Vidaurre, *Plan del Perú* (1823), 15n, 108n.

21 *El Centinela* (Buenos Aires), 24-IV–1824, in *Biblioteca de Mayo*, tome 9.2, 261 and following.

22 On this topic, see Margaret M. Bakos, "El antiguo Egipto en Brasil: historia de la egiptología y la egiptomanía en Brasil"; and Neldson Marcolin, "Los emperadores y las momias."

23 *El Sol del Cuzco*, facsimile, Caracas: Comisión Nacional del Sesquicentenario de las Batallas de Junín y Ayacucho y de la Convocatoria del Congreso Anfictiónico de Panamá, 1974, tome 1, year 1825, issue 49, Saturday 3-XII–1825, p. [210].

24 On these ideas for the Venezuelan case see Elías A. Pino Iturrieta, *La mentalidad venezolana de la emancipación*, 125, 126, 130, 147, 202, 234.

25 Geneviève Verdo, "Los patriotas rioplatenses frente a la Europa de Viena: entre cálculos estratégicos y filosofía de la historia," 89–90, 101.

26 "A la victoria del Maypo," 226.

27 Bolívar, "A las naciones del mundo" claim, 580; José Cecilio del Valle, Justificación de la independencia (1821), 33.

28 José Luis Lanuza, *Morenada*, 64.

29 Bolívar, letter to the editor of the *Gaceta Real de Jamaica*, in *Obras completas*, vol. 1, 181.

30 Felipe Lledías, Composition "Lima libre," on the occasion of the arrival of José de San Martín at Lima, 300.

31 Bolívar, to the governments of Colombia, Mexico, Río de la Plata, Chile y Guatemala, call for the Panama Congress, 7-XII–1824, in *Obras completas*, vol. 3, 739.

32 "Placed in a central position of the new Continent, still more favourable than that of ancient Tyre or Alexandria, she can accumulate in her bosom the perfumes of Asia, the ivory of Africa, the manufacture of Europe, the skins of the North, and the whale of the South. She can enjoy the commerce of China, Greenland, and Kamschaska, without encountering the dangers of Capes Horn and Good Hope"; article on *The Courant* (Jamaica), 27-IX–1815, whose opinions Bolívar considers "correct," and to which he replied on the *Royal Gazette* of the same city the following day, see both articles, in their Spanish and English versions, in *Escritos del Libertador*, vol. 8 (Caracas: Sociedad Bolivariana de Venezuela, 1972), 249–260.

33 Bolívar, Jamaica's Letter, 171.

34 José Toribio Medina, *Historia del Tribunal del Santo Oficio de la Inquisición en México* (1905), 443; *Gaceta del Gobierno del Perú*, 48.

35 Noelia Quintana Villasboa, "El Dictador Francia y sus influencias: Rousseau y el Conde de Volney," http://www.paraguayeterno.com/v1/el-dictador-francia-y-sus-influencias-rousseau-y-el-conde-de-volney/.

36 Alberto Miramón, 256–265.

37 From the Old World: the Amerian cultures are singularly excluded from Volney's critique.

38 See Jean Gaulmier, "Volney et ses Leçons d'Histoire," 54.

39 "Programa, objeto, plan y distribución del estudio de la historia," in Juan A. Ortega y Medina, *Polémicas y ensayos mexicanos en torno a la historia*, bibliographical notes and onomastic index by Eugenia W. Meyer, second edition, México: UNAM, 1992, 25–69, 28.

40 The essential documents (descriptions and different types of papers) are gathered thoroughly in Francisco de Miranda, *Colómbeia*. See Mehmet Necati Kutlu's study, "Reflexiones sobre el viaje de Francisco de Miranda al imperio otomano," 171–186. The reading of the Ottoman Empire section should be complemented with the one about his trip to Russia; that was the one that followed it: Catalina II had just conquered the Tartar Crimea, and her Muslim subjects were abundant. Miranda found some and made commentaries about them.

41 Miranda, *Colómbeia*, vol. 5, 294.

42 Arturo Uslar Pietri, *Los libros de Miranda*.

43 See Antonio Dougnac Rodríguez, "El pensamiento confuciano y el jurista Juan Egaña," 143–193.

44 His library included Antonio Conde's *Historia de la dominación árabe en España*, from 1820, and Reinhard Dozy's *Rechereches sur l'histoire des musulmans en Espagne*, used and criticized in his studies of medieval literature; Leonard Chappelow's *Elementa linguae arabicae*, 1730; a French collection of Moorish romances and a French history of the Ottoman Empire, both from 1825; Rollin's *History of Ancient Egypt*; Raffenel's 1825 *Histoire des Grecs modernes*; some minor Orientalist texts, see Barry L. Velleman's *Andres Bello y sus libros*, with a prologue by Pedro Grases, Caracas: La Casa de Bello, 1995, pp. 149, 154, 163, 165, 192, 242, 248.

45 With regard to these aspects of Bello's ideas, read Nadia Altschul, "Andrés Bello and the Poem of the Cid: Latin America, Occidentalism, and the foundations of Spain's 'national philology,'" 219–236; Francisco Javier Pérez, "Bello orientalista," 113–139.

46 Tomás Pérez Vejo, "La invención de una nación: la imagen de México en la prensa ilustrada de la primera mitad del siglo XIX (1830–1855)," 395–408.

47 Montserrat Galí Boadella, "Del orientalismo ilustrado al orientalismo romántico: Oriente en las revistas mexicanas de la primera mitad del siglo XIX," 615–639; Nancy Vogeley, "Turks and Indians, Orientalist Discourse in Postcolonial Mexico," 3–20.

48 Presentation of the translation of *Curso de filosofía* by Victor Cousin, published in installments in Buenos Aires, 1834, quoted in *El Salón Literario*, with a preliminary study by Félix Weinberg (Buenos Aires: Hachette, 1956), 21.

49 Axel Gasquet, *Oriente al Sur: el orientalismo literario argentino de Esteban Echeverría a Roberto Arlt*, 54–60.

50 Oliver Lubrich, "'Egipcios por doquier': Alejandro de Humboldt y su visión 'orientalista' de América," 75–101; and "A la manera de los beduinos: Alejandro de Humboldt 'orientaliza' a América," 11–29. Both articles say more or less the same.

51 Paulette Silva Beauregard, "Humboldt y la orientalización de Venezuela en los relatos de viaje a la Gran Colombia de William Duane y Gaspard Théodore Mollien"; Adolfo Prieto, *Los viajeros ingleses y la emergencia de la literatura argentina, 1820–1850*.

52 Rafael María Baralt, *Resumen de la historia de Venezuela desde el descubrimiento de su territorio por los castellanos en el siglo XV, hasta el año de 1797*, 407–408; Laureano Vallenilla Lanz, *Disgregación e integración* (1930), 342ss. Even in Vallenilla and Rómulo Gallegos, Silva Beauregard finds "a large chain of texts, from different genres that have direct and indirect dialogue with Humboldt's book"; see Silva Beauregard, "Humboldt y la orientalización de Venezuela", vol. 24.

53 Martín Bergel, *El Oriente desplazado: el Oriente y los orígenes del tercermundismo en la Argentina*, 31ss.

54 Reinhardt Koselleck, *Future past: on the semantics of historical time*; François Hartog, *Régimes d'historicité: présentisme et expériences du temps*.

55 José María Lacunza, "Discurso" (1843), 82.

56 Vicente Fidel López, *Memoria sobre los resultados generales con que los pueblos antiguos han contribuido a la civilización de la humanidad, con el capítulo del Curso de Bellas Letras, De las diversas escuelas de Historia Social*, and a preliminary study by José Luis Romero, Buenos Aires: Nova, 1943, pp. 73, 106–107. With regard to the ideas surrounding this López essay and his historical novel about Ali Bajá, see Daisy Rípodas Ardanaz, "Vicente Fidel López y la novela histórica: un ensayo inicial desconocido", *Revista de Historia Americana y Argentina* (Mendoza), year 4, vol. 7 and 8 (1962–1963), pp. 133–175.

57 About this subject, see: Ricardo Orta Nadal, "Presencia de Oriente en el Facundo," Anuario del Instituto de Investigaciones Históricas (Rosario, Universidad Nacional del Litoral), 5 (1961): 93–122; Carlos Altamirano, "El orientalismo y la idea del despotismo en el Facundo," 83–102; Ricardo Cicerchia, "Journey to the Centre of the Earth," 665–686; Isabel de Sena, "Beduinos en la pampa: el espejo oriental de Sarmiento," 69–89; Gasquet, Oriente al Sur, pp. 73–99; Roberto Amigo, "Beduinos en la Pampa: apuntes sobre la imagen del gaucho y el orientalismo de los pintores franceses", Historia y Sociedad (Medellín, Colombia), vol. 13 (2007), pp. 25–43; Elizabeth Garrels, "Sarmiento, el orientalismo y la biografía criminal: Ali Pasha de Tepelen y Juan Facundo Quiroga," 59–79; Françoise Perus, "'Orientalismo' y 'occidentalismo' en la escritura de Facundo de Domingo F. Sarmiento," 105–116; Christina Civantos, "Orientalism criollo style: Sarmiento's 'Orient' and the formation of an Argentine identity", in Erik Camayd-Freixas, ed., *Orientalism and Identity in Latin America: Fashioning Self and Others from the (Post) Colonial Margin*, Tucson: The University of Arizona Press, 2013, pp. 44–61.

58 Perus, "'Orientalismo' y 'occidentalismo,'" 113.

59 Domingo Faustino Sarmiento, letter to Juan Thompson, 172. Even if it was unconscious, Sarmiento was inspired by the phrase of the costumbrist Jotabeche, who had just written (1844) that "the Muslim has to peregrinate at least once in his

life to the sacred Mecca and visit the sacred places of their belief and traditions. The European painter is not a painter if they have not visited the Italian capitals and the Swiss landscapes. The antiquarian, to pass the aficionado category, needs to steal something from Athen's ruins, the pharaohs' tombs, or travel to Peru to exhume tombs. The fancy santiaguino that has not traveled to Paris to study his source, or to see full of life the kinds of fashion that we only get in prints here, should abandon all hope of gaining celebrity in his career"; see "El provinciano en Santiago" (1844), in *Colección de artículos de don J. Joaquín Vallejo, publicados en varios periódicos bajo el seudónimo de Jotabeche, 1841–1847*, with a biographical introduction by Abraham König, 223–234 (Valparaíso: Imprenta del Deber, 1878), 223. It can also be seen that in between the explorers that were looking to confirm their prestige they are also included the ones that searched to do it in Athens or Egypt.

60 Bergel, *El Oriente desplazado*, 14.

61 Domingo Faustino Sarmiento, "Segunda contestación a Un Quídam," 152.

62 Altamirano, "El orientalismo y la idea del despotismo en el *Facundo*," 90; Perus, "'Orientalismo' y 'occidentalismo,'" 106.

63 Daisy Rípodas Ardanaz, "Vicente Fidel López y la novela histórica: un ensayo inicial desconocido", *Revista de Historia Americana y Argentina* (Mendoza), año 4, núms. 7 y 8 (1962–1963), pp. 133–175.

    Elizabeth Garrels, "Sarmiento, el orientalismo y la biografía criminal: Ali Pasha de Tepelen y Juan Facundo Quiroga", *Monteagudo* (Alicante: Biblioteca Virtual Miguel de Cervantes), núm. 16 (2011), pp. 59–79.

64 Cicerchia pudo rastrear *L'Illustration, Le National, La Quotidienne, La France Algérienne, La Revue d'Afrique, Étude sur l'insurrection du Dhara, Lettre sur les affaires d'Algérie*, unas ilustraciones y un mapa, "Journey to the centre of the earth", 674 n. 28.

65 Sena, "Beduinos en la pampa," 86.

66 Cicerchia, "Journey to the centre of the earth," 681ss.

67 Domenico Losurdo, *Liberalism: A Counter History*.

68 It should be noted that the Argentinean liberals in exile that represented grand innovation for Chile had more rejection and disdain toward the Araucanians than the Chileans; see the polemics that this caused in Fabio Wasserman, *Entre Clío y la Polis: conocimiento histórico y representaciones del pasado en el Río de la Plata (1830–1860)*, 111–130.

69 Quoted in Leopoldo Zea, *El positivismo en México: nacimiento, apogeo y decadencia*, México: FCE, 1968, p. 330.

References

"A la victoria del Maypo." In *La Lira Argentina* (1824), facsimile reproduction in *Biblioteca de Mayo. Literatura*, tome 6. Buenos Aires: Senado de la Nación, 1960.

Altamirano, Carlos. "El orientalismo y la idea del despotismo en el Facundo" [1994]. In *Ensayos argentinos*, edited by Carlos Altamirano and Beatriz Sarlo, 83–102. Buenos Aires: Ariel, 1997.

Altschul, Nadia. "Andrés Bello and the Poem of the Cid: Latin America, Occidentalism, and the foundations of Spain's 'national philology.'" In *Medievalism and the Post/ colonial Perspective*, edited by Nadia Altschul and Kathleen Davis, 219–236. Baltimore: Johns Hopkins University Press, 2009.

Ardash Bonialian, Mariano. *El Pacífico hispanoamericano: política y comercio en el imperio español (1680–1784), la centralidad de lo marginal*, México: El Colegio de México-Colegio Internacional de Graduados-Entre Espacios, 2012.

Bakos, Margaret M. "El antiguo Egipto en Brasil: historia de la egiptología y la egiptomanía en Brasil." *Transoxiana* 9 (December 2004). http://www.transoxiana. com.ar/0109/bakos-egipto_brasil.html.

Bergel, Martín. *El Oriente desplazado: el Oriente y los orígenes del tercermundismo en la Argentina*. Bernal: Universidad Nacional de Quilmes, 2015.

Biblioteca de Mayo. Tome 9.2. Buenos Aires: Senado de la Nación, 1960.

Bolívar, Simón. "A las naciones del mundo" claim, Valencia, 20-IX–1813. In *Obras completas*, vol. 3, 573–580, Caracas: Pool Reading, 1975.

Bolívar, Simón. "Bolívar al Congreso de Colombia, 20-I–1830." *Obras completas*, vol. 3. Caracas: Pool Reading, 1975.

Bolívar, Simón. Jamaica's Letter, 6-IX–1815. In *Obras completas*, vol. 1, 159–175, Caracas: Pool Reading, 1975.

Bolívar, Simón. Letter to the editor of the *Gaceta Real de Jamaica*, September (¿) 1815. In *Obras completas*, vol. 1, 178–182. Caracas: Pool Reading, 1975.

Bolívar, Simón. To the governments of Colombia, Mexico, Río de la Plata, Chile y Guatemala, call for the Panama Congress, 7-XII–1824. In *Obras completas*, vol. 3, 738–740. Pool Reading, 1975.

Bonilla, Adolfo Bonilla. *Ideas económicas en la Centroamérica ilustrada 1793–1838*. El Salvador: FLASCO, 1999.

Carrillo Martín, Rubén. *La génesis de Sacheofú: Asia en las letras novohispanas de González de Mendoza a Fernández Lizardi (1585–1831)*. IN3 Working paper series, Internet Interdisciplinary Institute, Universitat Oberta de Catalunya, 2013.

Cecilio del Valle, José. Justificación de la independencia (1821). In *Textos fundamentales de la independencia centroamericana*, edited by Carlos Meléndez. Ciudad Universitaria Rodrigo Facio, Costa Rica: Editorial Universitaria Centroamericana (EDUCVA), 1971.

Cicerchia, Ricardo. "Journey to the Centre of the Earth." *Journal of Latin American Studies*, vol. 36 (2004): 665–686.

Dougnac Rodríguez, Antonio. "El pensamiento confuciano y el jurista Juan Egaña." *Revista de Estudios Histórico-Jurídicos* (Valparaíso), issue 20 (1998): 143–193.

El Sol del Cuzco, facsímile. (Tome 1, year 1825, issue 49, Saturday 3-XII–1825.) Caracas: Comisión Nacional del Sesquicentenario de las Batallas de Junín y Ayacucho y de la Convocatoria del Congreso Anfictiónico de Panamá, 1974.

Findlen, Paula. "De Asia a las Américas: las visiones enciclopédicas de Athanasius Kircher y su recepción." In Elisabetta Corsi, *Órdenes religiosas entre América y Asia: ideas para una historia misionera de los espacios coloniales*, 105–140. México: El Colegio de México, 2008.

Gaceta del Gobierno del Perú. Facsimile edition (issue 11, tome 8, p. 2, 7-viii–1825). Vol. 3. Government of Simón Bolívar (Lima y Trujillo), prologue by Cristóbal L. Mendoza, Félix Denegri Luna, preliminary word by Pedro Grases. Caracas: Fundación Eugenio Mendoza, 1967.

Galí Boadella, Montserrat. "Del orientalismo ilustrado al orientalismo romántico: Oriente en las revistas mexicanas de la primera mitad del siglo xix." In *Orientes-Occidentes: el arte y la mirada del otro*, edited by Gustavo Curiel, 615–639. México: iie-unam, 2007.

Garrels, Elizabeth. "Sarmiento, el orientalismo y la biografía criminal: Ali Pasha de Tepelen y Juan Facundo Quiroga." *Monteagudo* (Alicante: Biblioteca Virtual Miguel de Cervantes), vol. 16 (2011): 59–79

Gasquet, Axel. *Oriente al Sur: el orientalismo literario argentino de Esteban Echeverría a Roberto Arlt*. Buenos Aires: Eudeba, 2007.

Gaulmier, Jean. "Volney et ses Leçons d'Histoire." *History and Theory* vol. 2, issue 1 (1962): 52–65.

Gil, Juan. "Libros, descubridores y sabios en la Sevilla del quinientos." In *El Libro de Marco Polo anotado por Cristóbal Colón*, edited and with an introduction by Juan Gil, i–lxix. Madrid: Alianza, 1987.

Gómez, Antonio. "Ensayo político contra las 'Reflexiones' de William Burke" (Caracas, 2 de marzo de 1811). In *La libertad de cultos: polémica suscitada por William Burke*, preliminary study by Carlo Felice Cardot, 231–271. Caracas: Academia Nacional de la Historia, 1959.

Hartog, François. *Régimes d'historicité: présentisme et expériences du temps*. Paris: Seuil, 2003.

Javier Pérez, Francisco. "Bello orientalista." In *Andrés Bello y los estudios latinoamericanos*, edited by Beatriz González Stephan and Juan Poblete, 113–139. Pittsburgh: Instituto Internacional de Literatura Iberoamericana, 2009.

Joaquín de Mora, José. *Cuadros de la historia de los árabes: desde Mahoma hasta la conquista de Granada* (tome 1). Londres: R. Ackermann, Strand, 1826.

Koselleck, Reinhardt. *Future Past: On the Semantics of Historical Time*. Cambridge: mit Press, 1985.

Kutlu, Mehmet Necati. "Reflexiones sobre el viaje de Francisco de Miranda al imperio otomano." Espacio, Tiempo y Forma (Madrid, UNED), Serie IV, Modern History, Vol. 20 (2007): 171–186.

Lledías, Felipe. Composition "Lima libre," on the occasion of the arrival of José de San Martín at Lima. In *La poesía de la emancipación*, edited by Aurelio Miró Quesada Sosa (*Colección documental de la Independencia del Perú*, tomo 24). Lima: Comisión Nacional del Sesquicentenario de la Independencia del Perú, 1971.

Losurdo, Domenico. *Liberalism: a counter history*. London-New York: Verso, 2011.

Lubrich, Oliver. "A la manera de los beduinos: Alejandro de Humboldt 'orientaliza' a América." *Casa de las Américas*, vol. 232 (2003): 11–29.

Lubrich, Oliver. "'Egipcios por doquier': Alejandro de Humboldt y su visión 'orientalista' de América." *Revista de Occidente*, vol. 260 (enero 2003): 75–101.

Luis, Lanuza, José. *Morenada*. Buenos Aires: Emecé, 1946.

Marcolin, Neldson. "Los emperadores y las momias." *Pesquisa FAPESP*, edition 131 (January 2007). http://revistapesquisa.fapesp.br/es/2007/01/01/los-emperadores-y-las-momias/.

María Baralt, Rafael. *Resumen de la historia de Venezuela desde el descubrimiento de su territorio por los castellanos en el siglo XV, hasta el año de 1797*. Vol. 1. París: Imprenta de H. Fournier y Comp., 1841.

María Lacunza, José. "Discurso" (1843). In *Polémicas en torno a la historia*, edited by Ortega y Medina, 81–89. México, Universidad Nacional Autónoma de México, Instituto de Investigaciones Históricas, 1970.

Mariluz Urquijo, José M. "La China, utopía rioplatense del siglo XVIII." *Revista de Historia de América*, issue 98 (1984): 7–31.

Miramón, Alberto. "Los libros que leyó Bolívar." In *Miscelánea Lecuna: Homenaje continental*, tome 1, 256–265. Caracas: Cromotip, 1959.

Miranda, Francisco de. *Colómbeia*. Second edition, El viajero ilustrado, 1785–1786. Prologue, notes, and chronology by Josefina Rodríguez de Alonso. Caracas: Presidencia de la República, 1979.

Obra gubernativa y epistolario de San Martín (*Colección documental de la Independencia del Perú*, tome 13, vol. 1). Inventory and prologue by José A. de la Puente Candamo, Lima: Comisión Nacional del Sesquicentenario de la Independencia del Perú, 1976.

Osorio Romero, Ignacio. *La luz imaginaria: epistolario de Atanasio Kircher con los novohispanos*. México: UNAM, 1993.

Pérez Vejo, Tomás. "La invención de una nación: la imagen de México en la prensa ilustrada de la primera mitad del siglo XIX (1830–1855)." In *Empresa y cultura en tinta y papel*, edited by Laura Beatriz Suárez de la Torre, 395–408. México: Instituto Mora, 2001.

Pérez Vila, Manuel. *La biblioteca del Libertador*. Caracas: n/p., 1960.

Perus, Françoise. "'Orientalismo' y 'occidentalismo' en la escritura de Facundo de Domingo F. Sarmiento." *Cuadernos Americanos*, vol. 139 (2012): 105–116.

Pino Iturrieta, Elías A. *La mentalidad venezolana de la emancipación*. Prologue by Leopoldo Zea. Caracas: Universidad Central de Venezuela, 1971.

Prieto, Adolfo. *Los viajeros ingleses y la emergencia de la literatura argentina, 1820–1850*, 2nd edition. Buenos Aires: FCE, 2003.

Quintana Villasboa, Noelia. "El Dictador Francia y sus influencias: Rousseau y el Conde de Volney." http://www.paraguayeterno.com/v1/el-dictador-francia-y-sus-influencias-rousseau-y-el-conde-de-volney (2015).

Rodríguez O., Jaime E. *El nacimiento de Hispanoamérica: Vicente Rocafuerte y el hispanoamericanismo 1808–1832*, México: FCE, 1980.

Ruiz Martínez, Eduardo. "Catálogo de libros de la biblioteca de Santander." In *Santander y los libros: perfil biográfico y catálogo de la biblioteca que perteneció al general Santander* (tome 2), Luis Horacio López et al., 107–273. Santafé de Bogotá: Biblioteca de la Presidencia de la República, 1993.

Sánchez Concha, Rafael. "Athanasius Kircher: los caminos del saber erudito" (1990). in RSC, *Miradas al Perú histórico: notas sobre el pasado peruano*, 175–183. Lima: San Marcos, 2012.

Sarmiento, Domingo Faustino. Letter to Juan Thompson, January 2nd 1847. In *Viajes por Europa, África y América 1845–1847 y diario de gastos*, edited by Javier Fernández. Paris: UNESCO, 1993 (col. *Archivos*, 27).

Sarmiento, Domingo Faustino. "Segunda contestación a Un Quídam" (1842). En *Obras completas*, vol. 1. Buenos Aires: Universidad Nacional de La Matanza, 2001.

Sena, Isabel de. "Beduinos en la pampa: el espejo oriental de Sarmiento." In *Moros en la costa: orientalismo en Latinoamérica*, edited by Silvia Nagy-Zekmi, 69–89. Madrid-Frankfurt: Iberoamericana, 2008.

Silva Beauregard, Paulette. "Humboldt y la orientalización de Venezuela en los relatos de viaje a la Gran Colombia de William Duane y Gaspard Théodore Mollien." *Espéculo*: Revista digital, year 14, vol. 40 (2008–2009).

Taboada, Hernán G. H. "De la España africana a la América despótica: notas sobre el ideario de Simón Bolívar." *Cuyo: Anuario de filosofía argentina y americana* (Mendoza, Universidad Nacional de Cuyo) Vol. 28, Issue 1 (enero-junio 2011): 35–59.

Taboada, Hernán G.H. "La sombra del Oriente en la Independencia." In *Un orientalismo periférico: Nuestra América y el Islam*, 75–97. México: CIALC-UNAM, 2012.

Taboada, Hernán G. H. "La Gran China en el horizonte de la independencia." In *América Latina, el Caribe y China: relaciones políticas e internacionales*, edited by José Ignacio Martínez Cortés, 375–384. México: UNAM-Red ALC-China-UDUAL, 2015.

Toribio Medina, José. *Historia del Tribunal del Santo Oficio de la Inquisición en México* (1905), reprinted. México: UNAM–Miguel Ángel Porrúa, 1987.

Uslar Pietri, Arturo. *Los libros de Miranda*. Caracas: La Casa de Bello. 1979.

Vallenilla Lanz, Laureano. *Disgregación e integración* (1930). In *Cesarismo democrático y otros textos*, edited by Nikita Harwich Vallenilla. Caracas: Biblioteca Ayacucho, 1991.

Vázquez, José Antonio. *El doctor Francia visto y oído por sus contemporáneos*. Buenos Aires: Eudeba, 1975.

Verdo, Geneviève. "Los patriotas rioplatenses frente a la Europa de Viena: entre cálculos estratégicos y filosofía de la historia." *Historia y Política* (Madrid), issue 19, (2008): 75–102.

Vidaurre, Manuel Lorenzo de. *Plan del Perú* (1823). In *Plan del Perú y otros escritos*, edited by Alberto Tauro (*Colección documental de la independencia del Perú*, tome 1,

Los ideólogos, vol. 5). Lima: Comisión Nacional del Sesquicentenario de la Independencia del Perú, 1971.

Vogeley, Nancy. "Turks and Indians, Orientalist Discourse in Postcolonial Mexico." *Diacritics*, 35, 1 (1995): 3–20.

Wasserman, Fabio. *Entre Clío y la Polis: conocimiento histórico y representaciones del pasado en el Río de la Plata (1830–1860)*. Buenos Aires: Teseo, 2008.

Zea, Leopoldo. *El positivismo en México: nacimiento, apogeo y decadencia*. México: FCE, 1968.

Part II

New Directions in Asian-Latin American Comparative Philosophy

Breastfeeding in Between: A Lugonian Reading of Watsuji Tetsurō's *Rinrigaku*[1]

Allison B. Wolf

Yes, this is me sitting on a toilet feeding my sweet, Katalina Maria, after I was denied my right to breastfeed where I wanted to by a #marshalls employee. I was denied to breastfeed in a dressing room, instead I was directed to a bathroom stall to breastfeed. What a way to treat breastfeeding customers, shaming them for breastfeeding, making them feel embarrassed that you need to feed your child. I am angry, upset, but more so humiliated. My rights have been violated.[2]

—Katalina

There was a breastfeeding clinic at the hospital. I was the only black woman there, from East Oakland, which is challenging. I wasn't really making a connection with the women. I had resources if I needed them, but really had to go out of my community and wasn't exactly comfortable for me.

—Julia Chinyere[3]

I am an immigrant Dominican mother, with African American roots on my father's side. My husband is of Caribbean descent . . . I was certainly not prepared for the ongoing negativity that was associated with our decision for me to breastfeed. I am not the only one who shares this experience. Below are just some of the reactions I got . . .

   1- "You're going to kill your baby." . . .

   2- "You're still breastfeeding?!?" . . .

   3- "What? You can't afford formula?" . . .

   4- "You're just trying to be white." . . .

   5- "Your baby has teeth, that means it's time to wean." . . .

   6- "You're going to turn him gay." . . .

Imagine if your entire breastfeeding experience was framed by the
comments I listed above. How successful do you think you could be?[4]

—Carmen Castillo-Barrett

1. Breastfeeding

When most people think of it they imagine, maybe romantically, an easy, natural, experience where new mothers nourish their infants while forming a lifelong bond. Some reject breastfeeding because of its physical nature or perceived erotic connotations. And there is increasing attacking and shaming of breastfeeding women (as is clear from the brief accounts that begin this essay). I now see breastfeeding as a fraught, contested, and political practice.

Breastfeeding rates, support, and resistance are mediated by race, class, and education levels. According to a Chapman University Study, "black mothers were nine times more likely to be given formula in the hospital than white mothers."[5] The Centers of Disease Control (CDC) found that Hispanic women continue to breastfeed the most, with more than 80 percent initiating breastfeeding right after birth and 45 percent continuing at least six months later,[6] although white mothers breast-fed nearly seven weeks longer than did English-speaking Hispanic mothers.[7] The CDC and other studies "echoed earlier research that generally found lower breastfeeding rates in younger women, low-income women and those with less education. It also repeated findings that breast-feeding rates are lowest in black women."[8] Many black women face resistance when they do breastfeed and women of all races face public backlash when breastfeeding in public, though this too is augmented when the mother is not white.[9]

Watsuji Tetsurō's *Rinrigaku* (1996 [1937, 1942, 1949]) gives us a particularly apt framework for describing and assessing the breastfeeding relationship in its political aspects, *specifically because it is so focused on revealing the meaning(s) of what appear to be mundane, everyday, bodily, interactions.* Watsuji's work is often imagined to be a text that simply and uncritically seeks to preserve a pre-World War II Japan that has been lost. Some reject it fervently as a remnant of conservative, Japanese cultural and imperial values.[10] But, when we stop reading Watsuji in relation to Western, modern texts and colonial logic, and instead read him through Latina feminist philosophy, specifically the work of María Lugones, Watsuji's *Rinrigaku* is revealed as a tension-filled, complex, and fundamentally decolonial text. It is a project asserting the validity of Japanese ontology and ethics in the face of a Western, colonial ontology and ethics that had been gaining influence in Japan since 1854, including its ontology of the self. In this context, the West was seen as the modern, progressive, and innovative future, whereas traditional Japanese values were represented as dangerous and outdated relics of the past. The idea that Watsuji would present a Japanese ethic that not only challenged this Westernization, but asserted its validity and superiority, must be seen as the resistant move that it was.[11]

Sadly, modern, Western, colonial logic erases this aspect of his work, just as it erases the politically resistant nature of breastfeeding. As such, we lose Watsuji's decolonial, resistant aspects and their abilities to help us to better understand what appear to be simple, everyday, interactions in our own society, such as breastfeeding. Once it is revealed that the 'betweenness' in which these interactions occur is itself inherently a political space, then we are better able to see such everyday interactions as being squarely located within the realm of ethics and in need of more complicated scrutiny. In the end, then, bringing Lugones to bear on Watsuji's notion of betweenness will both enhance the complexity and value of Watsuji's scholarship within philosophy and demonstrate its continued relevance for evaluating and apprehending everyday interactions, like breastfeeding, in the complicated ways that they deserve. At the same time, a Lugonian reading of Watsuji's *aidagara* helps reveal the fact that even the most mundane interactions do not occur in a neutral "between", but rather in various, often political, betweens, that generate multiple meanings. Understanding this will then allow us to improve the quality of those interactions (be they between mothers and infants, mothers and mothers, or strangers and mothers) and the ways we can support each other in betweenness. This essay will defend these conclusions by exploring Watsuji's and Lugones' work, specifically their concepts of betweenness or *aidagara* (Watsuji) and liminality (Lugones).

2. Watsuji's ethics and the concept of betweenness

Betweenness consists of the various human relationships of our life-world. To put it simply, it is the network which provides humanity with a social meaning, for example, one's being an inhabitant of this or that town or a member of a certain business firm. To live as a person means, in this instance, to exist in such betweenness.[12] —Yuasa Yasuo

Watsuji Tetsurō begins his treatise on ethics, *Rinrigaku*, by declaring that modern Western philosophy is confused about the nature of ethics. This confusion is rooted in an erroneous ontology of human beings as atomistic and individualist, which then leads them to conceive of ethics exclusively as a problem of "individual consciousness."[13] Put differently, Western theorists wrongly think that ethics is about determining how individuals should behave, their duties to each other (assuming that others in fact exist), and saving themselves from sin. Watsuji attempts to correct this confusion.

For Watsuji, ethics is the study of *ningen*,[14] more specifically, it is "the study of *ningen sonzai* (human existence)."[15] This broader focus entails that ethics is "not simply a disciplined reflection on right and wrong, or on the proper ways of acting in social circumstances, but is about what it means to be a human in the world."[16] And this makes sense given the social and relational nature of *ningen*. As Robert Carter explains, *ningen* is composed of two characters: *nin* (人) and *gen* (間). *Nin* can be translated as "human being," "person," or, as James Mark Shields suggests, "two men supporting each other"[17] and *gen* (or *aida*) implies "between," "space," or "among."[18] Based on this, as Erin McCarthy states, "taken literally . . . *ningen* means a self 'between persons' . . . There is no characterization of individuality applicable to selves that can be understood without considerations of that individual's relations to others."[19] Individuals do not (and cannot) exist in isolation. Rather, they are defined by relationships. As Kazuhito Okuda explains: "*Rin* (fellowships) conceived of as 'ways of *ningen*' does not exist in general. It is found in a specific form of practical relationships among human beings."[20] And there is a moral rule that structures these relations that exists prior to the individuals entering into them. As Watsuji elaborates:

> Now it is not the case that father and son first all exist separately, and then come to relate to each other in this way later on. But rather, only through this relationship does the father obtain his qualification as father, and the son his qualification as son. In other words, only by virtue of the fact that they constitute 'one fellowship' do they become respectively father and son.[21]

So, individuals cannot exist outside of relationships; their relationality defines them. "To put it simply, it is the network which provides humanity with a social meaning, for example, one's being an inhabitant of this or that town or a member of a certain business firm."[22]

Ningen is not simply a social product, however. Instead, *ningen* has a dual nature that keeps it constantly in flux between individual and social existence. In essence, the idea is this: We know that there are individuals. In fact, many of us feel as if we are individuals with our own unique histories and circumstances. The only way we can really see ourselves in this way, however, is to negate the social and its influence on our identities. But, as we negate the group or the social, we simultaneously acknowledge the existence of said group; after all, if the social or group did not exist, what are we negating? At the moment that we admit to being part of a group or society, however, we simultaneously negate our individuality. And the cycle continues. Carter summarizes the crux of the relation as follows:

> Everything is deprived of its substantiality, nothing exists independently, everything is related to everything else, nothing ranks as a first cause, and even the *self* is but a delusory construction. The delusion of independent individuality can be overcome by recognizing our radical relational interconnectedness. At the same time, the negation must be negated, so our radical relational interconnectedness is possible only because true individuals have created a network in the betweenness between them.[23]

This process of constant double negation suggests that *ningen* is a fluid, dynamic being, continuously moving in between the individual and the social. As McCarthy says, actual lived human experience, for Watsuji, "is neither an individualistic experience *nor* an experience of being completely dissolved into society."[24] We are simultaneously individual and part of a community. Again, *ningen* is a "self between persons . . . it is 'a betweenness-oriented being.'"[25] And, if ethics is the study of *ningen*, then ethics is "concerned with those problems that prevail *between* persons."[26]

Watsuji discusses "betweenness," or *aidagara* (間柄), in two related ways. In one sense, betweenness refers to *ningen*'s everyday relationships and interactions. But, in another sense, it references the physical space in which interactions occur. "*Aidagara*" or betweenness refers to those relationships that connect us, as they occur in the place and space or *basho* between us and in which we associatively interact properly or appropriately."[27] Let's examine this in more detail.

Fundamentally, betweenness references connections between individuals. But, again, human beings exist in a network of relationships—child-parent, employer-employee, ruler-ruled, sister-brother, etc.—and where one stands in this network shapes who one is and becomes. As such, *ningen* is inherently a social-relational being who cannot be conceived of apart from interactions and interconnections. These relationships, these human interactions, are betweenness.[28] Carter summarizes:

> Simply speaking, we exist in our daily life in the being in betweenness. Moreover, this being in betweeneness is, from the commonsense standpoint, grasped from two angles. The first is that betweenness is constituted 'among' individual persons. This we must say that the individual members who compose it existed

prior to this betweenness. The second is that the individual members who compose this betweenness are determined by it as its members. From this perspective, we can say that antecedent to there being individual members, the betweenness determined they existed.[29]

We should be careful, however, that we do not misunderstand betweenness as merely a metaphysical condition, since it is also concrete, spacial, and physical. "We exist within a definite space, a spacial *basho* or 'place.'"[30] Human interactions occur in space and time; they are not abstractions. We move in the same spacial locations, and we are separated by physical space. Or, as Yuasa Yasuo put it, "To exist in betweenness is to exist in a life-space."[31] In short, as Watusji states: "All expressions that indicate the interconnection of the acts of human beings— for example, *intercourse, fellowship, transportation, communication*—can be understood with a subjective spatiality."[32]

The body is a core element of *ningen*'s physical space and, by extension, betweenness, as evidenced by Watsuji's own examples. In discussing early relationships between mothers and babies, Watsuji notes that the two rarely physically separate from each other, and have bodily cravings for the other.[33] We see this, for example, in breastfeeding. The infant's body craves the mother's when it is hungry, and the mother's breasts fill with milk in anticipation of the infant's bodily needs. Friendship also involves bodily attractions. Watsuji writes: "That one wishes to visit a friend implies that she intends to draw near to the friend's body. If she does go to visit a friend who is at some distance by streetcar, then her body moves in the friend's direction, attracted by the power of intimacy and oneness of body-mind."[34] So, in friendship we physically seek out others in space and time to create betweenness. And, we respond in bodily ways, for example hugging our friends, shaking their hands, or smiling according to social custom. For Watsuji, then, the relationship between two people "cannot be separated from the relation of their bodies."[35] And if this is the case, betweenness is inherently spatial, bodily, and physical.

We should note that betweenness is not simply a space of "meeting." It is also an active, dialogical, and communicative space. It is a space where *ningen* communicate with each other directly and indirectly via media, social arrangements, and culture through public languages, public networks of roads, accepted norms, and communication networks. In short, betweenness is an active, dynamic, physical space where people do not simply meet, but engage.

Recalling that Watsuji characterizes ethics as being about the study of *ningen*, which requires an exploration of what it means to be a human in the world, we can now see the central place of *aidagara* or betweenness in his ethics. Ethics is the study of what occurs "in between;" ethics explores the active, embodied, communicative, dynamic, physical spaces where *ningen* engages and creates meaning in her existence. These interactions are the focus of ethics. Proper ethical analysis, then, requires understanding *aidagara*.

3. Lugones's account of resistance, liberation, and liminality

Decades after Watsuji's lifetime, María Lugones began exploring the experiences of social and relational beings. Motivated by a concern about the challenges faced by women of color in the United States, she explores ontology to find a way to resist oppression and create paths to liberation. Understanding Lugones's work, especially as it relates to liminality, will shine light on Watsuji's work in important ways.

In her essay, "Structure/Anti-Structure and Agency under Oppression," Lugones explores "oppressed subjectivity and the subjective possibility of liberation."[36] Her concern is not so much with the nature of oppression or when oppression arises as much as with liberation from oppression in various forms and contexts. As such, she is worried about the fact that many theories (specifically Karl Marx's account of class oppression and Marilyn Frye's account gender oppression) portray oppression as inescapable.[37] And if oppression is, indeed, inescapable—practically and philosophically—there is no room for liberation. And this is a serious problem because "if oppression theory is not liberatory, it is useless from the point of view of the oppressed person. It is discouraging, demoralizing."[38]

When we shift our focus from oppression to liberation, we will realize that the ontological possibility of liberation depends on recognizing and embracing the reality of ontological pluralism.[39] Lugones maintains that we do not simply occupy and live in a singular reality. Rather, reality is plural and we inhabit multiple worlds. But, when Lugones is arguing that we live in multiple worlds, she is not referring to traditional understandings of this term. Lugones rejects the traditional Western philosophical understanding of "world" as the sum of all things, a worldview, a culture, a utopia or a possible world.[40] On the contrary, Lugones conceives of a "world" as:

A place inhabited by "flesh and blood people" an actual society, given its dominant or non-dominant culture's description and construction of life in terms of the relationships of production, gender, race, sexuality, class, politics, and so forth; a construction of a small portion of society; an incomplete, visionary, non-utopian construction of life; a traditional construction of life; a community of meaning.[41]

As Mariana Ortega summarizes, "a world in this sense is thus incomplete, and it is not monistic, homogenous, or autonomous."[42] In other words, worlds are intertwined; they overlap, interact with and affect each other, and stand in relations of power with each other.

Lugones's conception of a "world" is inextricably linked to her conception of selfhood and subjectivity.[43] In "Purity, Impurity, and Separation," Lugones details how the search for unity underlying the diversity is a long-standing philosophical quest. Rejecting this ontology as an exercise in futility and domination, Lugones proposes a multiplicitous self (or, more accurately, selves).

To help us understand this, Lugones explores two senses of the Spanish verb "*separar*," or "to separate." The first sense is an operation of purity, which requires the complete separation of a whole into its pure constituent parts. This sense of *separar* is illustrated by an exercise Lugones performed as a girl—separating egg whites from egg yolks. The separation needed to be total, complete—no yolky whites and no whitey yolks, just pure whites and pure yolks.

In contrast, there is another sense of *separar*: curdled separation. Curdling occurs when separate substances are mixed and, once combined, they cannot be separated again in their pure constituent parts. Instead, each element partially constitutes the other. For example, when we are making mayonnaise, we mix egg yolks and oil to make an emulsion. If the emulsion breaks down, it does not separate into the pure ingredients. Instead, it curdles, leaving you with oily yolk and yolky oil.[44]

When Lugones speaks of multiple selves, she refers to curdled-separate selves rather than purely separated; the selves are not separable in the first sense. Although one can identify distinct selves, once mixed they never separate in the purist sense; they always contain elements of each other. They are curdled. Important to note, again, is that Lugones is not referring to a multiplicitous self that travels, but rather to multiplicitous selves. We are plural. As Ortega states, Lugone's ontological pluralism posits "a multiplicity of selves as well as a multiplicity of worlds."[45] For Lugones, we are multiplicitous selves, different persons in different worlds; there is no underlying 'I'. And this is integral to Lugones's framework for resistance and liberation.

As Mariana Ortega explains:

[O]ntological pluralism is necessary so that oppressed people can have the open-endedness or the ability to know themselves in different realities in which they can be and act differently than the alternatives offered in those worlds in which they are oppressed and marginalized. It is necessary if the oppressed, marginalized people are to envision different possibilities and are to become resistant.[46]

If reality is singular and we only occupy one world, then oppression seems to be simply "the way it is." It appears inescapable. Under these circumstances, the best an oppressed group can do is attempt to survive. Even in cases where one may think that it is possible to change the system, then, at best, they are simply creating a reactive resistance program. So, there are few to no avenues to see differently. If there are no possibilities for conceptualizing new subjectivities and new ways of operating, then it is not possible to move beyond the mode of survival and reaction toward resistance.

One way the above ontology opens possibilities of resistance is via memory. We remember ourselves executing our wills and bringing desired actions to fruition in other worlds when we are being thwarted in a dominant one. Or we remember ourselves in other worlds where we defy the construction that is being imposed on us in the world we currently occupy. So, Lugones "prompts us to remember our experiences in other worlds so as to remind ourselves that we are not crazy and can move beyond survival to resistance."[47] Memory allows us to resist totalization of the dominant logic.

Still, memory will not be enough. There must be a place from which multiplicitous selves can see the dominant logic (and themselves) differently. Multiplicitous selves must have access to other worlds "in which the self is constructed differently and thus can see resistant possibilities that lead to resistant practices."[48] According to Lugones, this happens at the limen.

A core feature of multiplicitous beings—from Gloria Anzaldúa's *new mestizaje* and continuing to Lugones's multiplicitous, curdled, world traveler, to Mariana Ortega's multiplicitous self as being-between-worlds and being-in-worlds—is liminality. Inherent to multiplicity is traversing, traveling, and occupying the spaces in between worlds. The oppressed travel and inhabit liminal space(s) to create new meaning, new worlds of sense, and to resist.

Her account of liminality begins with Victor Turner's work. As Turner points out, "liminality" is a term that comes out of anthropologist Arnold van Gennep's investigation into rites of passage.[49] In this original meaning, the term referred to "the moment when the initiated is 'betwixt and between successive lodgments in jural political systems.'"[50] According to Turner, during the liminal period, "the characteristics of the ritual subject ... are ambiguous; he passes through a cultural realm that has few or none of the attributes of the past or coming state."[51] In other words, the liminal state frees the subject of the structured norms that usually construct her. Turner continues: "The attributes of liminality or of liminal *personae* are necessarily ambiguous since this condition and these persons elude or slip through the network of classifications that normally locate states and positions in cultural space. Liminal entities are neither here nor there; they are betwixt and between the positions assigned and arrayed by law, custom, convention, and ceremonial."[52]

The limen, then, for Turner, is a space of anti-structure; a location not structured by social and cultural norms and practices.

Lugones adapts this description to define the limen as "the place in between realities, a gap 'between and betwixt' universes of sense that construe social life and persons differently, an interstice from where one can most clearly stand critically toward different structures."[53] Again, like Turner, Lugones characterizes the limen as an anti-structure where selves "encounter possibilities of standing aside from one's social position."[54] But, for Lugones, unlike Turner, liminal beings exist between worlds, realities, and selves, rather than between life stages predetermined by a singular dominant social order. Lugones's limen, then, is a space outside of dominant logic and dominant worlds; it is a place between the spaces, between the logics, between dominant worlds. Within the liminal space, the multiplicitous subject does not stand in any defined or fixed relation to others in that liminal space because the limen is not constrained by the logic or rules of a specific world. It is a space between worlds, not a product of them.[55] And, it is because of this freedom from dominant social standards, structures, and logics that makes the limen a space that can open liberatory possibilities.

For Lugones, the limen is an active, productive space where multiplicitous selves meet and create or imagine liberating possibilities; a place "in which the self can attain resistant and resisting visions."[56] In the limen, in between worlds, inhabitants experience themselves shift as they move from one world to the liminal space and then to another, which allows them to shift their vision and see what was invisible from within a structural framework.[57] Using these new insights, they can see other possibilities of living, organizing, and furthering society, which opens up resistant possibilities.

In more recent work, however, Lugones cautions against viewing the limen so "barely," as if it were free of power. She is concerned that many of us operate on a presumption that "in the limen, to the extent that we lie outside structural descriptions, we are neither in the presence of power nor related to each other in terms of power."[58] But this is not the case; we do not simply enter the limen as if we are not produced and/or exhausted by structures of domination.[59] Moreover, inhabitants of the limen do not enter this space simply as oppressed. Instead, their journey to the limen is more complex and fraught. As a white, Jewish, bisexual woman, for example, I may animate oppression and domination in one self, but enter the limen and experience oppression in another.[60] As Lugones states: "in each of these journeys, the key that opens the door to the limen is not resistance to oppression *per se*, but rather resistance to particular forms of oppression at particular spaces. The spatialities and times of liminality are particular."[61] And, this means that we are not transparent to each other in the limen. Our communication to achieve liberation will often be a struggle.[62]

To emphasize this, Lugones shifts her view of the limen from one based on Turner to one based on Gloria Anzaldúa. Lugones begins discussing the limen as a borderland that "is also constituted *culturally* and *historically*."[63] In this conceptualization, "the limen is understood not just outside of power but outside of that particular version of power which dichotomized subject/object, male/female, reason/passion, nurturance/desire."[64]

When we combine the insights that we are multiplicitous selves traveling and moving within multiple realities with those that the limen is cultural and historical, we realize that: "there is not one limen where we get to meet as a matter of course as we resist oppression. Rather, the different journeys that we have taken to liminal sites have constituted each limen as a different way of life, not reducible to the other, resistant, contestatory ways of life."[65]

In other words, we should not speak of *the* limen, but rather of particular limens. Liminality, too, is multiplicitous.

As we follow Lugones's work, we see an increased emphasis on the historical and geographical nature of borderlands and liminal spaces—more specifically, the decolonial potential of such spaces. In part, this results from Lugones's insights into the coloniality of gender, which imposes dichotomous hierarchies into "the historicity of relations."[66] Colonial logic initially imposed a core hierarchy delineating human and non-human.[67] On this ontology, bourgeois white Europeans were civilized (i.e. fully human), while "the behaviors of the colonized and their personalities/souls were judged as bestial and thus non-gendered, promiscuous, grotesquely sexual, and sinful."[68] This initial hierarchy then set up a gender dichotomy of man/woman. But, "the gender system is not just hierarchical but racially differentiated, and the racial differentiation denies humanity and this gender to the colonized."[69] In other words, the colonial dichotomy of human/non-human was racially infused such that it produced the modern, colonial, gender system wherein only white, European, bourgeois,

Christians are fully human (and thus eligible to be assigned a gender) and non-whites are relegated to some non-human, exploitable, ontological state. The category of "colonized woman," then, is an empty one as there is no such thing as a being who could be both colonized and gendered. Lugones states:

> Indigenous peoples of the Americas and enslaved Africans were classified as not human in species—as animals, uncontrollably sexual and wild. The European, bourgeois, colonial modern man became a subject/agent, fit for rule, for public life and ruling, a being of civilization, heterosexual, Christian, a being of mind and reason. The European bourgeois woman was not understood as his complement, but as someone who reproduced race and capital through her sexual purity, passivity, and being homebound in the service of the white, European, bourgeois man.[70]

Definitions of humanity, gender, race, class, sexuality, and religion were then used to judge those who did not meet their standards and then create pretexts (such as the idea that Europeans were trying to help the indigenous peoples of the Americas and African slaves to become civilized) to simultaneously justify and mask "brutal access to people's bodies through unimaginable exploitation, violent sexual violation, control of reproduction, and systematic terror."[71]

These insights into the coloniality of power and the modern, colonial, gender system further elaborate Lugones's concept of liminality. Some limens are created at what Lugones calls, "the fractured locus," from the wound of colonial difference.[72] But, Lugones clarifies, she is "proposing a feminist border thinking, where the liminality of the border to a ground, a space, a borderlands, . . . not just a split, not an infinite repetition of dichotomous hierarchies among de-souled spectars of the human."[73] Liminalities both see the coloniality of gender and rejects and resists it. And, for reasons already outlined, they are fraught space that contain tense movements; "the tension between the dehumanization and paralysis of the coloniality of being, and the creative activity of be-ing."[74] In the end, then, there are a multiplicity of limens and liminal existences, all of which are populated with actual, multiplicitous, complex beings engaging in the demanding work of resistance and liberation.

4. The politics in between: A Lugonian reading of *Aidagara*

I imagine that few would place Watsuji and Lugones together. After all, Lugones is known for her liberatory, anti-colonial work while many have criticized

Watsuji for being a conservative who "contributed to the legitimacy of wartime 'emperor-system fascism.'"[75] Watsuji's account of betweenness describes a space that is common; it is not simply part of the dominant logic, it is valued for animating and reinforcing it. In fact, it upholds well-worn Buddhist styles of argumentation regarding non-duality and the self-emptying or self-negating function of emptiness.[76] In contrast, Lugones is describing a space between dominant logics that resists those logics. Watsuji accepts the idea of a singular social order, while Lugones both denies it and argues that trying to achieve such an order is an act of domination.[77] Watsuji's betweenness happens in everyday, common, experience, whereas Lugonian liminality occurs outside the view of the common/dominant experience. Lugones's limen is where oppressed people go to interact with each other outside of the dominant order, whereas Watsuji's between is a space of upholding societal rules and tradition through everyday interactions. And this suggests that for Watsuji, the between is a stable space resistant to change, while for Lugones the limen is a more creative space where new norms are generated and new histories are re-evaluated.[78] Despite these clear differences, however, reading Watsuji alongside Lugones reveals the deeply political and decolonial aspects of *aidagara* and Watsuji's general project.

First, Watsuji emphasizes that we exist in networks of relationships that form betweenness. These networks, however, are not neutral; the Japanese social order that Watsuji is touting is structured to maintain specific norms and values, for example, respect of family and ancestors, order, and valuing one's community over oneself. Beyond this, *ningen* is a political being. While Watsuji speaks about *ningen* as if it were universal, when we read Watsuji alongside Lugones it becomes clear that no such universal, embodied being exists. *Ningen* is gendered, raced, classed, and infused with history, contradiction, and diverse meaning. *Ningen* is a social and political being. Therefore, the betweenness that *ningen* construct with each other is political.

Second, the political aspect of *aidagara* is revealed when reading its communicative aspect via Lugones. While Watsuji speaks of communication in a relatively politically and morally neutral way (i.e. means of communication, dialogue between the individuals involved in the interaction, speaking and writing to share an idea or message), Lugones's work on complex communication in the limen shows that communication in between is not that simple. Communication and dialogue are neither politically neutral nor straightforward between these beings that are situated, raced, gendered, historicized, embodied in various ways. *Ningen* cannot simply shed all of those histories and locations once they enter betweenness. A white professional woman who has had her first child in her mid-thirties and does not know how to coax her to take the breast or feed with the "correct latch" neither easily communicates with her newborn nor sheds her desire to be competent at all things just because she is dealing with a newborn. Similarly, a black, Christian, conservative male and an Arab, Muslim, progressive, woman each bring their social constructions into the space in between, which helps creates interactions that are reflective of their distinct social locations. Any frictions that exist in society at large also exist in their interactive space. Betweenness, then, is often fraught with miscommunication, friction, and missteps produced by the relational, historical networks that produce *ningen*. So, while *aidagara* is a communicative space, Lugones's work reveals the challenging political nature of that communication.

These insights into the political nature of *aidagara* lead to larger insights about Watsuji's ethical project—its political subversiveness and decolonial nature. As previously highlighted, many critique Watsuji's deep conservativism in relation to Japanese tradition.[79] And, clearly, this is true to an extent—Watsuji defends a traditional, dominant Japanese social and political order that marginalized many and, arguably, supported domination and oppression. In fact, his discussion of what is required of *ningen*, to accept absolute emptiness, is reminiscent of telling marginalized groups to sacrifice themselves for the greater good. But, extending this reading too far can only hold if we read Watsuji through a Western, colonial lens.

Lugones's recent work on decoloniality of gender especially illuminates that Watsuji's point about the mistake of modern Western ethics beginning at the isolated individual was not simply him pointing out an error in that logic; he was resisting an imposition of colonial logic onto Japan and Japanese culture. As Isamu Nagami explains, it is obvious that Watsuji's main intentions in writing the books that preceded *Rinrigaku*, such as *Guzo Saikō* (*Revival of Idols*), were "to defend the values of Japanese culture against the overpowering influence of Western civilization."[80] More broadly, he was writing in a time of newfound Western influence in Japan. Nagami explains that after centuries of isolation from foreign powers, Japan opened its doors to Western civilization, which "resulted in the decline of the Tokugawa shogunate, the restoration of Meiji imperial authority, and finally the total adoption of Western institutions in Japanese life" led to periods of the deep influence of American pragmatism and, later, German ideology.[81] This "meant that any Japanese thinker has to distill his own thinking out of the conflict between his own traditional heritage and what he adopted from the Western mind. Tetsurō Watsuji ... [developed] his philosophical thought out of this struggle."[82] But we cannot see this within modern Western logic.

Aparicio and Blaser refer to ways of organizing the social, the cosmological, the ecological, and the spiritual that resist "modern, capitalist modernity that are in tension with its logic," as *non-modern*.[83] Lugones follows them in employing this terminology of non-modern to express that these other ways of organizing are not premodern, despite how modern colonial logic constructs them. On the contrary, Lugones maintains that, "the modern apparatus reduces them to premodern ways." So, non-modern knowledges, relations, and values, and ecological, economic, and spiritual practices are logically constituted to be at odds with a dichotomous, hierarchical, 'categorical' logic.[84] As a result of these logical constructions, she explains, the modern colonial logic dismisses those who resist the imposition of their logic as being backward and opposed to progress. Modern logic reduces non-modern to premodern ways, such that we read any attempt to preserve such norms as backward and conservative, rather than resistant. "Modernity attempts to control, by denying their existence, the challenge of the existence of other worlds with different ontological presumptions. It denies their existence by robbing them of validity and co-evalness."[85] From the modern Western colonial logic, we deny that Japan would have its own cosmology, ontology of humanity, and ethics. And, whatever they do have is clearly invalid (which is why the West is so noble to have shepherded them into the modern era post-World War II). But Watsuji challenges that—he is asserting that Japan has its own valid ontology and ethics. Reading Watsuji via modern logic, then (as has been done up to this point), will render us unable to see his decolonial project; we will see simply conservative nostalgia that hinders progress.

Lugones's work here reveals the truly subversive nature of Watsuji's project (and the mechanisms that hid it). According to modern Western colonial logic, the white, European, bourgeois man is the proper agent/subject to rule, to organize public life, etc. So, under this frame, *ningen,* who is social and relational and stuck in constant flux between his individuality and the social, cannot meet these standards. Thus, his colonization is justified. But Watsuji inverts this logic; *ningen is* the proper agent/subject to rule, to organize public life, and is the model of the ethical human, not the modern, Western, atomistic individual. This is not only bold and innovative but also subversive.

Contemporary understandings of breastfeeding are also influenced by modern, colonial logic. In the United States, for example, the woman and the newborn/infant are conceptualized as separate individuals who are self-interested, rational, and ontologically distinct. As such, they each have their own, sometimes mutually exclusive, interests (which is why there is a "fetal-maternal conflict"). Under this ontology, women will not freely give up their breast milk to their infant. After all, doing so sacrifices or gives some of her body to the infant without anything in return; the infant is literally sucking out the property of the mother and incorporating it for her or his own needs without giving anything back to her.[86] Breastfeeding then appears irrational. Under this logic, then, if newborns and infants require breast milk to survive, women must be either convinced or coerced into breastfeeding; for example, by claiming that a baby's health is in jeopardy without breast milk, shaming women who do not breastfeed, and/or defining a "good mother" as one who breastfeeds.[87] While there are countless issues here, my core point is that traditional Western metaphysics shapes our conceptualizations (and by extension, our discussions) of breastfeeding. However, when we change how we conceptualize subjects and breastfeeding to Watsuji's vision, our discussion changes.

Starting our explorations with Watsuji's ontology means that we begin with *ningen*, a social, relational being who meets other *ningen* in between. As Watsuji himself stated clearly, here we begin with the ontology where mother and child (including newborn and infant) are inherently *connected*. He states:

> A mother and her baby can never be conceived of as merely two independent individuals. A baby wishes for its mother's body, and the mother offers her breast to the baby. If they are separated from each other, they look for each other with all the more intensity.... To isolate them as separate individuals, some sort of destruction must occur.[88]

Mother and baby exist and do so in relation. The idea that the two have distinct interests becomes nonsensical; their interests are intertwined.

Because mother and baby cannot be separated, the debate neither pits women and their babies against each other in a conflict and competition for resources, nor does it focus on convincing or coercing. Instead, the discussion focuses on what would be needed to create a space where mother and child can interact. How can women and their infants meet in between so that they can bond and thrive and love? That is what matters.

5. Breastfeeding in between: A hopeful, potentially resistant, political act

Before concluding, I must point out one more way in which Lugones's work on liminality enriches Watsuji's project, namely that it provides hope. What I mean is that it could be possible to read Watsuji's description of *ningen* as being stuck, as never being able to win. *Ningen* cannot be an individual without subverting society but, at the same time, she cannot conform to societal expectations and structures and meet her destiny as an individual. *Ningen* seems to be in a metaphysical and practical double bind. No matter what *ningen* does, satisfaction eludes her. But, reading this ontological picture via Lugones demonstrates that its dim conclusions are only valid under a presumption of ontological singularity and unity. Luckily, Lugones shows us the error of this metaphysics. So, *ningen* may not be as stuck as it seems.

We know that *aidagara* is a political space populated by socially, historically, infused *ningen*. *Ningen* world-travels through various worlds, creating numerous *aidagara*. So, just as there is not one, singular limen (but rather many limens),[89] there are multiple "in-betweens."[90] And, *ningen* can retreat to and create these spaces to reevaluate and challenge society's norms (or even to create new ones). So, *ningen* can shift her geographical space to meet different beings in different betweens to create paths to resistance and liberation. In world-traveling in these ways, *ningen* recognizes her multiplicity; she does not have to choose between herself and society, she wins by embracing her ontological pluralism and the possibilities it brings. And, when she feels stuck, she can remember herself in other worlds and resist the way a particular space constructs her. After all, she is different in different worlds. In this way, *ningen* is in constant flux is not so much problematic as much as the ideal of trying to be a singular, unchanging, self. In accepting her constant flux as normal and good, *ningen* can find satisfaction.

Just as it seemed that *ningen* was in a double bind, so too it may appear that way for the breastfeeding woman. If she thwarts the norms of breastfeeding, then she is shunned and shamed. On the other hand, if she conforms to them, then she cannot fulfill her individual ambitions. But, just as was the case with *ningen*, the breastfeeding mother's practice is more complicated than that and there are places she can find satisfaction—in liminal spaces.

Women and their babies meet in between and breastfeed. But these betweens are far from politically neutral; they are infused with racism, sexism, heterosexism, Christianity, and colonial norms. So, while certain (usually white, middle- and upper-class) mothers can meet their babies in a loving, peaceful, between; others (often poor white women and women of color of all classes) meet in a place that is fraught with social critique (to borrow Carmen's examples above, that the mother wants to be white, wants to hurt her child, or will turn him gay, and so forth).[91] Some bodies do not even get the chance to meet in this particular space in between because hospital staff have given their newborn formula based on the race of her mother. Still, the women are resisting—they continue to find ways to breastfeed, even if that is in literal spaces, between bathrooms, cars, and offices.

In all of the examples that began this essay, we see the tension between women challenging racial, gender, and sexuality structures and those enacting or trying to enforce a colonial logic to perpetuate them. If the modern, colonial, gender system defines women as white and civilized, and civilization requires that breastfeeding be done in private to reproduce the white, European, bourgeois man's child, then doing so in public becomes uncivilized. This, then, is used to try to justify laws, policies, and practices that punish and violate women like Katalina above, who dare to breastfeed in public. This same logic is also used to justify disciplining women who breastfeed publically. After all, they are not acting like "real women," who maintain modesty and rules of civilization.

Julia's and Carmen's experiences demonstrate different ways that they are affected by and resist the modern, colonial, logic. If part of the modern/colonial gender definition of "woman" is to be a mother (specifically to reproduce white children) and part of being a good mother is to breastfeed those white children so that they can survive, then we need to support women (read white, bourgeois women) to do that effectively. Since, as Lugones pointed out, the colonized woman does not exist, then non-white women are not really women at all. As such, they do not require support to do "womanly" things, like breastfeeding their children. I would even go further to suggest that since women of color are denied the title of "woman" and all of its privileges, including the ability to reproduce,[92] then a woman of color who chooses to nurture her child via breastfeeding is herself a threat to the logic of the modern, colonial, gender system. Or worse, since she is characterized as "bestial and thus non-gendered, promiscuous, grotesquely sexual, and sinful,"[93] her breastfeeding is read as grotesquely sexual and/or sinful. As such, it must be stopped; she must be stopped from furthering her "inappropriate" behavior. Under that context, the mere act of breastfeeding is resistant. Beyond this, to leave one's own community, as Julia did, to demand support is to resist colonial gender-logic categories. She is claiming what the modern, colonial, gender system has denied her.

While Carmen's experience of claiming breastfeeding is also resistant in itself, her case is also clearly interwoven with multiple oppressive social structures— homophobia, racism, sexism, classism—that are all being resisted in her determination to breastfeed for as long as she wishes. For example, she is not falling prey to the homophobic baiting that her son will be gay or the class enticements of elevating one's socio-economic status by buying formula.

And she refuses to cede breastfeeding to white women. She is fighting. She is resisting. And she is subverting modern colonial gender norms as she suckles her son.

All of the above is occurring in the public spaces that characterize Watsuji's examples of betweenness. If a woman cannot breastfeed in public, then she does so in a new space. Or she takes over the public and takes pictures as she breastfeeds and posts them on social media. Regardless, she still meets her infant in the politicized Watsujian *aidagaras* that Lugones reveals. However, just as the modern colonial logic erased and obscured the subversive nature of Watsuji's project, so too did it erase the subversive nature of the breastfeeding occurring in *aidagara*.

Under a Lugonian reading of Watsuji's *aidagara*, then, we see that the apparently simple interactions, including those between mother and infant that Watsuji describes, are far from the uncomplicated interactions that some misread Watsuji as suggesting. On the contrary, like Watsuji's overall project, the interactions that occur within it are far more complex, politically infused, and subversive; including breastfeeding. So, bringing these two divergent philosophers together who seem to have little in common leads to a more interesting and richer philosophical analysis while helping us better understand and recognize *ningen* and all of the women—including Katalina, Julia, and Carmen—who are fighting to find satisfaction.

Notes

1 I want to express my deep appreciation to Jennifer Benson for helping me see the resistant nature of both these thinkers and the practice of breastfeeding and to Leah Kalmanson for introducing me to Watsuji Tetsurō's wonderfully rich and complicated, *Rinrigaku*, and for fostering my immediate comparisons to Maria Lugones's work in our invigorating Friday discussions.

2 Caroline Bologna, "Breastfeeding Mom Is 'Humiliated' after Being Told to Nurse in Marchalls Bathroom Stall," http://www.huffingtonpost.com/entry/breastfeeding-mom-is-humiliated-after-being-told-to-nurse-in-marshalls-bathroom-stall_us_55f6cf2ae4b063ecbfa4c92e.

3 Hatty Lee, "We Need to Support Moms Who Breastfeed, Not Shame Them," http://www.colorlines.com/articles/we-need-support-moms-who-breastfeed-not-shame-them.

4 Carmen Castillo-Barrett, "Why Black Breastfeeding Week is Important to Me," http://theleakyboob.com/2014/08/why-black-breastfeeding-week-is-important-to-me/.

5   Chapman University, "Breastfeeding Gaps between White, Black, and Hispanic Mothers in the US," http://www.eurekalert.org/pub_releases/2016–07/cu-bgb071216.php.

6   Mike Stobbe, "Hispanic Moms Breastfeed the Most," http://www.nbcnews.com/id/36039199/ns/health-childrens_health/t/hispanic-moms-breast-feed-most/#.V6ty5q6XLGs.

7   Ibid.

8   Ibid.

9   See, for example, the different responses to breastfeeding in graduation pictures by white and black women: Lisa Flam, "Breastfeeding Mom's College Graduation Photo Stirs Controversy," http://www.today.com/parents/breast-feeding-moms-college-graduation-photo-stirs-controversy–2D79780389; Kevin L. Clark, "College Graduate Breastfeeding Photos Cause Controversy," http://www.blackenterprise.com/news/college-graduate-breastfeeding-photos-cause-controversy/; and Caroline Bologna, "Internet Cheers for Photo of Mom Breastfeeding at Graduation," http://www.huffingtonpost.com/2014/11/05/breastfeeding-graduation-photo_n_6108164.html.

10 See, for example, Isamu Nagami, "The Ontological Foundation in Tetsurō Watsuji's Philosophy: Kū and Human Existence," 280; and James Shields, "The Art of *Aidagara*: Ethics, Aesthetics, and the Quest for an Ontology of Social Existence in Watsuji Tetsurō's *Rinrigaku*," 266.

11 Nagami, "The Ontological Foundation in Tetsurō Watsuji's Philosophy," 279.

12 Yuassa Yasuo cited by Robert Carter, "Interpretative Essay: Strands of Influence," 337.

13 Ibid., 9.

14 Watsuji Tetsurō, *Rinrigaku*, 9.

15 Kazuhiko Okuda, "Watsuji Tetsuro's Contributions to Political Philosophy" (unpublished working paper), 1999.

16 James M. Shields, "The Art of *Aidagara*: Ethics, Aesthetics, and the Quest for an Ontology of Social Existence in Watsuji Tetsurō's *Rinrigaku*," 272.

17 Ibid., 267.

18 Ibid., 267.

19 Erin McCarthy, *Ethics Embodied: Rethinking Selfhood through Continental, Japanese, and Feminist Philosophies*, 13.

20 Okuda, "Watsuji Tetsuro's Contributions to Political Philosophy."

21 Watsuji, *Rinrigaku*, 11.

22 Robert Carter, "Interpretative Essay: Strands of Influence," 337.

23 Ibid., 350.

24 Erin McCarthy, *Ethics Embodied*, 18.

25 Ibid., 14.

26 Watsuji, *Rinrikagu*, 12.

27 Carter, "Interpretative Essay: Strands of Influence," 341.

28 Watsuji, *Rinrigaku*, 34.

29 Ibid., 58.

30 Carter, "Interpretative Essay: Strands of Influence," 338.

31 Yuasa Yasuo, *The Body: Towards an Eastern Mind-Body Theory*, 39.

32 Watsuji, *Rinrigaku*, 157.

33 Ibid., 61.

34 Ibid., 62.

35 McCarthy, *Ethics Embodied*, 40.

36 María Lugones, *Pilgramages*/Peregrinajes: Theorizing Coalition Against Multiple Oppressions," 53.

37 Lugones does recognize that each theorist offers an account of liberation, but she goes on to claim "that the account of oppression itself leaves the subject trapped inescapably in the oppressive system" (ibid., 53).

38 Ibid., 55.

39 Ibid.

40 Mariana Ortega, *In-Between: Latina Feminist Phenomenology, Multiplicity, and the Self*, 65, 92.

41 Lugones, *Pilgramages*/Peregrinajes, 26.

42 Ortega, *In-Between*, 65.

43 To say that we all inhabit and travel between multiple worlds does not mean that we are all aware of the worlds, how they construct us, or how we interact with and construct others. For example, we could be myopically focused on performing a task, such as giving birth, than we do not realize that we are in a world at all, let alone, being constructed by it. We could be so focused on controlling pain that we don't realize that the context I am giving birth in shapes my options for accomplishing that goal. So, I may feel as if I made a choice to have an epidural without being cognizant of how I am enacting the syllogism the medicalized birth world constructed for me. So, merely inhabiting a world does not entail an awareness of that world or how it constructs us. But this lack of awareness does not negate the fact that we are all inhabiting multiple worlds and animating their constructs.

44 Lugones, *Pilgramages*/Peregrinajes, 122.

45 Ortega, *In-Between*, 88. This is important for Ortega because she contends that we can also have an understanding of a multiplicitous self. As Ortega explains in her recent book, *In-Between*, she rejects Lugones's claim that world-travel requires a shift of self in addition to an epistemic shift. To the contrary, Ortega proposes that there is a multiplicitous self that has a continuity of experience that provides it with a sense of being an "I" (78). So, we must note that Lugones is referring to multiplicitous, plural, selves rather than a multiplicitous self.

46 Mariana Ortega, *In-Between*, 96.

47 Ibid.

48 Ortega, *In-Between*, 99.

49 Victor Turner, "Liminality and Communitas," 94.

50 Lugones citing Turner (ibid., 60).

51 Turner, "Liminality and Communitas," 95.

52 Ibid.

53 Lugones, *Pilgramages*/Peregrinajes, 59.

54 Ibid., 20.

55 Ibid., 61.

56 Ibid., 59.

57 Ibid., 61.

58 Lugones "On Complex Communication," 76.

59 Ibid., 77.

60 Ibid.

61 Ibid.

62 And, for Lugones, this is done through complex communication rather than liberal conversation.

63 Lugones "On Complex Communication," 80. Specifically in this citation, she means that the borderlands is constituted by Anzaldúa as a recovery of memory. In addition, while I do not have space to get into this here, when we read this aspect of Lugones alongside of Watsuji, we see that there is a geography of the limen in a very literal sense that often goes unrecognized.

64 Ibid., 80.

65 Ibid., 83.

66 Lugones, "Toward a Decolonial Feminism," 743.

67 Ibid., 743.

68 Ibid.

69 Ibid., 748.

70 Ibid., 743.

71 Ibid.

72 Ibid., 752.

73 Ibid., 753.

74 Ibid., 754.

75 Shields, "The Art of *Aidagara*," 266.

76 Thank you to Leah Kalmanson for pointing this out to me.

77 See, for example, Lugones, "Purity, Impurity, and Separation."

78 Barry Decoster, personal conversation.

79 Nagami, "The Ontological Foundation in Tetsurō Watsuji's Philosophy: Kū and Human Existence," 280.

80 Ibid., 281.

81 Ibid.

82 Ibid.

83 Juan Ricardo Aparicio and Mario Blaser, unpublished manuscript, as cite in María Lugones, "Toward a Decolonial Feminism," *Hypatia*, 25:4, Fall 2010, 742–3.

84 María Lugones, "Toward a Decolonial Feminism," *Hypatia*, 25:4, Fall 2010, 743.

85 Ibid., 749.

86 Think here, for example, of the Lockean notion that our bodies are our personal property. As a result, we own our bodies and all products of our bodies. Under this understanding, then, a woman's breast milk is her property.

87 See, for example, Hanna Rosen, "The Case Against Breastfeeding," http://www. theatlantic.com/magazine/archive/2009/04/the-case-against-breast-feeding/307311/ and, from a writer at Crunk Feminist Collective, "Tough Titty: On Feminist Mothering and the Breastfeeding Doll," https://crunkfeministcollective.wordpress. com/2011/07/20/tough-titty-on-feminist-mothering-and-the-breastfeeding-doll/.

88 Watsuji, *Rinrigaku*, 61–2.

89 María Lugones, "On Complex Communication," 83.

90 And Watsuji, seems to agree, though he does not speak in these terms. For example, he discusses betweenness between readers and authors, surgeons and patients, and mothers and babies.

91 Carmen Castillo-Barrett, "Why Black Breastfeeding Week is Important to Me," http://theleakyboob.com/2014/08/why-black-breastfeeding-week-is-important-to-me/.

92 For a detailed account of racial logic that constructs women of color as those who should not reproduce, see Dorothy Roberts, *Killing the Black Body*.

93 Ibid., 743.

References

Anzaldúa, Gloria. *Borderlands/Las Fronteras: The New Mestiza*, 4th Edition. San Francisco: Aunt Lute Books, 2012.

Bologna, Caroline. "Breastfeeding Mom Is 'Humiliated' after Being Told to Nurse in Marchalls Bathroom Stall." *Huffington Post*. September 14, 2015. http://www. huffingtonpost.com/entry/breastfeeding-mom-is-humiliated-after-being-told-to-nurse-in-marshalls-bathroom-stall_us_55f6cf2ae4b063ecbfa4c92e.

Bologna, Caroline. "Internet Cheers for Photo of Mom Breastfeeding at Graduation." *Huffington Post*. November 5, 2014. http://www.huffingtonpost.com/2014/11/05/breastfeeding-graduation-photo_n_6108164.html.

Carter, Robert. "Interpretative Essay: Strands of Influence." In Watsuji Tetsurō, *Rinrigaku,* translated by Yamamoto Seisaku and Robert E. Carter. Albany: SUNY Press, 1996.

Castillo-Barrett, Carmen. "Why Black Breastfeeding Week is Important to Me." *The Leaky Boob*. August 26, 2014. Accessed August 10, 2016. http://theleakyboob. com/2014/08/why-black-breastfeeding-week-is-important-to-me/.

Chapman University. "Breastfeeding Gaps between White, Black, and Hispanic Mothers in the US." *EurekAlert*. July 12, 2016. http://www.eurekalert.org/pub_releases/2016–07/cu-bgb071216.php.

Clark, Kevin L. "College Graduate Breastfeeding Photos Cause Controversy." *Black Enterprise*. November 5, 2014. http://www.blackenterprise.com/news/college-graduate-breastfeeding-photos-cause-controversy/.

Crunk Feminist Collective. "Tough Titty: On Feminist Mothering and the Breastfeeding Doll." *The Crunk Feminist Collective*. July 20, 2011. https://crunkfeministcollective.wordpress.com/2011/07/20/tough-titty-on-feminist-mothering-and-the-breastfeeding-doll/.

Flam, Lisa. "Breastfeeding Mom's College Graduation Photo Stirs Controversy." *Today*. June 9, 2014. http://www.today.com/parents/breast-feeding-moms-college-graduation-photo-stirs-controversy–2D79780389.

Lee, Hatty. "We Need to Support Moms Who Breastfeed, Not Shame Them." *Colorlines*. June 11, 2013. Accessed August 10, 2016. http://www.colorlines.com/articles/we-need-support-moms-who-breastfeed-not-shame-them.

Lugones, María. Pilgramages/*Peregrinajes: Theorizing Coalition Against Multiple Oppressions*. Lantham, Boulder, NY, Oxford: Rowan & Littlefield Publishers, 2003.

Lugones, María. "On Complex Communication." *Hypatia* 21 (2006): 3.

Lugones, María. "Toward a Decolonial Feminism." *Hypatia* 25, No. 4 (2010): 742–759.

McCarthy, Erin. *Ethics Embodied: Rethinking Selfhood through Continental, Japanese, and Feminist Philosophies*. Lantham, Boulder, NY: Lexington Books, 2010.

Nagami, Isamu. "The Ontological Foundation in Tetsurō Watsuji's Philosophy: Kū and Human Existence." *Philosophy of East and West* 31, No. 3 (1981): 279–296.

Okuda, Kazuhiko. "Watsuji Tetsuro's Contributions to Political Philosophy." Unpublished working paper, Number 1 (1999).

Ortega, Mariana. *In-Between: Latina Feminist Phenomenology, Multiplicity, and the Self*. Albany: SUNY Press, 2016.

Rosen, Hanna. "The Case Against Breastfeeding." *The Atlantic*. April 2009. http://www.theatlantic.com/magazine/archive/2009/04/the-case-against-breast-feeding/307311.

Shields, James. "The Art of *Aidagara*: Ehtics, Aesthetics, and the Quest for an Ontology of Social Existence in Watsuji Tetsurō's *Rinrigaku*." *Asian Philosophy* 19, Issue 3 (2009): 265–283.

Stobbe, Mike. "Hispanic Moms Breastfeed the Most." *NBC News*. March 25, 2010. http://www.nbcnews.com/id/36039199/ns/health-childrens_health/t/hispanic-moms-breast-feed-most/#.V6ty5q6XLGs.

Turner, Victor. "Liminality and Communitas." *The Ritual Process: Structure and Anti-Structure*. Chicago: Aldine Publishing.

Watsuji Tetsurō. *Rinrigaku,* trans. Yamamoto Seisaku and Robert E. Carter. Albany, NY: SUNY Press, 1996.

Yasuo, Yuasa. *The Body: Towards an Eastern Mind-Body Theory*. Nagatamo Shigenori and T.P Kasulis translators. Albany, NY: SUNY Press, 1987.

6

Two Ideas of Education: Amano Teiyū and José Vasconcelos

Agustín Jacinto Zavala

In this paper I present two parallel cases that illustrate the manner in which a philosophy born from reflection on the cultural specificities of a philosopher's own culture becomes the basis for an educational project. Nishida Kitarō (1870–1945) tried to develop his own philosophy on the basis of his own Japanese culture, and his former student Amano Teiyū (1884–1980) sought to place it at the basis of his view and practice of education, planning to carry out his project while he was Minister of Education for Japan (1952–1953), and later as rector of the Peers' School (Gakushū-in). For his part, José María Albino Vasconcelos Calderón (1882–1959) tried to formulate a philosophy that would better reflect a worldview on the basis of some features of Mexican culture; and, being also a man of action, in the years 1921–1924, while Secretary of Public Education, he made changes to the Mexican educational system and cultural promotion that have been influential even to this day. From this twofold consideration, we may perceive the movement toward a world vision not constrained by national borders, in which Eastern and Western cultures complement each other in education provided by the state. Human culture is seen in its transregional dimension, and both society and individual human beings become creative in their continuous transformation.

1. Amano Teiyū

Amano Teiyū was born on September 30, 1884, in Kanagawa province. He graduated in 1909 from Preparatory School 1, whose Director was Nitobe Inazo. That same year, Amano entered the Faculty of Letters in the Philosophy Department at Kyoto Imperial University where he studied philosophy and philosophy of history and from where he graduated in 1912. Following graduation, he held a series of teaching positions[1] until leaving for Heidelberg in 1923 to study Kantian philosophy. After his return he was appointed assistant professor at Kyoto University in 1925, and promoted to professor in 1937 (this same year he was appointed Head of the Student Affairs Section). He taught at Kyoto until 1944.

After the war he worked as a teacher at the First Preparatory School in Tokyo. In 1949 he became Minister of Education in the third (1949–1952) and fourth (1952–1953) Yoshida cabinets. He was Deputy Minister of the Interior from 1950 to 1952, and from 1964 to 1969 he was the first president of Dokkyō University. After the end of his term, he became principal of Dokkyō Gakuen, a post he retained until his death on March 6, 1980.

One approach to Amano Teiyū's theory of education is through his relationship with Nishida Kitarō. I begin with the concept of creativity, which derives from Nishida's philosophy, in which both character training and creativity played important roles, and where the goal of education must be consonant with the mission of the nation in the historical world.[2] It is from this perspective that I would like to discuss some of the ideas of Amano Teiyū that were published in four compilations between 1935 and 1945. As we will see, they capture the thrust of Nishida's views on the themes I have chosen to examine in this text.[3] Concerning Amano's relationship with Nishida Kitarō, we have several references in Yusa Michiko's biography of Nishida,[4] but Amano himself makes other references to it in the books under consideration here.[5]

Although Amano Teiyū's direct contact with Nishida, both as a student and after his return from Germany, lasted for a considerable period,[6] his contact with the neo-Kantian group at Heidelberg University and his own work on Kant[7] have led to his being considered a neo-Kantian. In this paper, I present his views from the perspective of what Ueda Shizuteru calls "Kyoto Philosophy,"[8] though I prefer to call it the "Kyoto circle," which centered around Nishida Kitarō; in contrast to the "Tokyo circle" centered around Inoue Tetsujirō.

Creativity[9]

Despite all the suffering that survival entails, everyone wants to live. Compared to other living creatures, human beings are frail in body and mind. Even if they see good things, they sometimes choose evil, and even though they desire harmony and intimacy, these are not easily achieved, so their lives are full of such contradictions. But human beings are endowed with mind, and even though they are originally prisoners of nature and live in time and space, through their intelligence they are able to transcend those limitations and, through a judicious choice of means, realize their goals.[10] According to Amano, their teleological action involves form (foresight to perceive, transcending time and causality, goals, and the planning that leads to choosing appropriate means to achieve ends), the content of the goal (material or otherwise, its value, and its reason or *dōri*, 道理), and the possibility to choose both the means and the ends. Here, human beings face *dōri* (reason), which is an order of things they must bring about even at the cost of suffering. Human reason differs from natural law, but is not powerless, though it may lie dormant.[11]

Human beings, who are sensitive to values, respond to the demands of *dōri* through sincerity (*makoto* 誠). This brings to life what Amano calls the "sense of reason" (*dōri no kankaku* 道理の感覺), which is the sense that leads toward the reason for things (*mono no dōri* ものの道理), one that can only be apprehended and realized by human beings—to be mediators of reason (*dōri*) is their privilege and destiny. However, they can realize *dōri* only through effort, suffering, and the sacrifice of their own bodies (*kenshin gisei* 獻身犠牲). The call of *dōri* has no force without their consent or if it goes against their will. This is the daemonic and godly aspect of human beings. It is through this freedom to spontaneously decide their attitude that the true freedom of human beings is established, together with the responsibility that accompanies it. At the same time, the sense of reason (*dōri no kankaku*) cannot be externally restricted or touched by the force of authority. This privilege is also the source of human suffering and worry: "it is not easy to be a human being."[12] Even though they enjoy freedom, responsibility is its underside. Further, each human being is a microcosm through which reason is realized. But because an individual apart from the whole is just an abstraction that lacks real existence, the relationship between the individual and the whole is one of the most difficult of all philosophical problems.[13]

Amano analyzed the two prevailing solutions to this problem: individualism and totalism. Individualism considers the individual as existent and the whole as the group of individuals. The individual as an atom can exist separately from the whole or without it. The whole (be it society or the state) is constituted as the conjunction of these atoms and thus disappears when they are scattered. In this case, the whole exists for the sake of the individual. The antecedent of individualism is the emergence of individual self-awareness. But individualism was a peculiarity of modern culture that became highly abstract and now no one is supposed to advocate it. People have come to realize that by transcending our body—which undergoes change as we age—the environment, and so on, we enter social interrelations; the "we" comes to have the same importance as the "I," and their unity becomes internalized. In this way, individual consciousness, group consciousness (*dantai ishiki* 團體意識), and "integral" consciousness (*zentai ishiki* 全體意識) all attain self-awareness, realizing a unity that demands self-preservation. Amano recognized its most recent development in the nation state (*kokumin-teki kokka* 国民的国家).[14] This state is an autonomous reality into which people are born and which they leave upon their death. Individualism rings true insofar as it recognizes the freedom of the subject, and in this regard should not be rejected.[15]

Totalism, the second solution, has one Western and one Eastern direction, according to Amano. Western totalism in general is a negation of individualism and, as negation of negation, returns to a totality (whole) that includes the opportunity for the self-awareness of the individual. In contrast, Japan as a totality (whole) did not break away sufficiently from individual self-awareness.[16] "To negate without self-awareness the self-awareness of the individual just a little awakened is to eliminate individual self-awareness without having previously elevated it. It must be a regression to a substantial whole without having elevated it into a concretely self-aware totality (*gutai-teki jikaku-teki zentai* 具體的自覺的全體)."[17] Here, room remains for further development and "the totalism of Japan must be entirely Japanese and not a translation" of Western totalism.[18] In the meantime, there is no guarantee that egoism or materialism will not become the life principle of Japanese society. This is why "We must deeply savor the truth of the saying, 'when the Great Way declines, benevolence and justice appear (*daidô sutarete ningi ari* 大道廢れて仁義有り).'"[19]

Totalism can assume a variety of structures: economic, environmental, materialistic, geometrical, vitalistic, developmental, and so on. In every case, the totality (whole) is real and it becomes difficult to give life to the individual. When history or society are thought of in this way, the spontaneity of the individual is negated, there is no moral freedom and, consequently, no responsibility or morality.[20] For Amano, this was a problem that had yet to be solved by the Christian medieval worldview, Spinoza, or Leibniz. However, the philosophy of nothingness of Nishida Kitarō sheds light upon this difficult problem that cannot be solved with a philosophy of Being.[21] Amano says that while in Nishida's philosophy the individual is unique, it is never alone and is always in interaction with other individuals through a mediator, which is the environment, i.e., through a world that moves dialectically in three dimensions: "The movement of the world, in relation to matter is simple movement, in relation to living beings it is formation, but in relation to human existence it is *creation*."[22]

As for Nishida, so also for Amano the historical world is a world of creation, a world of production, and the individual is its creative element. When what is made becomes independent from its maker, true creation is being realized. Creativity is the essence and mission of human beings.[23] The world incessantly advances from the past to the future; but it also advances in space: it is temporal and spatial, fluid and solidified, linear and circular. This world of the self-identity of contradictories infinitely moves from the made into the maker in formative activity and dialectical development. And because in itself it is self-forming, there is concrete life in the world, a life that is constituted in the harmony of disharmony. Life thrives in this harmony of disharmony, and in its harmony the various forms are born. A species is a fixed form of this formative activity, a form of the mutual determination of individuals; consequently, the world is constituted from innumerable species. An individual can only work through its species, so it can be said that "the form of the work of the Japanese cannot be other than Japanese."[24] The self-formation of the world has the character of an instinctual species. And when an instinctual species enfolds the absolute, the world is constituted as a society in some region, and the formation of society must have a mythical-religious character. From another viewpoint, it can be said that society is a self-identity of contradictories: many≡one, matter≡spirit, instinct≡intellect, and so on.[25] And as individuals "we receive our life as creative elements in a creative world which goes on forming itself".[26]

The state as formation of the species must be passionate, while as a legal-moral formation it must be a realm of duty. It cannot lean in either direction. In its scientific aspect the state has the character of reality, and as religious and moral formation it must have authority. When a formation with the character of species enfolds the absolute, it takes on the character of a state, thereby becoming world-historical. The absolute, in turn, manifests itself in individual creation, and the world forms itself in individual creative activity. Nishida philosophy is a philosophy of nothingness in which the Way activates both totality and individual: by placing the totality as the universal of nothingness with the character of substance. This philosophy thinks the dialectical relation between the environment as object and the individual as subject in terms of the one and the many, and considers the individual as a creative element. Amano says that this is a brief exposition of his understanding of Nishida's philosophy, in which the absolute, the state and the individual determine themselves and, through this determination, a dialectical world is brought into existence.[27]

For Amano, as for Nishida, creativity is a prevalent characteristic in history: the individual is creative, the world is creative, and the absolute is creative. The individual can create through its capacity for sensing values, for planning and free action: "Creativity must really be the essence and mission of human beings. Our life is creation." [28] In its daily actions, the individual constructs itself. In this sense, habit has an important moral meaning and constitutes the meaning of training (*shugyō* 修業). This is well-expressed in Nishida's philosophy through the principle of "from the made into the maker." [29] The life course of the individual is a creative process that takes part in the creative activity of a national people as the creation of its culture. This culture, in turn, forms the people and, at the same time, is a world-creation. "The realm of culture, as a public *basho* (場所) of the world" [30] is a place of creation in which all peoples of the world can take part, and only through its mediation can the conflict among species be overcome. Creation "is founded upon the contradictoriness of the world." [31] It is the "historical activity of historical life" [32] and the essential and real activity of human beings, one that elevates the particular unto universal and mediates the universal in the particular. In a world full of contradictions, "suffering, fatigue, blood and tears become the life of creation and shine with eternal brilliance." [33]

It is from this perspective, inspired by Nishida's philosophy, that Amano approaches the problem of Japanese education, stating that "the present situation of education in our country not only cannot carry out its mission of promoting creativity but, on the contrary, has fallen into a resulting obstruction of creativity." [34] This is why the reform of education is a most urgent task. [35] The health of the school-age population is another problem, as tuberculosis afflicts not only the students but also their teachers. But the whole population must be healthy if people are to "shoulder the responsibility for the future prosperity of Japan." [36] Amano puts this succinctly by affirming that present-day education should be the basis for the progress of Japan. Education should be focused on promoting the creativity inherent in the Japanese soul, but based on living knowledge. He thought that the best way to achieve this was to simplify matters, beginning with the educational system itself: the status of educators (ranking, salaries, and so on), the curriculum (courses offered and class hours) and the examination system. In this manner, education would respond to the needs of the nation. [37]

This brings us back to Amano's view of creativity in human life. In order to survive in nature we must learn its laws, obey them, and receive their benefits. It is our obeisance to the laws of nature through human intelligence and wisdom that allows us to use it. [38] In order to properly conduct our actions in the world we must have a sense of reason (*dōri no kankaku* 道理の感覺) that tells us the order that must be realized. [39] It is only when human beings offer their own bodies in sacrifice that the control of *dōri* manifests itself. Only human beings can sense the call of reason, but it is up to each one of us to decide his/her response to it.[40] This is why our existence is moral, and we are persons. In this sense, even if we should lose our freedom of action, the sense of reason remains, and the basis for our self-respect is precisely the fact that we are still capable of freedom as a fundamental characteristic of our personality. Even though constrained bodily by nature, we can still set our goals and act: we still have the freedom to sense reason (*dōri wo kankaku suru* 道理を感覺する).[41] Both the environment and conditions present problems for us, but not their solution. For this we must depend on ourselves. The free individual has its own existential structure as a microcosm; it is a special individual that is not realized unless reason (*dōri*) is present.[42]

In this sense, Amano's understanding of creativity rejects either strict individualism or strict totalism. As noted above, Amano says that in Nishida philosophy, the individual exists and acts through its own self-determination but, at the same time, it can only exist in interrelation with other individual(s), which means that, while being independent of each other, they must have something in common as their mediator.[43] This mediator that enfolds the individuals is their environment, their world, which is a contradictory unity that includes the past and is pregnant with the future, and in which the present goes on determining itself. It is a world that moves from the made into the maker.[44]

An example Nishida used in order to present this idea concerns a sculptor who while making a statue decides that the following cut depends on the result of the previous one. Amano thinks this is deeply meaningful when applied to the life of human individuals. We are our own sculptors and continually create ourselves: one action of ours determines the next. In this way, what is historically made in turn determines its maker. This principle can be seen in or applied to our inquiry into reality, including the formation of the individual, of society, or of the state. In the case of the state, it can be said that it is constituted through the fact that a people enfolds the idea:

> the State does not simply have scientific reality but also has a religious moral authority. . . . And the formation of the species becomes world-historical through its enfolding of the Idea. Now, the State is born because a people enfolds the absolute: and it is through the fact that human individuals with the character of species–formation—i. e., through the state—reflect the absolute, that they can become concrete personalities. This is the meaning of "constructively hearing the voice of God as creative elements"

of a creative world. And if unity is to be sought, it must be sought in the creation of culture.[45]

The creativity of the Japanese people is inherent to them, not only as individuals but as a people. Through their creativity as the practice of reason (*dōri*) they take part in the creation of the world, contribute to the increase of individual and social enlightenment, and ensure the survival of the imperial country. Creativity cannot be evaluated from the outside, and it is not easy to decide what kind of life is creative and real. "The gist of it is for each one of us to exhaust *makoto* [誠を盡す, to do one's best] ... [because] true creation means for those who are constituted in *makoto*, to enfold the Idea and to possesses eternity."[46]

Education

Amano's views on creativity inform his approach to education. Amano says that an educator should keep in mind that appreciating the naturalness of human beings is part of education. This implies the problems of body-education (*tai-iku* 體育), which is a material basis for the practice of virtue, and the social use of knowledge.[47] Amano says that "education cannot be carried out without a denial of self in view of the *Ōyake* [公].... [and] this academic spirit, according to the theory of professor Nishida Kitarō, is also the Japanese spirit."[48]

The whole life of a person should be a process of education; starting from the womb, human education and development are achieved through home education, school education, social education, and self-education. The influence of nature is also important in this process. Education is the development and cultivation of the character and talents of each person. Nature has entrusted us with our human education. We receive talents that require development and cultivation. Even though we are restricted by nature and society, we still have the freedom to create ourselves and the voice of conscience to guide us. This condition leaves enough room for spontaneity. In spite of natural and social restrictions, our growth and development are possible. As Nishida's philosophy explains, that which has been made determines its maker. This teleological process, which may be viewed as a poietic process, can be transcended through our human freedom.[49]

Whenever an individual, characterized by its spirit and natural capacities, is born into a society, a new and peculiar element that enriches humanity is added to the world. But this new element needs education to develop itself: its capacities, character, knowledge and personality must be developed and cultivated. Even though the educational process tries to instill 'sincerity in public service,' it is still very difficult to appropriate the spirit of such an objective element as the *Ohoyake* (Amano here uses おほやけ).[50] Moral education encounters great difficulties due to individual attitudes, natural inclinations and the influence of society. But the educational endeavor, which is like the creation of works of art amid material limitations, should promote the self-perception of each individual. Here, human freedom and creativity play a great role. Our true self becomes manifest through our spiritual effort: to bring about its manifestation and growth through education is our responsibility. This is why "education consists in this creation."[51]

Without good individuals society cannot be good, and without a high-level social foundation, superior individuals will not be formed. Education comprises the intellectual, moral, and bodily aspects, each of which should contribute to the cultivation of "wisdom, humanitarianism and courage [智仁勇],"[52] which Amano names as the three main Eastern virtues; or to the cultivation of the four Platonic virtues, "wisdom, moderation, courage and justice [智慧、節制、勇気、正義]."[53] But virtue can only be appropriated through practice, which turns it into flesh and blood, and marks our *praxis*. We cannot master knowledge, virtue, or our bodily condition unless, unconditionally yielding to the requirements of each, we practice and this practice conforms our *hexis*. Not only is intellectual education at the same time moral education, but bodily education is also moral education.[54]

The goal of bodily education, rather than being the perfection of the body, is training in the respect for rules and the cultivation of group spirit. But we cannot master the rules unless we practice them. This can be observed easily in sports, whose reason for existence is to cultivate the spirit of cooperation. Both individually and as a whole, participants must play their part and give their best (*makoto wo tsukusu*) in their position.[55] There are few other opportunities, other than sports, to learn in fact and reason that to die for the whole is to live for it. This is why sports competitions have an educational meaning, as can be seen in sports like *jūdō* (柔道), *kendō* (劍道, Japanese fencing) and *kyūdō* (弓道, archery), in which our spirit is refined through the mediation of these arts.[56]

The spirit of cooperation requires the self-perceptive operation of each personality, which lives through dying so that the whole may become a true whole. We reach this spirit of cooperation "through the comprehension in lived-experience of the relationship between individual and whole."[57] We must understand alumni associations in the light of this ideal of cultivating the spirit of cooperation. Through all their activities and organs, educational organizations develop and educate the human side of their students.[58] Their activities entail restrictions, but also creation: "education should be creation."[59] When we look at present-day educational institutions in Japan, it is most regrettable that the examination system obstructs the independence of schools.[60]

For Amano, ideally, all educational institutions should be independent but, at the same time, form a system. Unfortunately, "they have lost their independence and have become expedients for examinations, with the result that ultimately true education cannot be carried out".[61] Instruction is given, but not education, and study has become a means for passing examinations. The result is that intellectual and moral education cannot be conducted. As a result, we should worry about the future of the state.

> Liberating grade school students, at least, from the suffering of examinations is a nodal problem for Japanese education. An indispensable countermeasure is to include middle schools in the regional system, because this problem cannot be solved no matter how the method of entrance examinations is conceived. This implies a great expense that is inevitable for the future prosperity of Japan.[62]

Furthermore, entrance examinations have a negative effect on the students who fail to pass them because they feel their dignity is lost, while passing them does not necessarily mean a bright future and could, instead, induce an arrogant attitude. Instead of entrance examinations, other countries (Germany for example) have state examinations for different professions.[63] The reform of this unhealthy educational system should begin from its simplification: the courses, the examination system, the number of class hours, and the discrimination in teachers' allowances. "The reform of Japanese education! The advance of Japan must start from here."[64] There are additional problems that afflict the Japanese educational system, but, for Amano, one of the greatest is the lack of the promotion of creativity: "All cultural activities, including politics and economics, should be creative." But we should keep in mind that if the flight of the spirit is curtailed, creativity does not arise.[65]

Basically, "virtue is power" (徳は力である): both intellectual and bodily strength proceed from virtue. In this sense, intellectual education is moral education. Our entire life is a continuous moral education. But the kernel of virtue emerges in our self-transcendence and arises in the denial of self for the Ōyake (公). In order to reach an understanding of this we must start from the realm of the objective and cultivate the spirit of devoted sacrifice (*kenshin gisei* 獻身犠牲) to it, and doing one's own best (*makoto wo tsukusu* 誠を盡す) for it. And this means that "the foundation of education must be the lived experience of our comprehension of the fact of living through dying."[66]

Teaching morality

Amano writes that in recent times (the 1930s) emphasis has been placed throughout society on the promotion of moral education. "No one would oppose this since education is, in the final analysis, moral education. We could even say that life itself is an educational process whose objective is human perfection (*ningen kansei* 人間完成). There is no need for words to understand the importance of moral education."[67] However, when intellectual and moral education are seen as opposites and one or the other is emphasized, several problems arise. Another difficulty is how to promote such moral education. Promotion itself is not easy. "If we think that anti-moral and irrational things are prevalent in real-life society, it will be clear that moral education is very difficult. In a society in which lies, hypocrisy, and immorality are rampant, ... morality lacks authority."[68]

There are several reasons for its lack of power. First, it is due to "the structure of morality itself."[69] For Amano, moral—that is, personal—values are not like objective values or those related to material things; rather they are values related to our action and to the activity of our will. Though it is not impossible to pursue them intentionally, it is extremely difficult to do so. The first reason is that moral values do not depend on materiality, as can be seen in the fact that generosity is not measured by the amount of money given away. Moral value accrues to material value, and yet is independent of, and free from, material value.[70] The second reason for the difficulty of moral education is that for Amano moral laws differ completely from natural laws in regard to their realization. From their very origin, natural laws absolutely control nature but moral laws do not. Virtues such as love, justice, honesty, faithfulness and so on do not control reality as natural laws do, nor do they determine the morality of actions or the activity of the will, as a basis for the control of reality. Being guided by one's own conscience does not necessarily apply to mundane affairs, even though in real life there is respect for morality. But moral laws do not control human life or society in the way natural laws control nature.[71] Amano states, "It is possible that even under the shadow of the highly proclaimed Clarification of the Kokutai (*Kokutai meichō* 国體明徵), private gain and desire extend their roots".[72] These difficulties, inherent in the structure of moral values themselves, present at least three obstacles to teaching morality.

The first reason is that texts on morality (*shūshin* 修身)—containing models of the sayings and actions of excellent persons—are used in primary and middle schools to elucidate moral themes, teach ordinary admonitions, and concretely explain them. This is a good way to teach morality, but it only teaches the formalities of moral action and is deficient in its consideration of the circumstances of the lives of students. Models are always idealized and it is not easy for real living people to meet such special cases; indeed, even if they are encountered it is doubtful whether the model will be applicable. Reality is continually changing and each person's circumstances differ. There is no use in simply learning the models of a past epoch and of extraordinary people by heart. Occasionally, it helps to know a model, but in the case of morality it is also dangerous to know the form without knowing its animating spirit. Even though in extreme occasions people just carry out the outward models of morality, such practice invites the criticism of ordinary people as pharisaic. In this sense, *shūshin* courses need other resources, otherwise they will form pharisaic students. In short, the best can easily be accompanied by the worst. If values are altered they become anti-values and bring about great disasters. *Shūshin* courses are important, but their danger is great: for Amano morality is the highest value but hypocrisy is the worst.[73]

The second reason concerning *shūshin* courses is the danger that through *shūshin* texts students may learn so many themes and moral sayings and actions that their moral sense becomes blunted and they lose the freshness of their feelings toward morality. Depending on the manner of teaching, a feeling of opposition can also be provoked in the students. People lose their sensibility toward customary things, even if it's the majestic Mount Fuji. But moral sensibility is a human privilege and the center of personality, and although *shūshin* courses are responsible for polishing it, they can also destroy it.[74]

A third danger of *shūshin* courses is that the teachers responsible for them think that *shūshin* is their exclusive possession, or consider themselves as technicians in a course for which they are not responsible, forgetting that school education contributes to the perfection of the personality (*jinkaku kansei* 人格完成) of the students.[75]

If one maintains that moral education should be promoted, the aforementioned difficulties cannot be overlooked. One experience is worth a hundred explanations. "The purest form of moral education is constituted *in direct personal interaction*,"[76] and the realization of moral values through the actions of the teachers is the highest form of moral education. The reason is that the actual experience of virtue is the best way to lead students toward an understanding of virtue. Furthermore, the moral value of an action resides in its motive, its purpose aided by its material side, as in the case of a selfless action. This is the reason why it cannot be said that there is no moral education unless its direct purpose is the morality of the students. A practical method is needed in this case and this is where intellectual and moral education can meet.[77]

A classroom situation in which the teacher forgets him/herself in concentrating solely on elevating the students' knowledge is a good example of this. Although the teacher is not directly interested in moral education, his/her self-forgetful dedication in the classroom is a good example of it. "The axis of moral education is to convince the students of the moral order".[78] But a strict conscience sometimes is a disadvantage in the struggle for survival, and we need a strong conviction concerning moral order if we want to practice benevolence while forgetting ourselves.[79]

Moral education must keep the moral order of the world within its vision. The study of history through the eyes of reason can help us in this task because in current society there are many instances of immorality and irrationality, which could lead us to despair. In this way, we can see that the acquisition of knowledge nourishes our moral convictions, and that it is only through intellectual education that moral education reaches its completion. Conversely, science teachers should cease to be mere technicians and become contributors to "the perfection of the students' personality, [which means] the cultivation of knowledge and virtue."[80] Without training there is no teaching, and true moral education is not achieved unless teachers realize their true mission. In this sense, according to Amano, at the time education in Japan was not truly independent.[81]

Amano points out two great pressures that greatly constrained Japanese education in the 1930s and 1940s. The first was that military instructors were responsible for the education in primary and secondary schools, while parents and people in general thought that their children were receiving an excellent instruction in being trained as the military. The second was that the administrative structure of the education system was in the hands of people lacking pedagogical knowledge and experience, which resulted in a lack of independence at the school level. The result of these two pressures was the distortion of primary and secondary education. Amano points out the need for regaining the independence of the school system, for education to be "in the hands of people who have knowledge and experience in education [and] feel education as a vocation," and for educators to assume the responsibility "to overthrow the present subordinate status of education."[82]

As part of the solution to these problems, Amano states that educators should become aware of the subordinate position in which the education system had been placed; that they should abandon their internecine disputes "and unite against this common enemy."[83] He points out that people in other occupations "acquire great social power through group formation, [and that] officers and teachers can also attain it because originally both are well trained and education is no less important for the State than the military."[84] If teachers form local associations throughout Japan, their profession would become strong, stable and acquire social influence.[85] Amano called for a great educational reform carried out from the inside by professional educators. He writes that he is not in favor of "people involved in educational work who are unconcerned with social justice [and] who, in fact, are an obstacle to the emergence of educational reform ... Unless educators themselves become strong, nobody will free education and educators from their social shackles."[86]

As the discussion above shows, we have been able to see how Amano incorporated into his own thinking some concepts that are central in Nishida's philosophy, in both its theoretical and practical aspects. Although before the end of World War II Amano never held a government position and was highly critical of the educational situation in Japan, we can perceive two sides to his position. On the one hand, as an academic philosopher interested in education, Amano opposes the control of education by military and government officials who lack educational experience. On the other, once the war began, he sought methods to streamline Japanese education that would strengthen the state. In the first case, he was silenced by the authorities and one of his books was banned. In the second, his proposals influenced or at least coincided with, those of the movement of middle-school teachers. Indeed, as the war situation worsened, the military government made changes that paralleled some of the ideas contained in his published texts; in the post-war period, he became Minister of Education (1952–1953).

As we will see in what follows, José Vasconcelos shares many of the concerns that inspired Amano's educational reforms, including the focus on the role of educators in the active training of whole persons in both body and mind, and the role of the state in supporting education as a means to realizing a more just and moral society.

2. José Vasconcelos's educational ideas and practices

Vasconcelos was born in 1882 in the city of Oaxaca. In 1899 he entered the National Preparatory School and after graduation he studied law at the National School of Jurisprudence. He was appointed rector of the National University by President Adolfo de la Huerta in 1920. In 1921 he became Secretary of Public Education, a post he held until 1924. This is the period that interests us here. In what follows, we will examine how Vasconcelos's philosophical, political, and social ideas influenced his approaches to educational theory and practice.

Philosophical ideas

Vasconcelos developed a system that emphasized aesthetic intuition and called it "aesthetic monism,"[87] in which Bergsonian creative evolution[88] and Kantian aesthetic intuition result in a form of Plotininan (aesthetic) monism. The kernel is an aesthetic a priori that through a coordinating method is active, just as rhythm, melody and harmony are active in a musical symphony. His monism was based on a humanism that emphasized the diversity and continuous transformation of human beings, society, the state, and the world. This is the reason why for him a philosopher is someone who has arrived at a worldview in which beauty and aesthetic emotion become knowledge. True knowledge is aesthetic knowledge because even though it is acquired through the senses, imagination, and the intellect, it is through emotion that knowledge translates into practice. Knowledge is put into practice through selfless service to society and state, in view of the highest ideals that result in the active union of the true, the beautiful, and the good. The active school induces this practice through occupational training centered on the essence of the fatherland, which, for Vasconcelos, included both indigenous and Hispanic origins.

Political theory

Vasconcelos's graduation thesis was titled: "A Dynamic Theory of Right" ("Teoría dinámica del derecho" 1905), and centered on the dynamic development of right[89] and the idea of natural justice. Dynamic right means the free interplay of all individual energies in constant dynamic change. This allows for a scientific approach to the concept of right and of law as the verbal expression and praxis of right. For Vasconcelos, the state is a political morphology, which is born as self-expression of a society that maintains a dynamic and unstable equilibrium with its environment. Right is the manifestation of the law of the distribution of energy proportionate to causes or needs and is in constant dynamic change.[90]

His position translates into a democratic liberalism strongly influenced by vitalism, which justifies a dynamic view of legislation to address three great national problems: (1) the absence of pluralism that homogenizes the citizen; (2) the lack of opportunities for the free participation of all individual and social forces within the state; and (3) the poor development of legislation that does not include new rights and their diverse modalities.[91]

Social theory

For Vasconcelos, the formation of society rests on the following five main points: (1) a theory of cosmic, social, and political rhythm; (2) a theory of the revulsion of energy that disrupts ossified structures and dynamizes the people and the country; (3) the cycles of the transmutation of energy; (4) the theory of aesthetic monism; and (5) the relationship between the transmutation cycles and the praxis of an ideology.[92]

Starting from his conception of culture, Vasconcelos describes the strata of Mexican culture—as in the typology of Eduard Spranger's *Lebensformen* (*Life-forms*)—the ideal of Mexican culture, and the place of the indigenous ethnic groups in Mexico.[93] This viewpoint can be seen in his *Estudios Indostánicos* in which he presents the task of cultural synthesis that would result in multiculturality.[94]

Vasconcelos calls for a unifying ideology that would include his views on language, religion, and racial mixing (mestizaje, miscegenation). His proposal translates into: mestizo, Latin American and Catholic, based on his view of contemporary society. He considers that this ideology is based on reality, but can disappear unless consciously formulated and put into practice through the Mexican Revolution as a requirement for social justice. And in order to keep it alive, the state must promote education for the whole nation so that every citizen would be able to take part in the transformation of society and the state.[95]

Educational theory

Vasconcelos named his educational proposal as "constructivist education," also named "structuring education." It can be described under five headings: (1) free, non-doctrinal education as a function of the government; (2) humanistic ("aesthetic") education for the integral development of the human being as the essential function of culture; (3) education that covers the four main aspects of the physical, technical, social, and "spiritual";[96] (4) nationalistic education that would be imparted in view of the state's highest aspirations; and (5) education in accordance with one's own culture that would lead to the realization of the ultimate values of the "cosmic race."

His structuring pedagogy aimed, beyond scientific training, for the attunement of the teaching activity to a given view of life, in order to lead the spirit toward its full development. This development took place in the material, intellectual, spiritual, and socio-cultural life forms, each with its own view of life and, in this sense, the school should be "the guide of society," providing the basic conscious experience through its activities.

Educational practice[97]

During his period as Secretary of Public Instruction (1921–1924), Vasconcelos aimed for a nationalistic education of the citizen even while maintaining a multicultural approach through the above-mentioned dynamic theory of right that would bring about the final stage of humanity in the cosmic race.

This resulted in a new position within Mexico's educational history: after more than three centuries of educational control by the Catholic church; after a period of liberalism in which the main emphasis was on freedom of education (in 1861 this was a responsibility of the Ministry of Justice and Public Instruction); and after a period of positivism in education (under President Benito Juarez in 1867 and 1869, the Organic Laws of Public Instruction were passed), which lasted until 1910.

After Vasconcelos was appointed in 1921 to the Secretary of Public Instruction and Fine Arts, he petitioned for the modification of a section of Article 73 of the 1917 Constitution, and his role was renamed Secretary of Public Education. Under this legal framework he organized its educational activities through the School Department, the Library Department, and the Department of Fine Arts.

The School Department not only supervised ordinary primary, middle, and high schools, and universities but also oversaw programs for indigenous education, technical education, teachers' colleges, and rural normal schools. Through this department, Vasconcelos established the Alphabetization Campaign, cultural missions, and vocational schools for technical education. During his administration, the following schools were established: School of Construction Masters, Technological School for Teachers, Technical School of Arts and Crafts, National School of Graphical Arts, Technical School for Shorthand Specialists, and Housing School for Young Women.

Through the Library Department, a library system was established and promoted the publication of world classics.[98] Although he planned a National Library, it did not materialize, but other projects, such as mobile libraries, rural libraries, school libraries, urban libraries, technical libraries, and public libraries, were installed throughout the country.

Lastly, through the Department of Fine Arts (Departamento de Bellas Artes), he created the National Institute of Fine Arts and promoted the artistic movement known as "muralismo" in which Diego Rivera, José Clemente Orozco, and David

Alfaro Siqueiros participated. He was responsible for the construction of theaters for dramatic representations, poetic recitals and musical performances. And he also favored the promotion of gymnastics.[99]

In light of the above discussion of Vasconcelos's theories and practices, there are several aspects that call for attention in his view of education, and I would like to mention six of them:

1. The change in mentality away from the nineteenth-century positivism, and a turn toward a creative transformation of the world, society, and the individual;
2. An education based on new philosophical premises, such as Bergsonian and neo-Kantian;
3. The Active School movement inspired in the New School of Johann Heinrich Pestalozzi, Fichte, and Georg Kerschensteiner, which sought to overcome dichotomies, such as mind/body, intellect/emotion, learning/ practice, and so on;
4. A turn toward multiculturalism and universalism led by the educational activity of the state;
5. A new emphasis on education addressed to the body, emotion, and intuition;[100]
6. The final aim of education is to give human beings a value-based form of life,[101] and to form them as good patriotic citizens following the political ideas of Simón Bolivar.[102]

As Vasconcelos described his view of the future, "The world will be divided into four or five great powers that will collaborate in everything good and beautiful, each one expressing the good and the beautiful in their own manner," among which he mentions the Ibero-American race in the South and the "Russian and Japanese in Asia."[103]

3. Conclusion

Both Amano and Vasconcelos called for a radical change of direction in education. Amano was primarily interested in the administrative aspect and the manner in which the fundamentals of education should be attended to. And, instead of a militaristic training (that had appropriated the teaching of *shūshin* morals through the examples of military exploits; led to the oversight of the moral aspect of education; and emphasized a chauvinistic worldview), Amano envisaged the formation of a moral citizen within an open, internationalist world. Amano pointed out that the examination system was a nodal problem at the time (a problem that is still present and is popularly known as "examination hell") that required an entrance examination for secondary, preparatory, and university studies. The system was expensive for the country and had a negative effect on the students (both for those who passed and became arrogant, and those who did not and became despondent). His proposal was a state examination system for the professions, just as he had seen it at work in Germany. On his part, Vasconcelos presented a new ideal of education that would contribute to the formation of a multicultural and universalistic mentality among citizens.

Their shared emphasis on creativity and holistic pedagogies deserve explicit mention here. Both Amano and Vasconcelos pointed out the need for the promotion of creativity in students, so that they would be creative in all their endeavors: cultural, political, economic, and so on. This would have positive repercussions for the nationalism of the citizen. In the case of Vasconcelos this is also strongly supported through a dynamic conception of right and the legal system. Moreover, taking their inspiration from the Greeks and from the New School movement, both Amano and Vasconcelos laid emphasis on the integral training of the student (putting aside dichotomies such as mind/body, intellect/ emotion, human beings/nature, and so on) to promote a holistic vision of the human being within nature, society, the state, and international relations. This holistic vision, which is nowadays imperiled by one-sided views of reality, is needed for a full and peaceful life in our present world. Hence, these are among the most important aspects of their educational proposals that can and should be incorporated into our contemporary educational theory and practice.

Notes

1   He was appointed assistant to the seminar on ethics in the philosophy department at Kyoto Imperial University. In 1915 he became professor at Preparatory School 7 in Kyushu. Then in 1920 he was appointed professor at Gakushūin University, where he taught for three years.

2   Jacinto Z. Agustín, "Nishida Kitarō's Views on Education: 1895–1935," *Nishida Tetsugakkai Nenpō* No. 13 (2016): 191–171.

3   Since there are few publications on Amano's writing in Western languages in relation to the influence of Nishida philosophy, my paper is largely a paraphrase of several selections from the period 1935 to 1945.

4 Yusa, Michiko, *Zen and Philosophy: An Intellectual Biography of Nishida Kitarō* (Honolulu: University of Hawaii Press, 2002), 10, 120, 126, 192, 197, 198, 200, 212, 216, 233, 290–291, 292–293.

5 For the context of Amano's activities in the aftermath of WWII in Japanese education I relied, among other works, on Satō Kesao (ed.). *Sengo kyōiku no sōgō hyōka* (A Comprehensive Evaluation of Post-war Education). See References.

6 As can be seen in Nishida's diary and letters, his contact with Amano included extracurricular activities while the latter was a student. Later, from 1913 to 1914, through Nishida's intervention, Amano met Konoe Ayamaro, Harada Kumao, and Kido Kōichi. Nishida became interested in Amano's translation of Kant, and invited him to the philosophy department in 1925.

7 Between 1921 and 1931, Amano translated and published Kant's *Critique of Pure Reason* in three volumes.

8 Ueda Shizuteru, ed., *Zen to Kyoto Tetsugaku* (Kyoto: Tōeisha, 2006).

9 Nishida became interested in creativity primarily through Bergson's *Creative Evolution* (1907). On January 3, 1925, Nishida asked Amano to send him, from Germany, Anselm Rohner's, *Das Schöpfungsproblem bei Moses Maimonides, Albertus Magnus und Thomas von Aquin* (Munster: Aschendorff, 1913). However, in both the old (NKZ, XVII, 404) and new (NKZ, nXVIII, 109) editions, the first name of the author is omitted, his last name appears as "Rohmer", and the title as "d. Schöpfungsproblem." The references are to the *Nishida Kitarō Zenshū* (西田幾多郎全集, The Complete Works of Nishida Kitarō). Tokyo: Iwanami shoten, 1966–1967, second edition. I use NKZ, followed by the volume number in capitals, and page number. In the references to the volumes in the new edition (2004–2005) the volume number is preceded by an "n".

10 Amano, *Dōri e no ishi* (Tokyo: Iwanami shoten), 202, 205–206.

11 Ibid., 206.

12 Ibid., 214.

13 Amano, *Dōri e no ishi* (Tokyo: Iwanami Shoten), 215–217.

14 Ibid., 220.

15 Ibid., 221.

16 Ibid., 220–221.

17 Ibid., 221.

18 Ibid., 222.

19 Ibid., 223.

20 Ibid., 224.

21 Ibid., 225.

22 Ibid., 227–228.

23 Ibid., 228.

24 Ibid., 230.

25 Ibid., 228–230.

26 Ibid., 231.

27 Ibid., 230–233.

28 Ibid., 234–235, 237.

29 Ibid., 235.

30 Ibid., 236.

31 Ibid., 237.

32 Ibid., 239.

33 Ibid.

34 Ibid., 240.

35 Ibid., 242.

36 Ibid., 241.

37 Ibid., pp. 242–243.

38 Amano, *Gakusei ni atauru sho* (Tokyo: Iwanami Shoten, ([1939] 1940), 206.

39 Ibid., 208.

40 Ibid., 210–211.

41 Ibid., 212.

42 Ibid., 213–214.

43 Ibid., 219.

44 Ibid., 219–221. He restates his position in *Dōri e no ishi*, 226.

45 Ibid., 225–226.

46 Ibid., 229–230.

47 Amano, *Dōri no kankaku* (Tokyo: Iwanami Shoten, [1937] 1945), 205–206.

48 Amano, *Dōri e no ishi*, 152–153. Here Amano follows Nishida's *The Problem of Japanese Culture* (日本文化の問題).

49 Amano, *Shinnen to Jissen* (Tokyo: Iwanami Shoten, 1944), 383–387.

50 Ibid., 387–388.

51 Ibid., 389–392.

52 Ibid., 393–394.

53 Ibid., 396.

54 Ibid., 397.

55 Ibid., 398.

56 Ibid., 398–399.

57 Ibid., 400.

58 Ibid., 400–401.

59 Ibid., 401.

60 Ibid., 400–401.

61 Ibid.

62 Ibid., 401–402.

63 Ibid., 402.

64 Amano. *Dōri e no ishi*, 242–243.

65 Ibid., 403.

66 Ibid., 403–404. Cf. *Dōri e no ishi*, 210.

67 Amano. *Dōri no kankaku*, 238. Here follows a three-part critique of the *shûshin* education which began in the 1890s and in time became the core of militarist values up to the Second World War.

68 Ibid., 239.

69 Ibid., 240.

70 Ibid., 240–242.

71 Ibid., 243–245.

72 Ibid., 247.

73 Ibid., 247–248.

74 Ibid., 249–250.

75 Ibid., 250.

76 Ibid., 252, emphasis added.

77 Ibid., 251–253.

78 Ibid., 256.

79 Ibid., 255–257.

80 Ibid., 259.

81 Ibid.

82 Ibid., 259–260.

83 Ibid.

84 Ibid., 262.

85 Although at the time this seemed a good proposal, we should note that the creation in 1947 of the 日本教職員組合 *Nihon Kyōshoku'in Kumiai* (Japan Teachers Union or *Nikkyô-so*) resulted in other kinds of problems for national education.

86 Amano. *Dōri no kankaku*, pp. 262.

87 "I aspired to a monism, to a coherence between experience and vision. In science itself I would find the way towards the divine presence that sustains the world." Vasconcelos, *Obras completas* Vol. I, 485.

88 "We accepted the new French philosophy (Bergson, Poincaré, and so on)." Ibid., 54; see also 41, 48–49, 70–71.

89 "I wrote concerning right as the power and internal dynamism of social relations", Ibid., 509.

90 See References, under Jacinto Z., "La teoría de la formación de la sociedad en José Vasconcelos", and "La Teoría Dinámica del Derecho de José Vasconcelos".

91 Jacinto Z., "La *Teoría Dinámica del Derecho* de José Vasconcelos," *Crónica Legislativa* Año V, Nueva Época, No. 7 (febrero–marzo 1996): 99–108.

92 Jacinto Z., "La teoría de la formación de la sociedad en José Vasconcelos," *Revista Relaciones* 46, Vol. XII (1996): 99–127.

93 Jacinto Z., "Las etnias y la cultura mexicana en José Vasconcelos," *Revista Relaciones* 91, Vol. XIII (2002): 163–192.

94   Jacinto Z., *"Estudios Indostánicos* de José Vasconcelos y la multiculturalidad,"* in
     Escritores y escritos de la revolufia, edited by Álvaro Ochoa Serrano (Zamora, Mich.:
     El Colegio de Michoacán, 2004), 167–192.

95   Jacinto Z., "Nishida Kitarō y José Vasconcelos," *Revista Relaciones* 30, Vol. VIII
     (1987): 60–87.

96   Here we can point to Kerschensteiner's inclusion of the "spiritual" and the "saintly"
     among the absolute values that education should inculcate. Ernesto Meneses
     Morales, *Tendencias educativas oficiales en México, 1911–1934* (México: Centro de
     Estudios Educativos, 1986), 10–11.

97   For a detailed account of Vasconcelos's educational ideas, collaborators and
     activities during his tenure as Secretary of Public Education, see Meneses,
     Tendencias educativas oficiales en México, 1911–1934, 311–442 (Chapters VIII and
     IX). For some documents concerning Mexican education, see www.yumpu.com/es/
     document/view/1285861/educacion-en-el-desarrollo-historico-de-Mexico II.pdf
     (accessed 3xii2016).

98   Vasconcelos declared that he copied this educational novelty from Lunacharsky.
     Vasconcelos, *Obras completas*. Vol. I, 1187.

99   Alicia Molina, ed., *Vasconcelos, José: Antología de textos sobre educación* (México:
     SEP 80/8, 1981) 19–30, 290–303.

100 Roberto Luquín Guerra, "La intuición originaria en la filosofía de José Vasconcelos,"
     Signos filosóficos Vol. VIII, No. 16 (julio–diciembre 2006): 97–124.

101 Meneses, *Tendencias educativas oficiales en México, 1911–1934*, 11.

102 Rosado Zacarías, *José Vasconcelos* (Fundación Ignacio Larramendi: Madrid, 2015),
     22–26.

103 Vasconcelos, *Obras completas* Vol. I, 303. However, as Taboada says, in later years
     Vasconcelos distanced himself from the Orient. See Taboada "Oriente y mundo
     clásico en José Vasconcelos," *Cuyo: Anuario de Filosofía Argentina y Americana*
     No. 24, (2007): 103–119.

References

Amano Teiyū. *Gakusei ni atauru sho* 学生にあたうる書 [*A book for the students*].
     Tokyo: Iwanami Shoten, (1939) 1940.

Amano Teiyū. *Dōri e no ishi* 道理への意志 [*A will to reason*]. Tokyo: Iwanami Shoten,
     1940.

Amano Teiyū. *Shinnen to Jissen* 信念と実践 [*Conviction and practice*]. Tokyo: Iwanami
     Shoten, 1944.

Amano Teiyū. *Dōri no kankaku* 道理の感覺 [*A sense of reason*]. Tokyo: Iwanami
     Shoten, (1937) 1945.

Jacinto Z., Agustín. "*Estudios Indostánicos* de José Vasconcelos y la multiculturalidad." In *Escritores y escritos de la revolufia*, edited by Álvaro Ochoa Serrano, 167–192. Zamora, Mich.: El Colegio de Michoacán, 2004.

Jacinto Z. "Nishida Kitarō y José Vasconcelos." *Revista Relaciones* 30, Vol. VIII (1987): 60–87.

Jacinto Z. "La *Teoría Dinámica del Derecho* de José Vasconcelos." *Crónica Legislativa* Año V, Nueva Época, No. 7 (febrero–marzo 1996): 99–108.

Jacinto Z. "La teoría de la formación de la sociedad en José Vasconcelos." *Revista Relaciones* 46, Vol. XII (1996): 99–127.

Jacinto Z. "Las etnias y la cultura mexicana en José Vasconcelos." *Revista Relaciones* 91, Vol. XIII (2002): 163–192.

Jacinto Z. "Nishida Kitarō's Views on Education: 1895–1935." *Nishida Tetsugakkai Nenpō* 西田哲学会年報 No. 13 (2016): 191–171.

Jacinto Z. "Inoue Enryo: Towards a Hermeneutics of the Imperial Rescript on Education." *International Inoue Enryo Research* No. 4 (2016): 1–65.

Kōyama Iwao. *Bunka ruikeigaku* 文化類型学 [A Typology of Cultures]. Tokyo: Kōbundō shobō, 1939.

Kōyama Iwao. *Bunka ruikeigaku no kenkyū* 文化類型学研究 [Research on the typology of cultures]. Tokyo: Kōbundō shobō, (1942) 1940.

Luquín Guerra, Roberto. "La intuición originaria en la filosofía de José Vasconcelos." *Signos filosóficos* Vol. VIII, No. 16 (julio–diciembre 2006): 97–124.

Meneses Morales, Ernesto. *Tendencias educativas oficiales en México, 1911–1934.* México: Centro de Estudios Educativos, 1986.

Mishima Kenichi. "Der Tennō–Diskurs bei Watsuji Tetsurō und Amano Teiyū—Die Instrumentalisierung des Wortschatzes des deutschen Idealismus zur politischen Stabilisierung in der unmittelbaren Nachkriegszeit." *Bunron—Zeitschrift für literaturwissenschaftliche Japanforschung,* Heft 3 (2016): 1–19.

Molina, Alicia, ed. *Vasconcelos, José: Antología de textos sobre educación.* México: SEP 80/8, 1981.

Nishida Kitarō. *Nishida Kitarō Zenshū* 西田幾多郎全集 [*The complete works of Nishida Kitarō*]. Tokyo: Iwanami Shoten, 1966–1967, 2nd edition; new edition, 2004–2005.

Rosado Zacarías, Juan Antonio. *José Vasconcelos.* Edición digital. Fundación Ignacio Larramendi: Madrid, 2015. E-book. Accessed 28xi2019. www.larramendi.es/i18n/catalogo_imagenes/grupo.cmd?path=1021540.

Satō Kesao. *Sengo kyōiku no sōgō hyōka-Sengo kyōiku kaikaku no jitsuzō* 佐藤今朝夫(Ed). 戦後教育の総合評価ー戦後教育改革の実像 [*A Comprehensive Evaluation of Post-war Education—A True Image of Post-War Educational Reform*]. Tokyo: Kokusho kankō-kai. 1999.

Taboada, Hernán G. H. "Oriente y mundo clásico en José Vasconcelos." *Cuyo: Anuario de Filosofía Argentina y Americana* No. 24, (2007): 103–119.

Ueda Shizuteru, ed. *Zen to Kyoto Tetsugaku* 禅と京都哲学 [*Zen Buddhism and the Kyoto School*]. Kyoto: Tōeisha, 2006.

Vasconcelos, José. *Obras completas*, Vol. I. México: Libreros Mexicanos Unidos, 1957.

Yusa, Michiko. *Zen and Philosophy: An Intellectual Biography of Nishida Kitarō*. Honolulu: University of Hawai'i Press, 2002.

7

Confucius and the Aztecs on The Mean

Sebastian Purcell

It is a common feature of our lives that we search for apt expression in our actions and thoughts. We say of an outfit that it has too little color, and so is overly somber for an occasion. Or we might remark that a translation is stiff, rendered with too much formality. Of course, what holds in our practical lives generally holds in our ethical lives especially. We wonder whether we have given too little to charity, or whether our criticism of another's action has been too strong. It is this sort of aptness that we can recognize as common to our practical and moral lives.

A notable feature about the ethics of the Confucian tradition and the Aztec *tlamatinimê* (philosophers) is that this concern for aptness plays a capital role. Because it is apt expression that is neither too little nor too much which is at stake, both traditions used a metaphor to express their thoughts on the topic; they called it the "mean" (*zhong*), or "middle" way (*tlanepantla*). As the *Florentine Codex* (6, 231) says: "The mean-good is required".[1] Or, as is written in the *Analects* 6:29: "Supreme indeed is the mean as virtue".[2] Given the centrality of mean or middling expressions in our lives, and the prominence of the concept in these two ethical traditions, the purpose of this chapter is to take a first step toward a comparative philosophic dialogue on the mean.[3]

Ultimately, the Confucian tradition and the Aztec *tlamatinimê* understand the mean to have three central features that make it ethically significant. First, both take the mean to be a way of conduct that enables an agent to lead the good life. Second, they both maintain that one must distinguish the mean as a sort of state or disposition "internal" to the agent from the realization of that disposition "external" to the agent in real circumstances. Finally, both hold that practical wisdom plays the role of discerning what was in fact the "middle" for a situation, though they differ at this point on the structure of the relation. Given the complexity of the discussion, I begin with a brief review of the good life for both traditions and its relation to virtue.

1. The good life and virtue

In the Confucian tradition of philosophy, the *dao* or "way" is understood to express the good life. Specifically, it is held to be the ultimate goal after which one should strive. This is why it is stated at one point that "If one has heard the Way [*dao*] in the morning, it is alright to die in the evening."[4] The *dao*, so understood, is not a metaphysically teleological notion, but is rather a deliberative one. Moreover, is not intrinsically connected with pleasure, or elevated emotional states, and so while its achievement qualifies as leading a good life, it would be inaccurate to think of one who follows the *dao* as "happy" in the colloquial sense of the English word. It might be better, as is the case with the Aztec conception of the good life, to think of a life led following the way as a worthwhile one.

Though not metaphysically teleological, the *dao* does find its source in the way things are. Confucius is explicit in understanding it as a mandate from heaven (*tian*). He writes: "It is a long time since the Way prevailed in the world, but Heaven is about to use your Master as a wooden [tongue for a] warning-bell."[5] I follow Jiyuan Yu's analysis of these statements, and so take them to indicate that the *dao* is rooted in *tian ming*, the mandate of heaven.[6] Here again one must be careful not to read too much into Confucius's statements. The word "*tian*" literally means "sky," and was the source of religious reverence in the early Zhou (1122–256 BCE). It was understood both as an impersonal ordering force, and as a guarantor of moral value. Yet it did not indicate some transcendent realm or being. The same sort of ambiguity applies to heaven's mandate (*ming*), which was understood both as command—as from a ruler—and as a sort of destiny—the pattern in the way things inevitably turn out. For many ancient Chinese philosophers, and Confucius is one, these senses exist juxtaposed, and were not systematically organized. What matters for our analysis, then, is that Confucius takes the *dao* to follow *tian*, and he seeks to recover the human *dao*, which he holds has been lost since the Zhou period.

Of course Confucius's aim is not primarily a cognitive task, but a practical one. Confucius hopes to lead others in effecting the *dao*, and this is accomplished by developing virtue (*de*) in a specific way. He writes: "Set your heart on the Way [*dao*], base yourself on virtue [*de*], rely on humaneness [*ren*], and take your relaxation in the arts."[7] While *de* ("virtue," or more literally "power") was broadly accepted in Chinese culture as the means for effecting the *dao*, Confucius innovates by suggesting that human virtue should be *ren*. The word "ren" is often translated as "humaneness" and also "benevolence," because the origin of the graph consists of "man" plus "two," and the idea is that this is the way that humans should treat each other. On Confucius's account, then, one could say that *dao*, *de* and *ren* are inseparable at least for the way humans should lead their lives. *Dao* is effected as *de* and *ren*.

For the Aztecs, or more appropriately, the Nahuas, who were the pre-Columbian peoples who spoke Nahuatl, the good life is not understood to be a mandate of the divine (*teotl*), but does respond to the way humans lead their lives here on Earth.[8] At the end of the sixth volume of the *Florentine Codex* (*FC*) one finds a compilation of common sayings among the Nahuas with brief explanations of each. One of these expresses a very broadly held understanding about the human condition. It reads: "Slippery, slick is the earth [*tlalticpac*]."[9] The explanation for the saying states: "It means the same as the one just mentioned [in the *FC* above]. Perhaps at one time one was of good [*qualli*] life; later he fell into some wrong, as if he had slipped in the mud."[10] The point is that life on Earth, on *tlalticpac*, is difficult, and that, despite one's intentions, one is likely to "slip and fall," to err.

That *tlalticpac* is a place where errors are likely to happen leads naturally to the second aspect of our condition here, namely that it is not an unmixed good. In the *Huehuetlatolli*, or the *Discourse of the Elders*, which is recorded earlier in the same sixth volume of the *FC*, a mother addresses her daughter as follows.

> "O my daughter, O my child, the earth [*tlalticpac*] is not a good place [*haieccan*]. It is not a place of joy or contentment. It is said merely that it is a place of joy-fatigue, of joy-pain on earth [*tlalticpac*];" so the old went saying. "In order that we may not live weeping forever, may not die of sorrow, it is our due that our lord gave us laughter, sleep, and our sustenance, our strength, our force, and also carnal knowledge."[11]

The earth, *tlalticpac*, is thus a place where humans are prone to error, and where circumstances will not favor our plans. It is a place where joy comes only with pain and fatigue, and where the gods have given us a few diversions so that we will not live entirely in sorrow.

Some of the terminology of this passage is important for understanding the basic terms for goodness and virtue in Nahuatl. The word *ha-yec-can* (*haieccan* as it is recorded in the *FC*) consists of three parts.[12] The first functions like the Greek alpha privative to negate the term that come afterwards. The last *can* portion of the word indicates a place, as in famous archaeological site *Teotihuacan* near Mexico City, which means the place (*can*) of birth for the gods. The root of the word is *yec*, from *yectli*, which means something straight, right or with rectitude.[13] It is one of two words generally used to indicate goodness. The other is *qualli*, which is used even more broadly. The root meaning of *qualli*, however, indicates that something is edible, and so will not cause harm and is healthful.[14] In Nahuatl new terms are often composed in one of two ways, either by compounding, as one finds in the above passage with the terms "joy-fatigue" (*ciauhca-pacoaia*) and "joy-pain" (*chichinaca-pacoaia*), or with what Angel María Garibay called *difrasismo*, meaning a phrase composed of two principle words that expresses a single idea.[15] The phrase *in xochitl in cuicatl*, or with flower and song, is a paradigm case of *difrasismo*, and it indicates what we might call "poetry." Another is *in qualli in yectli*, the good and the straight, and might be best translated as "the excellent" or "the virtuous."[16] The tenth volume of the *FC* is entitled *The People*, and it contains a set of descriptions of various social roles, and what makes people good or bad in fulfilling those roles. In the description of the "good" daughter, for example, one finds the following description: *ichpuchtli in iectli in qualli, in qualli ichpuchtli* which might be translated as "the excellent daughter, the good daughter."[17]

Having noted the character of the human condition, of life on *tlalticpac*, the general response of the Nahuas was to find a way to be rooted on the earth, to avoid slipping as much as is possible. One finds this attitude expressed quite widely. For example, a piece entitled "Flower-Song" recorded in the *Cantares Mexicanos*, was composed and recited for the meeting of wise men and poets in the house of Tecayehautzin. The author asks about what might be lasting or true on earth. He writes the following:

> Now do I hear the words of the *coyolli* bird
> As he makes answer to the Giver of Life.
> He goes his way singing, offering flowers.
> And his words rain down
> Like jade and quetzal plumes.
> Is that what pleases the Giver of Life?
> Is that the only rootedness (*nelli*) on earth (*in tlalticpac*)?[18]

The idea is that in order to avoid the slipperiness of the earth, one must take root. The good life for the Nahuas, as a result, consists in finding rootedness, which as an abstract substantive is *neltiliztli*.[19]

On *tlalticpac*, then, one aims to achieve rootedness in one's body, psyche, in society, by means of completing rituals and effectively executing one's social role, and in *teotl*, which is the divine as the single entity of existence—the Nahuas were pantheists of a sort. One ought to aim for this sort of life, they held, because a life led this way is just what it means to lead a life as a human being, and not as "a lump of flesh, a lump of flesh with two eyes."[20] *Neltiliztli*, then, is the highest good for humans in its performance, but like the Confucian *dao* it is not necessarily a "happy" life. Such pursuits would be considered a pointless and misguided aim among the Nahuas, since *tlalticpac* is just not the sort of place where pleasure, joy and contentment are to be achieved without their opposites.

If Confucius connects the good life, the *dao*, with virtue (*de* and *ren*) as the means to effect or lead a life by the Way, then do the Nahuas do the same? The argument so far suggests that they would be committed to such a position conceptually, and there is textual evidence to support that contention. In the description of the "good daughter" in volume ten of the *FC*, for example, these terms are all directly connected. Since the matter is critical, I provide a word-by-word translation and commentary.

yn tecuheuh yn ichpuchtli	One's daughter [who is]	This indicates that the daughter is addressed by both her father and mother.
quiztica, macitica, vel,	unspoiled, perfect, good,	These terms are all difficult to translate, because Christianity had already influenced the meaning of the words. Yet, none of them in Nahuatl have a fundamental connection to Christian understanding of virginity, which is another translation for "vel."
nelli,	rooted,	Dibble and Anderson omit this word in translation, as it fits poorly with the Christianized interpretation of the Nahuatl description.[21] It is the root of *neltiliztli*.
ichpuchtli in iectli in qualli,	[who is] the excellent daughter,	There is no sentence break in the Nahuatl, so the idea is continued: the rooted daughter is the excellent one ...
in qualli ichpuchtli ...	the good daughter ...	the good one, *et cetera*.[22]

One here finds a description of the "good" daughter as one who is rooted, who is leading the best life possible, and one who is excellent in doing so. The passage in the *FC* is a difficult one to analyze and translate, because some Christian influence was present at the time the *FC* was recorded, but it does nevertheless indicate that the Nahuas thought to connect virtue (*in yectli in qualli*) and rootedness (*neltiliztli*). The best life available on earth, in short, is one that is performed excellently.

2. Two sorts of mean: Inner and outer

If the above suffices for the general frame of ethical thinking in the Confucian and Aztec traditions, I need now to locate the role of the mean within that broader domain. Unfortunately the relation between the mean and virtue for both Confucius and the Nahuas is often misunderstood, because the mean is conflated with moderation. The difficulty here is that the English word "moderation" is informed by the history of Latin Christendom. In ethical discourse the word is used as a translation for the Latin *temperantia*, as one finds it in St. Thomas for example, which is itself a translation of Aristotle's Greek *sōphrosynē*. One source of the confusion appears to stem from the fact that there is a relation between the mean and moderation in Aristotelian (and Thomist) thought, though they are distinct concepts. Briefly, for Aristotle the mean (*meson*) is a middle with respect to the amount of feeling one has in response to a circumstance. For example, one might have too much (excessive) or too little (deficient) anger. Moderation, on his reasoning, is a specific virtue that enables one to act at the mean between poles of excess and deficient feeling. It is, in short, the ability to act with self-discipline and hit the mean, but is not the mean itself.[23]

In looking for appropriate moral terminology, one finds translators of Nahuatl and classical Chinese using moderation and the mean in a way that is inexact. The general statement that opens this chapter, for example, is recorded in Nahuatl as: "*tlacoqualli in monequj*," which Dibble and Anderson render as "moderation is required."[24] Instead, I have chosen to render it as "The mean-good is required." Dibble and Anderson translate "*tlacoqualli*" as "moderation," and yet I think this is a little misleading for ethical purposes. The term "*tlacoqualli*" is a composed of the two words "*tlaco*" and "*qualli*." The first of these, "*tlaco*," is generally used to indicate the middle, mean, or center of something, while "*qualli*," as noted above, is the broadest term to indicate something good. What is meant, then, is something rather different from Aristotelian "moderation." The gloss which follows the statement, using Dibble and Anderson's own translation, supports my analysis. It reads: "We shall not put on us very tattered things, neither shall we dress magnificently; only modestly shall we adorn ourselves as to clothing."[25] The idea is that something in the middle of two poles, dressing magnificently or in tattered things, is to be chosen. It is a matter of apt expression, as illustrated in the introduction of this chapter, not a matter of self-discipline to act at the mean.

With translations of the *Analects* one finds similar difficulties. For example, on Lau's translation we read: "The Master said: 'Supreme indeed is the mean as virtue.'"[26] This statement seems to go so far as to identify the mean with virtue itself: the mean *as* virtue. Dawson's translation inserts the indefinite article "a" before the word "virtue" to make the mean a specific virtue. It reads: "Supreme indeed is the Mean as a virtue."[27] On Dawson's interpretation, then, the mean would be some particular virtue, like moderation. The difficulty here is that the Chinese is not clear on the way one ought to translate the statements. This would not matter much if one took moderation and the mean to be similar notions, and I think that Dawson has taken this looser approach, but for ethical purposes one must recognize that while related, they are distinct notions. To decide which translation is correct, one might consider another statement a little later in the *Analects*: "The Master said: 'having failed to find the man who walks in the middle way [*zhong xing*] for associates, one should, if there were no alternative, have to turn to the undisciplined and the over-scrupulous. The former are enterprising, while the latter will draw the line at certain kinds of action.'"[28]

I have used Lau's (more literal) translation here because it clearly indicates that one must find friends who also walk the middle way. In Dawson's translation, we read: "The Master said: 'If one does not get hold of moderation to associate with ...'"[29] The meaning of the sentence is strained in English, because on Dawson's reading one is to associate with a virtue, moderation, not another person who walks the middle way. It makes sense, then, to understand Confucius to be discussing the mean as something distinct from moderation, just as one finds with the Nahuas.

Two further sources of confusion seem to emerge from misunderstanding what the mean could be, if it is not moderation, and how it is realized. With respect to the first difficulty, my suggestion all along has been that the mean is a sort of apt expression by a virtuous agent. Moderation is another virtue. For Aristotle, it was a sort of self-discipline, especially with regard to bodily pleasure. For both Confucius and the Nahuas, though I cannot develop this point here, it appears to have been a matter of balancing. This is to say it was a matter not of drinking only one beer in order to avoid intoxication, but a matter of drinking several beers, to the point of inebriation, at the right time and place, say on a festival day.[30] In any case, moderation and the mean are distinct. This point is, I take it, supported by the above analysis.[31]

With respect to how the mean is realized, both Confucius and the Aztecs hold that this occurs in a double way: with regard to an inner state or disposition, and with regard to an outward state of affairs. Confucius's *Doctrine of the Mean*, develops this double role rather plainly. In the first chapter we read: "Before the feelings of pleasure, anger, sorrow, and joy are issued, one is in a state that is called the mean [*zhong*]. When these feelings are issued, and each and all hit due measure and degree [*zhongjie*], one is in a state that is called harmony [*he*]."[32] In his commentary on the passage Jiyuan Yu argues that one can find here the basic structure of the mean in Confucian thought, which he calls the *zhong-he* structure. The mean (*zhong*), on the one hand, concerns a state that one is in, a state of feelings, pleasure, anger, etc. This is the "inner" or dispositional feature of the mean. Yet this disposition must also be issued or realized in the world, which is the "outer" feature of the mean. When this last "hits" the due measure from an inner mean, one achieves a state of harmony (*he*). In short, harmony does not emerge merely when one's actions realize a mean or middle way in the world, but rather when that middle way realized externally is from an inner dispositional state, which is also at the mean.

For the Nahuas, one finds a similar understanding, even if the points are not presented all in a single statement. The gloss on the common saying "the mean-good is required" already provides an example for how the mean is to be realized with due measure in an external state of affairs. There are two poles with respect to dress, or any similar other matter the gloss suggests, between too much, e.g., magnificent clothing, and too little, e.g., tattered robes. In quite a number of other statements, especially the discourses of the elders, one finds cases of the need for an inner mean. For example, a noble mother to her daughter urges the following.

> Take heed. On earth [*in tlalticpac*] it is a time for care, it is a place for caution. Behold the word [*tlatolli*]; heed and guard it, and with it take your way of life, your works. On earth [*tlalticpac*] we live, we travel along a mountain peak. Over here there is an abyss, over there is an abyss. If thou goest over here, or if thou goest over there, thou wilt fall in. Only in the middle [*tlanepantla*] doth one go, doth one live.
>
> Place this word [*tlatolli*], my daughter, dove, little one, well within the chambers of thy heart. Guard it well. Do not forget it; for it will become thy torch, thy light, all the time thou art to live on earth.[33]

The word for "middle" in this case is "*tla-nepantla*." The prefix "tla-" indicates an indeterminate object, while "*nepantla*" was understood as a sort of middling activity.[34] The idea is that with respect to anything, one is to go middling. What the mother suggests is that the daughter is to take this *tlatolli*, discourse or word (the meaning is surprisingly close to the Greek *logos*), and place it within the chambers of her heart. It is to become part of who she is, for her entire life on *tlalticpac*. The middle way, then, is to become an inner state, a steady disposition, to be realized in external matters like dress, or drink, or anything else.

For both Confucius and the Nahuas, these points suggest first that the mean is distinct from moderation, even if moderation is critical for realizing virtue, and second that the mean has a double structure. It is to be realized in external circumstances as the result of an internal state or steady disposition to act in a certain manner. Yet how is one to determine what the mean is in a specific situation? In response, one finds that the Nahuas and Confucius appear to depart somewhat, for the Nahuas appear to maintain a rather direct relation between practical wisdom and the mean, while in the Confucian tradition the mean appears to be set by tradition and ritual (*li*), which practical wisdom as *yi* then addresses. I turn to these points now.

3. Practical wisdom and The Mean

One of the more interesting features of the Nahua and Confucian virtue ethical traditions is that they both devote a significant amount of thought to the role of ritual and tradition. Yet, at least as the matter is presented in the *Huehuetlatolli* (*Discourses of the Elders*), the relation between the mean and practical wisdom appears to be rather direct. The noble father to his son, for example, states the following which recapitulates what the mother said to her daughter, but also explicitly introduces a connection to practical wisdom:

> Right here is a word or two which merit being taken, being guarded, being grasped, which our forefathers went putting in their coffers, in their reed chests; for all courtesy, all prudence [*in nematcaiotl, in nematiliztli*] come from [and] are taken from this.
>
> They went saying that on earth [*in tlalticpac*], we live along a mountain peak. Over here is an abyss, over there is an abyss. Wherever thou art to deviate, wherever thou art to go astray, there wilt thou fall, there wilt thou plunge into the deep. That is to say, it is necessary that thou always act with discretion [*in quexqujch*] in that which is done, said, seen, heard, thought, etc.[35]

There are two important concepts here which connect the middle way with practical wisdom, or what might be called the virtue of discernment. In this retelling of the wisdom of the mountain peak the father does not tell the son to go middling, *tlanepantla*. Rather he states that he should act with discretion, *in quexquich*. The word *quexquich* is more commonly used in interrogative statements which ask after a quantity. For example, *quexquich ipatiuh?* means "how much does this cost?" Similarly, *quexquich ca in Coyohuacan?* asks "how much further to Coyohuacan?" The father, then, is instructing his son to act in such a way that his actions assess how much is appropriate in this case.

This kind of assessment is related to the *difrasismo* above: *in nematcayotl in nematiliztli*, which are translated as courtesy and prudence respectively. Both words ultimately have the same root, *mati*, which means to know, though the former stresses a certain urbanity, while the latter stresses ability. Taken together they mean knowledge of the ways of social decorum with knowledge of how to effect ends. What is at stake, then, appears to be a virtue that one might call discernment. It assesses what is appropriate in a situation, aware of social rites and roles, as well as how to be effective in achieving those ends. The mean, then, is discerned by a sort of practical wisdom.

For the Confucian tradition, practical wisdom does not appear to be explicitly connected to the mean in the way that it is for the Nahua *tlamatinimê*. While "*zhong*" means both the "middle" and what is "appropriate," it does not mean a faculty for discerning appropriateness. This faculty, rather, is *yi*, and it is the sort of excellence that one finds in the following statement: "In his dealings with the world the excellent person is not invariably for or against anything. He is on the side of what is appropriate [*yi*]."[36] This excellence, however, does not act directly on the mean as a faculty which discerns what is appropriate. Rather, it would be better to state that the trajectory is through social rites (*li*). To understand how it functions, then, I shall need to say a little more about social rites in Confucian thought.

For Confucius, *ren* is possible only by observing social rites (*li*). We read, for example, the following: "Yan Hui asked about humaneness [*ren*]. The Master said: 'To subdue oneself and return to ritual [*li*] is to practice humaneness [*ren*].'"[37] The term *li* has been variously translated as "rites," "rituals," "ceremonies," and "manners." As it is used in the *Analects*, *li* tends to range from detailed regulations on social and political behavior, including the relation of rulers to subjects and how to support one's parents in a funeral, to general norms for ceremonies.[38] In brief, one might state that *li* covers the entire range of socially recognized behaviors, customs, and institutions.

For ethical purposes *li* comes to function in two ways for Confucius. In a first way, these rites serve to habituate agents into virtuous internal dispositions, and in this regard they are rather like many of the ritualized behaviors one finds attested in the Nahua literature. In a second way, however, these social rites operate with *yi*, the faculty for discerning what is appropriate. The relation between *yi* and *li*, however, is unclear in the *Analects* and scholars offer divergent interpretations. Chad Hansen, for example, proposes that there are two sorts of objective criteria at work: *li*, which concerns social mores, and *yi* which discerns moral reality.[39] On this understanding, one is to follow *li* where appropriate, but *yi* provides an overriding standard for *li* where those mores are inapposite.

Jiyuan Yu offers a different and, I think, more compelling analysis. He suggests that "[i]n Confucian ethics, the regulations of social rites (*li*) are of a general nature. Appropriateness (*yi*) adjusts the generality of social rites and brings them to bear on particular circumstances."[40] The idea is that because there is a difference between social rites and what is appropriate, it requires an intellectual quality (*yi*) to discern just what to do in each circumstance. Of course social rites may be inapplicable in some circumstance, so that one should not thoughtlessly follow customs, but it is precisely the job of an agent with *yi* to discern just this inapplicability. *Yi* then works with *li* to effect those rites in the right way, and as a result does not stand as a separate objective criterion for right action.

One can now more clearly identify the difference Confucius has with Nahua thought on this topic. The Nahuas also held that social rites played a critical role in "assuming a face," or character formation, but their understanding differed in two ways. First, with respect to content, the Nahuas and the Confucian tradition clearly had different social roles and rites, even different conceptions of which roles were fundamental to a good society. Second, the Nahuas appear to have conceived of the structural relation between discernment and social rites differently. There does not appear to be a sense for the Nahuas that discernment (*in nematcayotl in nematiliztli*) worked by means of realizing social rites in each circumstance. It did certainly work to realize one's social role where applicable, but elders and philosophers discussed a wide range of topics for discernment that were unrelated to social roles and social rites. The virtue appears to have functioned, then, in a more general way than it does for Confucius.

Despite these differences, there is a final point of similarity. Mencius, a significant figure in the Confucian tradition, develops a specific term for the process of assessing what is appropriate: *quan*. Social rites, for example, prescribe that a man and woman should not touch each other, but Mencius argues that one should help to pull out a sister-in-law who is drowning.[41] *Quan* is like the use of *in quexquich*, since it originally suggests weighing objects, and comes to serve as a metaphor for weighing circumstances to find an appropriate decision. Yu even suggests that one could translate it as "discretion."[42] The basic idea, then, is that *yi* or appropriateness is the virtuous result of a process of "weighing" the circumstances of a social rite, so that one may then act at the mean. If the Nahuas and the Confucian tradition are at odds on the relation of the mean to practical wisdom, then these points suggest the difference is not so great.

4. Concluding thoughts

The present chapter has taken a first step in the comparative task of understanding the Confucian and Nahua traditions of virtue ethics on the mean. Both traditions have a specific understanding of the good life, and interestingly both divorce that conception from elevated emotional states like pleasure. While in the Confucian tradition the intrinsic link between the *dao* and "happiness" is simply unremarked, in Nahua thought the mere pursuit of happiness would be considered foolish, and the mark of someone who lacked practical wisdom. If many of the premodern traditions of ethics appear to have been committed to a form of virtue ethics, Confucius and the Nahuas developed ethical accounts that centered on leading worthwhile, rather than "happy" lives. For Confucius, this is done through actions and dispositions which exhibit *de* and *ren*, while for the Nahuas this is accomplished by leading a life of excellent (*in qualli in yectli*) actions guided by similarly excellent internal states.

For both Confucius and the Nahuas, actions at the mean are those which are excellent. But this is not to say that all such actions are moderate. A misunderstanding conflates moderation and the mean, since moderation appears to be a related, but distinct notion. In fact, one finds that many of the most prominent passages concerning the mean for both Confucius and the Aztecs do not mention moderation in any way. Rather, the mean in both cases is taken to be a matter of apt expression or action. Moreover, for both the mean has a common twofold structure: it is exhibited externally in states of the world as "middling" (*tlacoqualli*) or "appropriate" (*zhong* as discerned by *yi*), as the result of an inner disposition (*tlanepantla* or *zhong*). A small difference here is that Confucius is clear that when both are accomplished, the result is harmony (*he*), while I find no similar term for the Nahua *tlamatinimê*.

How, finally, does one know that one has acted at the mean? The answer is that practical wisdom must play a role, though here again there is a slight difference. In Aztec thought *in nematcayotl in nematiliztli*, the virtue of discernment, assesses how much is too much, or what sort of action is one with discretion. For the Confucian tradition, *yi* acts to make social rites (*li*) appropriate to the situation, and so acts indirectly on the mean.

If these are the fruits of research, I should like to close by remarking on a few points about its value. I began this chapter by noting how pervasive that reasoning about too much or too little—reasoning about the mean—is to our practical and moral lives. I also noted that one of the strengths of the philosophical reflection one finds in the Confucian and Aztec traditions is that an understanding of the mean plays a central role, giving voice to this pervasive experience. Surprisingly, at least given the broad cultural and temporal differences at root in these two traditions, this investigation has revealed a number of rather specific agreements about mean. Yet as the brief review above suggests, this investigation has also touched on four other topics for philosophic disagreement that might be greater. One might put them in the following questions:

1. If the good life does not have to involve elevated emotional states, i.e. "happiness," then just what are the key features that make that sort of life worthwhile? A life led following the *dao* and one which aims at *neltiliztli* seem to be rather different conceptions of a good life. Are the differences so great, and if so which account is more accurate?

2. Practical reason (*yi* and *in nematcayotl in nematiliztli*) is thought to play a pivotal role in relation to social rites, but does that role consist in realizing those rites—a fully role-based virtue ethics as Confucian thought appears to be—or does it range over something wider as the Aztecs appear to hold?

3. If social rites and rituals are essential to a flourishing life and society, as the Confucian and Aztec traditions hold, just which ones are they? Is it a specific content that is needed, or is there a sort of formal characterization that must be satisfied?

4. Both the Confucian and Aztec traditions hold that moderation as a virtue should be understood more along the lines of balancing than self-discipline. Just what does this alternative approach look like, exactly? Is it a matter of following seasons, festivals, personal accomplishments, or something else still?

The value of studying the Greeks of classical antiquity, Bernard Williams has written, is that "[t]hey are among our cultural ancestors, and our view of them is intimately connected with our view of ourselves."[43] This cannot be the value, or at least primary value, of studying Confucius and the Aztecs. Rather, this sort of investigation has the potential to reveal topics and concerns that have, for cultural and historical reasons, been ignored or, possibly even, unimagined in those cultures primarily influenced by Latin Christendom. This is precisely what I hope this investigation (and by extension the present anthology) has accomplished.

While a discussion of the mean is a pervasive feature of our lives, the present chapter has addressed the topic in a way that is divorced from a discussion of mean feelings, as one finds it in Aristotle. Similarly, the four points for further research just highlighted point not only to fruitful avenues of reflection, but also to new questions in ethical philosophy. They are questions that would have never arisen had the Hellenistic philosophers of classical antiquity served as the primary axis of comparison. They become clear only with these sorts of "non-Western" to "non-Western" comparative investigations. The present sort of study, as a result, is thus what one might hope would be a beginning both for new scholarship, and, since the study of ethics is intended to be practical, for better-lived lives.

Notes

1   *The Florentine Codex* was originally compiled by Bernadino de Sahaghún in the immediate post-conquest era (i.e., mid-1500s) in both Nahuatl and Spanish. The twelve volumes of *The Florentine Codex: General History of the Things of New Spain*, in English and Nahuatl were edited and translated by Charles Dibble and Arthur Anderson (Salt Lake: University of Utah Press, 1953–82). In what follows I cite this work by the volume number and page number. Moreover, the translation is that of Dibble and Anderson unless otherwise noted. In the present quotation, however, the translation is my own.

2   Confucius, *Confucius: The Analects*, trans. D.C. Lau (Hong Kong: The Chinese University of Hong Kong Press, 1979). The other translation I shall use is Raymond Dawson's *The Analects*, (New York: Oxford University Press, 1993). Both are cited below as *Analects* by the chapter and statement number. If the translation is Lau's I shall also note that in the citation.

3   This essay was helped considerably by the comments of Leah Kalmason and Stephanie Berruz Rivera. I thank them both for their careful reading of this piece, and their gentle, if quite needed, suggestions.

4   Confucius, *Analects*, 4:8.

5   Ibid., 3:24.

6   I am here only outlining the account one finds in Confucius and his followers like Mencius, so I shall not develop the more intricate connections between *tian* and *dao*, or the ontological grounds for the *dao*. For those interested, I suggest chapters one and five of *The Ethics of Confucius and Aristotle: Mirrors of Virtue* by Jiyuan Yu, to which the present account of the Confucian tradition is greatly indebted.

7   Confucius, *Analects*, 7:6.

8   What follows is only a brief review of the points developed at length in my "*Eudaimonia* and *Neltilitztli*: Aristotle and the Aztecs on the Good Life," forthcoming in the American Philosophical Association *Newsletter on Hispanic / Latino Issues in Philosophy*.

9   Sahagún, *The Florentine Codex*, 6, 228. This translation is my own.

10 Ibid., 6, 228 modified.

11 Ibid., 6, 93 modified.

12 What follows is a slight simplification of the word's components.

13 As a note, Nahuatl lacks a standard orthography, though scholarship has tended in the twentieth century to use what might be called a modernized Franciscan method, while *The Florentine Codex* does not. In the *Codex* "i" often appears in the place of a (modern) standardized "y," and "j" for an "i," while the appropriate accents indicating breathers and glottal stops are omitted, or variously introduced using an "h." The *Codex*'s lexigraphy, then, is unique, and not the way that Nahuatl is written for contemporary scholarly purposes. It may help the reader to bear this in mind, given the variances this text and others (like the *Cantares Mexicanos*) introduce.

14 Rémi Siméon's entry for *"tlaco"* in the *Diccionario de la lengua Nahuatl o Méxicano* (trans. Josefina Oliva De Coll, Mexico City: Siglo Veinuiuno Press, 1981) reads: *"Mediano, que ocupa el centro, que está a la mitad, en medio."* One might also note that the root metaphor of *"qualli"* is that the item under consideration is edible, so that ingestion will not cause harm. Nevertheless, the meaning of *"qualli"* is almost never used in this restricted or metaphorical sense.

15 Garibay, Angel María, *Llave del Náhuatl, Colección de Torzos Clásicos con Gramática y Vocabulario, para utilidad de los Principiantes,* 112. Miguel León-Portilla also makes use of this analysis in multiple places in his *La Filosofía Náhuatl: Estudia en sus Fuentes* and *Aztec Thought and Culture: A Study of the Ancient Nahuatl Mind,* trans. Jack Emory Davis.

16 For "excellence" or "virtue" in the abstract form one might write, *"in quallot in yecyotl,"* since the *-yo* suffix indicates an abstract form similar to the English *-ness*.

17 Sahagún, *The Florentine Codex*, 10, 2. These translation, obviously, are my own. Dibble and Anderson render the entire phrase merely as "the good daughter."

18 *Cantares Mexicanos: Songs of the Aztecs,* fol. 9v. The present translation is adapted from Miguel León-Portilla's in *Aztec Thought and Culture,* 75.

19 More exactly, this is an abstract derived noun. The word *nelyotl* would be the abstract substantive. It does not appear, however, that this form of the word is attested in Nahua texts of the time, at least not for this use, and so I have chosen to make use of the abstract noun derived from the verb. The difference is also more consistent with the way in which the Nahuas thought of the good life as a performance, and not an achieved state of affairs.

20 Sahagún, *The Florentine Codex*, 10, 11.

21 To be fair to Dibble and Anderson, one purpose of their translation was to stay close to, or at least in contact with, the insights that informed the Spanish, which Sahagun rendered in his original transcription. If Sahagún interpreted the Nahuatl in a specific way, then their task was to make that known in English as well. My goals, clearly, are different ones.

22 Sahagún, *The Florentine Codex*, 10, 2.

23 See Aristotle's *Nicomachean Ethics* at 1106a-b for his statements on the mean, and 1107a-b and 1117b–9a on moderation. The topic is, of course, more complex than I can present here. For the interested, Rosalind Hursthouse has a nice review of the various difficulties facing interpreters of Aristotle's sense of the mean in "The Central Doctrine of the Mean."

24 Sahagún, *The Florentine Codex*, 6, 231

25 Ibid., 6, 231

26 Confucius, *Analects* (trans. Lau), 6:29.

27 Confucius, *Analects*, 6:29.

28 Confucius, *Analects* (trans. Lau) 13:21.

29 Confucius, *Analects*, 13:21.

30 Sarah Mattice in "Drinking to Get Drunk" makes the case that this practice was similarly observed in Chinese culture. I surmise that the common approach to life by way of a "balanced" view would yield this sort of analysis.

31 It is also underscored in the analysis that follows.

32 Confucius, *The Doctrine of the Mean* in *A Sourcebook in Chinese Philosophy*, 98.

33 Sahagún, *The Florentine Codex*, 6, 101–2.

34 James Maffie in *Aztec Philosophy: Understanding a World in Motion* has developed the metaphysical significance of *olini*, *malinalli*, and *nepantla* at length in the entire course of the book. They serve something like three sorts of causes, as opposed to the Aristotelian account of the four causes. The most important, holding a place similar in value to Aristotle's *telos*, is *nepantla*. Those interested in further points should look there, but I note this since these terms are used explicitly here in connection with these ethical matters. There is, in short, a deep metaphysical backdrop to the present discussion which I cannot address here.

35 Sahagún, *The Florentine Codex*, 6, 125. Translation modified.

36 Confucius, *Analects* (trans. Lau), 4:10.

37 Confucius, *Analects*, 12:1.

38 See for example Confucius, *Analects*, 3:18 and 2:5.

39 Chad Hansen, *A Daoist Theory of Chinese Thought*, 82.

40 Yu, *The Ethics of Confucius and Aristotle*, 156.

41 Mencius, *Mencius*, 4a/17.

42 Ibid.

43 Bernard Williams, *Shame and Necessity*, 3.

References

Aristotle. *Nicomachean Ethics*, trans. H. Rackham, Cambridge: Harvard University Press, 1929.

Cantares Mexicanos: Songs of the Aztecs, ed. and trans. Johnathan Bierhorst. Stanford, CA: Stanford University Press, 1985.

Confucius. *The Doctrine of the Mean* in *A Source Book in Chinese Philosophy*, trans. and ed. Wing-Tsit Chan, 97–114. Princeton, NJ: Princeton University Press, 1963.

Confucius. *Confucius: The Analects*, trans. D.C. Lau. Hong Kong: The Chinese University of Hong Kong Press, 1979.

Confucius. *The Analects*, trans. Raymond Dawson. New York: Oxford University Press, 1993.

Garibay, Angel María. *Llave del Náhuatl, Colección de Torzos Clásicos con Gramática y Vocabulario, para utilidad de los Principiantes*, Mexico City: Otumba, 1940.

Hansen, Chad. *A Daoist Theory of Chinese Thought*, New York: Oxford University Press, 1992.

Hursthouse, Rosalind. "The Central Doctrine of the Mean," in *The Blackwell Guide to Aristotle's Nicomachean Ethics*, ed. Richard Kraut, New York: Blackwell Press, 2006.

León-Portilla, Miguel. *Aztec Thought and Culture: A Study of the Ancient Nahuatl Mind*, trans. Jack Emory Davis, Norman: University of Oklahoma Press, 1963.

León-Portilla, Miguel. *La Filosofía Náhuatl: Estudia en sus Fuentes*, Mexico City: UNAM Press, 1959.

Maffie, James. *Aztec Philosophy: Understanding a World in Motion*, Boulder: University of Colorado Press, 2014.

Mattice, Sarah. "Drinking to Get Drunk: Pleasure, Creativity, and Social Harmony in Greece and China," in *Comparative and Continental Philosophy*, vol. 3 (2011): 243–253.

Mencius. *Mencius*, in *A Source Book in Chinese Philosophy*, trans. and ed. Wing-Tsit Chan, 49–83. Princeton, NJ: Princeton University Press, 1963.

Purcell, Sebastian. "*Eudaimonia* and *Neltiliztli*: Aristotle and the Aztecs on The Good Life," *Newsletter on Hispanic/Latino Issues in Philosophy*, 2016: 10–21.

Sahagún, Bernadino. *The Florentine Codex: General History of the Things of New Spain*, vol. 1–12, trans. and ed. Charles Dibble and Arthur Anderson, Salt Lake: University of Utah Press, 1953–1982.

Siméon, Rémi. *Diccionario de la lengua Nahuatl o Méxicano*, trans. Josefina Oliva De Coll, Mexico City: Siglo Veinuiuno Press, 1981.

Williams, Bernard. *Shame and Necessity*, Berkeley, CA: University of California Press, 1993.

Yu, Jiyuan. *The Ethics of Confucius and Aristotle*, New York: Routledge Press, 2007.

Part III

Comparative Philosophy from the Anti-colonial Perspective

Is Anarchy a False Hope? Latin American Revolutionaries Knew *Dhamma* and *Saddha*

Susan E. Babbitt

"Anarchy" means unmediated people power. It is defiant decentralization, resistance to hierarchies, radical freedom. Or so we are told. The slogan—and it is a slogan—is that there is power within each person to choose their own destiny. The power to give or to withhold consent to authority is supposedly waking from a long slumber.

This power doesn't exist, at least not as described. It is a seductive idea, but false. Yet it is hard to make this point because of what the twentieth-century playwright Eugène Ionesco called rhinoceritis. It is a disease identifiable as such only when cured, at least in part. The slogans of anarchism and liberalism are misleading at two levels: the political and how to think about the political. I explain below, starting from beyond the North Atlantic.

1.

Two hundred years ago, in Cuba, independence activists noticed a fact about thinking. It is a simple insight at first glance, but profound in its implications, politically.

It is about cause and effect. Lenin knew this truth.[1] He cited it explicitly, although much later than José de la Luz y Caballero and Felix Varela in the early-nineteenth century, and the Buddha 2,500 years ago. It goes like this: all thinking, even the supposedly most private, depends upon universals. Universals are general terms like "love," "tree," and "freedom." They depend upon social practices.

Thinking may be private, but universals are not. They are the result of the cause-and-effect relationship between how we think and how we live. Mind and body are connected. As we act in the world, the world acts upon us. We encounter patterns, and form expectations. We expect one thing to be like another as a result of experience.

In the analytic philosophical tradition, we refer to *kinds*.[2] They are general terms unifying particular instances. For example, two books are of the *same kind* although of different colors, shapes, sizes. To know an entity, we need to know its *kind*. Otherwise, we may not see it.[3] We rely upon patterns of behavior. They are not just ours. Any act of deliberation, moral and non-moral, depends upon kinds, which determine what we understand and how we act.[4] When you fall in love, you have feelings. You name those feelings. But why call them "love" and not something else? It is because of stories you have heard, perhaps what you saw on TV?

Lenin made the connection to freedom: people are confused about freedom when they overlook *kinds*.[5] Every entity is at the same time an individual and a universal: Fido is a dog, the leaves of the tree are green. When you think, "I want this. I need this. I dream such and such," you rely precisely upon society. This means you are not free *just because* you rely upon your *self*, supposedly independent of authority figures or government.

Thinking from "within," you are already interfered with. You respond to hierarchies. You even express such hierarchies. If your most intimate choices depend upon social practices, you express the very power structures you aim to resist, probably without knowing. You rely upon beliefs and values you did not choose. You may not understand or even identify them.

Some are philosophical. Everyone thinks philosophically sometimes. They wonder how to live a good life, or be a good friend, or whether their life is a good *human* life. To do so, they rely upon universals, unchosen. This point about understanding is evident to those who study nature and notice cause and effect. It is not an homogenization to suggest it has been evident to indigenous peoples. The question is how it was not noticed by European liberal philosophers who equated autonomy with listening to an "inner voice".

Latin American independence activists, José Carlos Mariátequi and José Martí both commented that Latin American indigenous peoples relied upon a more sensible conception of understanding than the view of knowledge more prevalent in European philosophers. The point here is not that indigenous peoples in general had a view of knowledge. Rather, it is that Europeans had a view that was distinct in its denial of causal connections. José Martí, who led Cuba's third independence war against Spain, and Che Guevara, who helped lead a revolution later, cared about epistemology as part of their political project: independence. Indeed, for Martí, independence required rejecting the 'false erudition' of Europe and North America.[6] It was a *vision* of erudition they rejected: The idea that to think freely I should look to my *self*, as if thinking is somehow unaffected by cause-and-effect relations between body and mind, and between body, mind and the world.

The point was evident to the Buddha. His entire philosophy emphasizes cause and effect. Just as no Christian would deny that Jesus Christ taught love for our neighbors, no Buddhist will deny the Buddha's emphasis on cause and effect, or dependent origination: precisely to the extent that we know cause and effect, we understand the nature of our reality, including human reality. I return to this point below.

2.

Cuba in the 1830s was the site of fervent philosophical debate—about universals. Cuba was threatened by four global institutions:[7] Spain took Cuba to define its "national integrity"; slavery was a "necessary evil"; the U.S. considered Cuba its manifest destiny; and England was gaining influence in the Caribbean. All four implied Cuba's submission. All four were dehumanizing, undermining even the imagination of real human freedom.

Varela and Luz knew imperialism's logic.[8] Varela (1788–1853) was a Catholic priest who taught physics, chemistry, and philosophy at a Havana seminary. Luz (1800–1862) was one of many students influenced philosophically and politically by Varela. They knew the point just made: institutions, or social practices, give rise to ways of thinking. It means imperialism affects thinking. For imperialism creates institutions, generating rights, roles, and ways of behaving. Martí wrote later that the tiger of imperialism crouches behind every tree, waiting to pounce.[9] He was referring to colonization of the mind.

The tiger walks on velvet paws: it shapes how people see themselves. It explains *kinds*. And it does so unnoticed: "When the prey awakens," Martí wrote, "the tiger is upon him."[10] The threat to Latin American independence, he went on to argue, is not just the U.S.: it is Latin Americans' identification with the U.S.; unnoticed and pervasive. This was an important part of the message of his famous "Our America."

European colonialism was not illogical: if the 'natives' are judged non-human, their brutal exploitation does not contradict humanist values. Jean-Paul Sartre explained this to Europeans in his introduction to Frantz Fanon's *Wretched of the Earth*.[11] Part of Sartre's point was that Europeans could not understand Fanon simply by reading him. They had to understand the "logic" that was not just a subject of Fanon's text but also informed how Europeans read that text.

Sartre's point is urgent today.[12] He was writing in the 1960s, telling Europeans it is not enough to just read Fanon. Sartre was expressing, in effect, Martí's view that the possession of knowledge does not equal education. Knowledge is not power because we have to know what it explains, or might, and this requires imagination, and caring.[13] Sartre urged Europeans to "enter in," to immerse themselves, to receive, to be changed, even if it means becoming confused, unstable. Academics today talk about "epistemic injustice," the jargon now applied to the question that concerned Varela and Luz more than 200 years ago. However, it is not clear that it is anything more than an academic debate. We return to this point below.

Latin American activists, like Martí and Guevara, preceded by Varela, Luz and their colleagues, knew the point about logic. They started with it. They knew that political action, like any action, depends upon kinds. This means it depends upon philosophy. Under imperialism, Cubans were non-persons. Varela and Luz knew this. They also knew that every thought, no matter how intimate, depends upon universals that are context-dependent. Understanding systemic discrimination and understanding universals, Varela and Luz knew Cubans' very thoughts were a vehicle for oppression. Universals arise from circumstances and conditions that are dehumanizing. *Human* liberation, Martí insisted later, required more adequate "forms and ideas."[14] Thus, extraordinarily, the Montecristi Manifesto (1895), the political statement of the Cuban Revolutionary Party, names "the nature of ideas" an objective of the liberation war.[15]

Martí did not assume that humanness was known, although he knew it was *thought* to be known, by Europeans at least. Thus, he claimed that independence was not about "civilization and barbarity" (or, in today's terms, "developed" and "developing"). Instead, it was against the "false erudition" that claims to tell us what these are.[16] A radical political movement was explicitly addressing the nature of knowledge. Martí writes that "weapons of ideas are more powerful than weapons of steel."[17] This includes ideas about human beings. Political freedom required reconceiving human beings, and how to live as such. He urged "*una nueva cultura*"—a new way of being.[18]

The Philosophical Polemic of 1838–40 was a remarkable debate across the entire Cuban island.[19] Its participants were philosophers and priests committed to independence. They are credited by historians with teaching Cubans how to think.[20] The backdrop was European liberalism, insisting that individuals possess power to determine their identity, and that we live best when we think "from the inside."[21] Luz argued at length that it justifies imperialism. Individuals by themselves possess no power to determine their destiny as human beings, at least not in a dehumanizing world. They need conceptual tools to do so. Such tools result from social collaboration and organization. More adequate universals, under imperialism, require political transformation.

3.

The Cuban philosophers mentioned above recognized what might seem to be a simple fact about how we are in the natural world: Human beings are not discrete entities. We are thoroughly interconnected and dependent upon others, including for our thinking. This was Marx's view, and Lenin's. It was not the view of European liberals, which was a matter of concern for the philosophers mentioned above. Such concern was a central part of their anti-imperialist theory and practice, as I've noted.

That human beings, minds and bodies, are part of nature was also the Buddha's view, millennia ago. Thus, the Buddha told his followers that nothing matters more to achieving happiness and well-being than choice of friends.[22] The human mind is not a hermetically sealed unit, emerging from a fountain of individuality. Its potential unfolds or withers under influence.

The word "*dhamma*" in the ancient Pāli language of India has several meanings. The teachings of the Buddha are called the *dhamma*. The word also means laws of nature and sometimes cause and effect. Insisting on *dhamma*—cause and effect—the Buddha's *dhamma*, or teaching, provides philosophical context for the anti-liberalism being discussed here. This *dhamma* is empirically based. The Buddha observed reality, like a scientist. He was an empiricist, through and through. He noticed that reality constantly changes. It consists of tiny particles, always moving. In order to act freely, we should know that reality. The Buddha did not conceive the mind as somehow separate from the world. Mind and body are in the world, connected. He urged us to know that world, starting in the body. Observe the body, quietly, to know the world.

The Buddha urges acceptance of reality "as it is," *yathabutha*. Emotional or experiential understanding is a higher form of understanding than analytical because analytical understanding depends upon intellectual traditions. Universality, the Buddha insisted, originates within the body, specifically in direct experience of cause and effect. Every act, no matter how simple, has an effect within the body. Every thought has an effect. With awareness of sensations, we are aware of such effects and better understand motivation.

The Buddha did not teach Budd*hism*.[23] He taught *dhamma,* or the laws of nature, that is, cause and effect. He did not teach Budd*hism* because cause and effect is not particular to any tradition. Intellectual understanding is explained by traditions; however, awareness of cause and effect is experiential, independent of traditions. Analytical understanding is constrained, to use a modern term, by kinds. Thus, discovery of how to live requires feelings because feelings are not similarly constrained, at least not in the first instance. The Buddha's insistence on experiential understanding of cause and effect was in effect an appreciation of the role and nature of universals.

In the *Mahāsatipatthāna Sutta,* for example, the Buddha refers to ardent, continuous awareness: *ātāpi sampajanō satimā.*[24] Disciplined awareness, though, is not of what one is doing or seeing, as is often thought. Rather, it is of cause-and-effect relations within the body—the rising and passing away of every aspect of mental and physical experience. Everything within the framework of the body is constantly changing. *Aniccia* is the Pāli word for constant change. It is the law of nature.

The Buddha departed from other Buddhas (the term "Buddha" just means "enlightened one") through his emphasis on sensations of the body, that is, on the experience of cause and effect:

> If a mediator abides observing the impermanence of pleasant sensation within the body, its decline, fading away and ceasing, and also observing his own relinquishing of attachment to such sensation, then his underlying conditioning of craving for pleasant sensation within the body is eliminated. If he abides observing the impermanence of unpleasant sensations within the body, then his underlying conditioning of aversion toward unpleasant sensations within the body is eliminated.[25]

Unfreedom is blind reaction to sensations, pleasant or unpleasant, caused by habit patterns. You see someone you dislike and react with avoidance. You think you decided but you actually reacted to (unpleasant) sensations. With greater awareness, you could judge, rationally, whether to act on the conditioning expressed in the body. Without awareness, you are enslaved by habit patterns, mental and physical. If we don't know our minds, we react, in ignorance, to the body. Desire arises, or hatred, or fear. You feel sensations. Thus, the body says "I want" or "I hate". You react, blindly. It is not freedom. It is the opposite.

Martí knew this same unfreedom: enslavement to unexamined, mostly inherited desires and fears; the same ones that make up a sense of self, glorified by liberalism into a mistaken source of freedom. It is an idea that is confused, as

Lenin noted, about the origins of every aspect of that self, which is the society into which we happen to have been born.

Therefore, without "spiritual freedom ... political freedoms will not long endure,"[26] Martí wrote. In a remarkable statement at the beginning of the "gilded age,"[27] Martí denounced values that were hedonistic, hypocritical, boring, and false:

> Contemptible times, these: when the only art that prevails is that of piling one's own granaries high, sitting on a seat of gold and living all in gold, without perceiving that ... the only result of digging up external gold is to live without gold inside! ... To the poets of today neither the lyric nor the epic mode comes naturally and calmly, nor is any lyric acceptable but that which each person draws from within, as if his own being were the only matter of whose existence he has no doubt, or as if ... there could be no theme better, more stimulating or conducive to depth and grandeur than the study of oneself.[28]

His comment is relevant today. We are urged to "get the most out of yourself, which means putting yourself in a job that is spiritually fulfilling, socially constructive, experientially diverse, emotionally enriching, self-esteem boosting, perpetually challenging and eternally edifying."[29] Such "higher selfishness" assumes "choice is a good thing ... and the more of it we have, the happier we are."[30] It may not be so.

Martí warned Latin Americans that they were "beginning with even more shameless degradation, to be the slaves of Liberty."[31] Political freedoms cannot constitute human freedom, he insisted, if Latin Americans were slaves in their thinking. From the time we are in the cradle, Martí wrote, we are swaddled and bound by "philosophers—or the religions, the parents' passions, the political systems" so that we become like blinkered horses.[32] And we do not know. We think we are free from within. But such a view robs us, not just of liberation, but of life. Like an underground river, life's real energy is submerged and hidden, and our lives flow by invisibly.[33] We do not act. We *react* to habit patterns, formed by society, in ignorance.

The person who looks to himself is like "an oyster in its shell, seeing only the prison that entraps him and believing, in the darkness, that it is the world."[34] Instead, Martí argued for "double redemption."[35] Political liberation, he insisted, requires liberation from the shell of the self, not glorifying it, as liberalism was doing. He urged Latin Americans toward "*una nueva cultura*" (a new way of living), as noted, but this was not about lifestyle. It was a "revolution in thinking."[36] Lifestyles can change without affecting how we think about ourselves. I can live an apparently revolutionary lifestyle while still thinking like an oyster in its shell, ignorantly insensitive to cause and effect.

Our most intimate deliberations can be our severest imprisonment. Or so thought Martí and the Buddha. They were not alone, by any means, as I've argued elsewhere.[37] Che Guevara made the point in 1965, responding to criticisms that the new Cuban government was repressing individual freedoms. It might be, Guevara acknowledged, but if so it is not due to strong central government. Such a view assumes that people without strong government and leadership are not already repressed. This is false. Repression results from beliefs and values making up the social fabric. We adopt them unwittingly. It is not always bad. But if a society is deeply unjust, dehumanizing even those who benefit materially, we cannot be free ignoring the "invisible cage."[38]

Individuals seek freedom, Guevara wrote, doing "our own" thing. I leave an alienating work environment and go home, for instance, to create art. But such a solution contains the "germs of the same sickness."[39] I pursue creativity within a cage—the oyster's shell.

4.

The Buddha saw a way out of the cage. We can look inward to know cause and effect. Still, it is not enough to observe the reality inside, "arising and passing away."[40] We should understand its essential characteristics: *dukkha*, *anattā*, *anicca*.[41] Of these, *anicca* or "impermanence" is most important because if one understands transience, fully recognizing the constantly changing nature of one's entire mental and physical structure, then one understands *dukkha* and *anattā*. In the *Meghiya Sutta* of the *Udana*, the Buddha says, "In one, Meghiya, who perceives impermanence, the perception of selflessness is established. One who perceives what is selfless wins the uprooting of the pride of egotism in this very life."[42] His view is simple: observe, without reacting, the constantly changing nature of the entire mental and physical structure. Mental states occur in the body.

A quiet mind is like water poured on a fire. Feelings, at first overwhelming, lose their grip. When feelings arise, mostly unnoticed, we usually react, even without choosing. We react to stimulus in the body, ignorantly. Yet if we observe without reacting, with a calm mind, we withhold fuel from the fire. And it loses its force. It may take a while, but eventually the fire diminishes.

Sometimes, it is only when the fires of fear, resentment, and strong desire are gone, that we know they were there all along. This is what the Burmese monk,

Ledi Sayadaw, calls the "kingdom of *saddha*."[43] *Saddha* is often translated as "faith." It is where proper effort to concentrate the mind provides the energy to continue doing so. It is not belief. It is a feeling of enthusiasm, arising from mental silence.

The Buddha taught simple, direct observation of cause and effect in the body. One observes systematically sensations occurring throughout the entire body. One observes constant, uncontrollable, rapid change. To do this, one must practice concentration. The mind wanders, chaotically, without logic. It can be trained, with persistence and patience.

A strange thing happens, over time. The more one practices, the more one desires training the mind, to be still, to be silent. The world of mental quiet is hidden in the modern world, submerged under a rumble of never-ending talk. But if one enters there, one discovers motivation, indeed compulsion, to go further. It takes work, and perhaps courage. But as one works, one gains confidence.

The Buddha considered *saddhā* a principal cognitive faculty. It is one of the five *indryas* or controlling faculties, allowing mastery of the mind.[44] It is also among the five *balas,* or mental powers. *Balas* are like generals, or commanders, engaged in destroying the "hostile kingdom of personality belief,"[45] discussed further below. Today, typically, faith is considered a hindrance to cognitive capacity. In early Buddhism, *saddhā* is drive or energy that arises as one performs certain actions, aiming for specific qualities: awareness and equanimity. One experiences the consequences. If they are beneficial, one continues.

Saddha is motivational. Indeed, it is sometimes identical to *virya* or effort.[46] It does not depend upon future vision. We don't need something to look forward to in order to have reasons. In answering a question (*Kalama Sutta*) about how to know which (ethical) path to follow, the Buddha suggested the following: first, examine the life of the person who teaches. If that person's life is free of hatred and greed, examine the arguments. If the arguments are compelling, you have reason to test them, by living. But only if, having lived those ideas, you experience benefits, is there reason to continue.[47]

Martí had a similar view of reasons. In discussing authenticity, Martí describes discovering his voice, his individuality, not "from my mind, warmed over, artful and beautified" but instead from "tears springing from the eyes or blood spurting out from a wound."[48] His was an embodied view of reason.[49]

In a statement that might puzzle North American readers, Martí wrote, simply, "To think is to serve."[50] It means that to think about the world *as it is* and not just as we expect it to be, given background beliefs and values, we should engage in a specific way: for the benefit of others. We must receive back from the world in a human sense, physically, intellectually, and socially. Martí was an essentialist, as was Marx, committed to the idea of essentially human capacities. We know these as we exercise them, and promote their realization in others. The statement—"to think is to serve"—is part of Martí's most famous, often cited, article, "Our America." But it is missed, unsurprisingly, by scholars in the North Atlantic.[51]

This statement about knowledge is key to a vision of who we are as human beings. It is a naturalistic, realist, essentialist view. By this I mean that it is a vision of human beings as part of the natural world, capable of knowing that world, as it is, at least in part, and not just how we believe it to be. And it is a view that recognizes that our humanity has to be discovered, that it is not automatically accessible, especially in societies that are dehumanizing.

Martí's conception of human beings is not unusual. It is present, as I have suggested above, in many traditions. It is, however, not a philosophically liberal conception. By this I mean that it is not a view that sets human beings outside the natural world as if our thinking is not affected by causal interrelations exactly as our bodily actions are. It is not a view proclaiming that individuals have power to seize our destiny, by ourselves, as if knowing that destiny is not itself a collaborative act, depending upon concepts whose meanings are radically contingent upon social, political, cultural, and economic conditions.

We do not have this supposed power to seize our destiny because we don't think alone. Karl Marx said human beings are "herd animals" not because we live in communities but because of how we think: "The human being is in the most literal sense a political animal, not merely a gregarious animal, but an animal that can individuate itself only in the midst of society."[52] We depend on others not just for cooperative activity but for awareness of ourselves as human and of our activities as humanly worthwhile.

Fidel Castro stated that anyone who reads Martí becomes a Marxist.[53] And yet many read Martí and are far from being Marxist (in a sense reflecting Marx's actual philosophy). There are two reasons. One is that they don't grasp Martí's philosophical vision.[54] The other is that they don't grasp Marx's philosophy.[55] In both we find the view that, to put it simply, the body thinks. It says that the proper functioning of my intellectual capacities depends upon relations. We are not discrete entities; rather, we are dependent creatures, with the capacity and need to receive back from people and the world. Serving others is one way in which this happens and it is a particularly reliable way, epistemically, as regards the human condition. "To think is to serve" is a statement of human interdependence. If I want my thinking to be guided by concepts reflecting human existence, I must engage with that existence, properly.

Martí was not a Marxist. He admired Marx but mentions him only a few times. He does not discuss class struggle. However, Martí was a dialectical materialist. He shared with Marx (and other philosophers) a naturalistic, realist, essentialist view of human nature and of how we discover the world, including its peoples and ourselves.

Martí rejected the fact/value distinction according to which value-claims, unlike factual claims, are not justifiable. Every cause has an effect. This means that when I act for the good of others, I benefit, and when I act to harm others, I suffer damage in some form. Thus, for Martí, "all the moral and physical truths are contained in each other."[56]

On a wall in eastern Cuba, a statement, clearly Martían, reads: *Al valor no le faltara la inteligencia; a la inteligencia no le faltara el valor* (there is no virtue without intelligence, no intelligence without virtue). It goes against the grain. Typically, we describe people as smart but not good, or kind but dumb. Not Martí: if someone is truly intelligent and not just possessing "false erudition"[57]— that is, knowledge without sensitivity—she will also be good. For she cannot become genuinely intelligent in the first place without being adequately responsive to others, as we've seen. And if someone is truly good—not just cultivating virtue for the sake of ego—she will also be intelligent. This is because she cannot be good in this sense without properly understanding and responding to relations with others, with nature.

When I interact with others, there are effects. Of course, I might not notice. When I kill a mosquito, because I can and because I want to, I experience effects. Killing other beings, needlessly, is not just, or most interestingly, a moral concern of the naturalistic view expressed above. Even the smallest act of harm creates agitation in the mind. The smallest act of good will brings partial relief from such agitation. I can know such effects, experientially, with training, with patience.

It is why some misunderstand Martí on science. He admired science.[58] Yet he denied that "reason alone is capable of penetrating the mystery of life ... The scientist sniffs like a dog, but like a great condor the spirit crosses the abyss in which the engrossed naturalist wanders."[59] His view, clearly expressed throughout his entire work is that without sensitivity and awareness, reason, understood intellectually, is limited. It is because of the nature of thinking: reason depends upon universals, which depend, as we saw above, upon institutions and social practices.

Early Buddhist philosophers referred to *sakkāyadiṭṭhi*, or personality belief. It is the beliefs about ourselves that we rely upon, day by day, to interpret our lives.

It includes such universals as national identity, opinions, loyalties, as well as petty likes and dislikes. Such beliefs are derived from traditions and from social practices. Ledi Sayadaw considered *sakkāyadiṭṭhi* a deep and pervasive evil,[60] preventing freedom: we invest ourselves in personality belief, expecting it to ground human well-being, non-morally at least, and it cannot do so. It is impossible, for it is explained by parents, teachers, social context, and the media, among other factors. Investment in *sakkāyadiṭṭhi* expresses ignorance of cause and effect. The Buddha, like Martí, had no truck with the supposed fact/value distinction: precisely as I understand the nature of reality as constantly changing, I begin to understand myself and others. I understand cause and effect. And when I engage with others out of good will, I understand causal connectedness.

Sakkāyadiṭṭhi is a deep and pervasive evil because I don't understand that it is caused. I value it precisely because it is *mine,* not for any other reason. I try to make it consistent so I can depend upon it for security and comfort. It provides neither, realistically. Reasons are derived from life plans, which we evaluate, occasionally, according to a self-concept which itself results from pursuing such life plans. It generates absurdity: I identify the importance of choices and actions by presuming the importance of my choices and actions, for me. It's a view that looks inward. Martí likened the holding of such a view to being an oyster in its shell, as mentioned above. Now, to be sure, the Buddha urged us to look inward also, but not at the conscious mind. He urged us to observe, objectively, the rising and passing away of sensations in the body. We learn through observation of the body that the world is constantly changing.

Martí's view was similar in that it urges us to look outward at the world and how it works. It urges us to take seriously the cause-and-effect nature of the entire universe, including the lives of human beings. He wrote:

> Men must know the composition, enrichment, changes and applications of the material elements from whose development they derive the healthful pride of one who works directly with Nature, the bodily strength derived from contact with the forces of the land, and the honest and secure wealth produced by its cultivation. Men need someone to stir their compassion often, to make their tears flow, and to give their souls the supreme benefit of generous feelings; for through the wonderful compensation of Nature whoever gives of himself grows; and whoever draws within himself, living for small pleasures and afraid to share them with others, thinking only of greedily satisfying one's own appetites, will gradually change from a man into pure solitude, carrying in his heart all the gray of wintertime. He becomes within—and appears to others—an insect. Men grow, they grow physically and visibly, when they learn something, when they

begin to possess something, and when they have done some good ... To be humane is the only way to be free. To be cultured is the only way to be free.[51]

Thus, in Martí's view, we know the world, when we do, because we "derive the healthful pride of one who works directly with nature." We need nature, including other people, to stimulate an emotional response so that we can receive the "supreme benefit of generous feelings."

Sakkāyadiṭṭhi is a fabrication. It cannot deliver truth about human well-being. It can only tell us what we already know, or think we know, from the perspective of a society arising at a point in time. For Martí, in contrast, freedom involves a "Herculean struggle" against our own selves.[62] Nothing is more difficult, for any human being, he argued, than distinguishing that which has been imposed upon us by society from that which springs from essential humanness. We do not discover humanness through intellectual study; at least not alone. In the same article in which he describes the plodding nature of science ("Emerson"), he points to a different sort of cognitive capacity: intuitions. It is, he writes, "When the mind falls silent ... [that] intuition bursts forth like a caged bird certain of the sky."[63]

5.

In the two final sections, I emphasize the distinctive focus of Martí and the Buddha: how to know and how to know that I know. It is this that explains why anarchism offers false promises.

Some will read the above discussion and find therein a comforting view of human connection. Relations and connectedness are popular. There is a health value. Usually, such talk is about how to live: sharing circles, nature experience, cooperative living. It is not about how to know. Properly understood, the point above is hard. It involves renunciation, as I now explain.

The belief that we think alone persists despite science. The explanation is simple: We do not consider evidence against beliefs that are well established. If a belief is presupposed in day to day activity, including in my self-concept, I explain away the counter-evidence. This is well known to philosophers of science.[64] For instance, if I release an object and it does not fall, and I make a sophisticated argument against the law of gravity, no one will study my argument. No one will check my evidence. It is because my claim is implausible.[65] Reason works like this. If the lights go out, and someone blames invading aliens, no one investigates. If someone did investigate, she would be considered a bit crazy. We consider evidence for claims that are plausible, and plausibility depends upon expectations arising from social practices. If a belief's truth is expected, as we expect gravity, we dismiss counter-examples, rationally.

The liberal/libertarian/anarchist view of freedom is expected. We assume we live best from "within", fulfilling desires, preferences, and life plans, within specified limits. We follow dreams, not because they are good but because we have them; because they are ours. Freedom is, roughly, not being prevented (including by government) from doing what we want. Accordingly, we expect that the conscious mind represents the real self. French philosopher René Descartes, had this view in 1641: my self is my mind. His view is disputed, widely. It is almost a cliché to refer to the Cartesian view of the self as mistaken, and not just in philosophy. It ignores the unconscious mind. It ignores social conditioning that explains how we think.

But the appeal of the "inner voice" persists. It is the voice of the self, the expression of the narrative we tell about ourselves throughout an entire life. We struggle to make that narrative consistent, for our comfort and security. Political philosophers claim, without argument, that it is uncontroversial that we live best "from the inside", meaning the self; no one lives well following beliefs and values from "outside."[66] Or so it is claimed, usually without argument. The so-called negative view of freedom says we are free if we do what we want. It gets dressed up. Essentially, though, my conscious mind is the best resource for controlling my life. Or so they say.

There are other views. We've been discussing them. They are not expected, just as the failure of gravity is not expected. They take more argument. Even so, just as my arguments against gravity would be dismissed, no matter how compelling, arguments against philosophical liberalism are often dismissed, even mocked.

In the 2000s, I introduced a philosophy course for credit at my university; taught at the University of Havana by Cuban philosophers. I wanted students to know that ideas, not just culture, come from Cuba. The ideas are about human beings, about how to live, and the nature of reality. The course was quickly moved to Development Studies, a social sciences department. It was as if a course in Cuba could not be philosophy. It had to be geography or sociology.

In the end, the course was renamed as a course on culture, although I invented it to counter the stereotype that ideas come from the North, and culture from the South. When North Americans talk about freedom, we are talking about the human condition. When Latin Americans talk about freedom, it is about Latin Americans. It gets studied, if it does, as ethnography or, as in Martí's case, poetry. In the more than twenty years I have gone regularly to Cuba, I can't remember a single researcher among those with research grants from North Atlantic universities in Cuba who knew its philosophical traditions. It is as if the existence of such traditions is not plausible.[67]

Mostly, I wanted students to know they could think differently about themselves, as human beings. At the Summit of the Americas in 2015, at which Cuba was present for the first time since expulsion by the U.S. in 1962, President Obama wanted to bury the past. Argentinean president Cristina Fernández disagreed. Cuba was at the summit, she proposed, not because of negotiations but because Cuba has fought for more than sixty years with unprecedented dignity. Cuba's history, she suggested, is morally unprecedented.

Even U.S. political conservatives know Cuba's difference. When Castro resigned in 2006, many predicted chaos. Yet Julia Sweig, U.S. Rockefeller senior fellow, noted a "stunning display of orderliness and seriousness," indicating the Cuban Revolution rests upon "far more than the charisma, authority and legend of [Raul and Fidel Castro]."[68] The "far more" is philosophical, as well as political. In 2014, the *Wall Street Journal* reported that "[f]ew have heeded the call [to fight Ebola], but one country has responded in strength: Cuba." Cuba responded without hesitation, sending more than 450 doctors and nurses, chosen from more than 15,000 volunteers, by far the largest medical mission sent by any country. Why did 15,000 medical workers volunteer to risk their lives for the suffering people of West Africa? There is an explanation.

It is supported by capitalist economists.[69] It turns out that we are not, after all, mostly motivated by material incentives. Instead, we derive reasons from what we receive back from activities, personally. We receive back from our actions, and even from our thoughts. It is a fact about the universe, governed by causation, known to sensitive, intelligent thinkers for millennia. Many such thinkers have noted the universal connectedness of all life. They have noted, as did Martí, that, "through the wonderful dispensation of nature, whoever gives of himself grows."[70]

Cuban history makes such motivation believable. Cuban presence in Angola, according to historian Richard Gott, was "entirely without selfish motivation."[71] Cuba sent 300,000 volunteers between 1975 and 1991, more than 2,000 of whom died, to push back and eventually defeat apartheid South Africa. In Pretoria, a wall of names commemorates those who died in the struggle against apartheid. Cuban names are there. No other foreign country is represented.[72]

The U.S. claimed Cuba was acting as a Soviet proxy. Yet according to U.S. intelligence, Castro had "no intention of subordinating himself to Soviet discipline and direction."[73] He criticized the Soviets as dogmatic and opportunistic, ungenerous toward Third World liberation movements, and unwilling to adequately support

North Vietnam. Former U.S. secretary of state Henry Kissinger wrote in his memoir twenty-five years later that Castro was "probably the most genuinely revolutionary leader then in power."[74] U.S. Intelligence even identified the real motivation for Cuba's costly involvement. Castro, it reported, "places particular importance on maintaining a 'principled' foreign policy ... [and] on questions of basic importance such as Cuba's right and duty to support nationalist revolutionary movements and friendly governments in the Third World, Castro permits no compromise of principle for the sake of economic or political expediency."[75] In 1991, Cuba's "great crusade" led Nelson Mandela to ask, "What other country can point to a record of greater selflessness than Cuba has displayed in its relations to Africa?"[76]

Cuba's internationalism continues. Cuba began exporting doctors in 1963 to the newly independent Algeria. After Hurricanes George and Mitch devastated Haiti, Honduras, and Guatemala in 1998, Cuba sent 2,000 doctors and other health professionals. They were replaced by other Cubans willing and able to work where no health services previously existed. After Hurricane Katrina, Cuba offered to send, at no cost, 1,586 medical personnel and 36 tons of emergency medical supplies to the U.S., an offer that was turned down.[77]

Visitors to Cuba ask why a poor country spends such resources on foreigners. Tour guides at the Latin American School of Medical Sciences, offering full scholarships to foreigners not otherwise able to train as doctors, explain that Cubans believe in sharing what they have, not what they have left over. The answer elicits skepticism, even derision: a nice idea but not realistic.

It is realistic. Or so argued Martí, in sync with the Buddha. Human beings are part of nature, and we depend upon nature, including other human beings, even and especially for our thinking. On such a view, there is no mystery that so many medical workers would volunteer to fight the deadly Ebola virus: we live better, and freely, when others live better, and freely. We think better. It is not about morality but about the nature of reality. It is about cause and effect. It is about thinking.

6.

But there is a cost. Renunciation is the idea that we must sometimes lose or give up what matters in order to gain in another sense. The idea exists in the work of religious philosophers such as Ivan Illich and Thomas Merton.[78] We lose life to gain life. It also exists in Marx, who thought we must change the world that changes us.[79] Change is loss.

Cuba's medical internationalism is often presented as moral achievement.[80] It is thereby diminished: anyone can do the same, if they're good. Presenting it that way ignores Martí's "revolution in thinking." If human beings are interdependent, causally connected, then learning, if it is really discovery, is like a passage through dark waters, as Lenin said.[81] You do not undertake such a passage without reason. But confidence arises when you know it is necessary. You know it is necessary when you know how the world works: cause and effect.

The picture of knowledge in Martí and the Buddha involves loss. It is an implausible idea in modern societies. I see this in university education. It is about gain. Students know a relatively rich, protected lifestyle cuts them off. And so they do many *things,* one after the other. They claim to have lived in this or that way, to have experienced hardship, simplicity, poverty, insecurity. Maybe. But it's presented as something done and accomplished, a feat to be listed along with other feats. It's a possession, a step to *somewhere,* unrelated to the experience they just had.

Knowledge and education are *possessed.* Martí, as already noted, made the remarkable claim that the biggest barrier to independence was a view of knowledge: "false erudition." It is the idea that education is knowledge, which is possessed. Recognizing cause and effect, *dhamma,* means we learn when the process of knowing acts *upon* us, changing even our idea of learning and why it matters. And this means that if we want to learn, that is, if we want to discover what was previously unimaginable, we should expect loss. The goals of research should change, in some way, as we research, including when that goal is ourselves.

Martí argued that "reason alone is [not] capable of penetrating the mystery of life and bringing peace to man and putting him in possession of the means to grow."[82] He was not against science, as noted. Neither was the Buddha. They both recognized that knowledge, no matter how much we possess, does not prevent ignorance and confusion.

Romanian-French playwright Eugène Ionesco made this point graphically. His 1959 play *Rhinoceros* is about a small town where people turn into rhinoceroses. At first, everyone is horrified by the rhinoceroses but eventually the change becomes seductive. Even the town's logician becomes a rhinoceros, happily, wanting to "move with the times."[83] In the end, Berenger is the only human remaining and now he is a monster. Berenger, reminds himself that "[a] man's not ugly to look at, not ugly at all!" However, a few sentences later he says, "I should have gone with them while there was still time."[84]

Berenger can know he is human. He can access his intuitions and build his awareness of social practices explaining false beliefs. But rhinoceritis is now the fabric of his society. It means Berenger's beliefs that he is human can be dismissed, *rationally,* just as any rational person would dismiss my arguments against gravity, without examining them. They are implausible, given social expectations. Reason works this way.

Rhinoceritis was the concern of the early Cuban activists and later Martí. Reason and knowledge cannot respond to imperialism, the disease of dehumanization, at least not alone. Hence Martí's warning about "false erudition". As long as education is gain, synonymous with the possession of knowledge, there would be no independence for Latin Americans. Reason and the possession of knowledge do not answer rhinoceritis. They depend upon it. They depend upon universals, as Varela and Luz, and the Buddha before them, well knew.

It is tempting to separate Martí's heart-warming view of connectedness from his "revolution in thinking" and its implications for political organization. The author of the Cuban single-party system is, after all, Martí, not Lenin. In "Our America," he argues that good government requires bringing about "by means and institutions . . . the desirable state in which every man knows himself and is active."[85] That is, *government* must bring about conditions for adequate self-knowledge. Fundamental institutions need to be transformed in order that individuals think better about their own lives. Thinking better, more humanly, at least in a dehumanizing world, requires political organization, broad theoretical vision, and leaders.

The Buddha, of course, was not political. Yet his view has political implications. This is because it is about thinking. It involves *saddha. Saddha* is not compatible with the pursuit of comfort. *Saddha* is the motivation that arises when we live our awareness of cause and effect. It is not possible to fully understand cause and effect, *and* to live one's life following petty likes and dislikes. To try to do so involves a contradiction. Awareness of cause and effect, *anicca,* is awareness of *dukkha* and *anattā.* It is not possible to be experientially aware of impermanence while at the same time being motivated by petty likes and dislikes. Understood properly, as ephemeral, such likes and dislikes cannot motivate. They dissolve.

Ionesco said that the only antidote to rhinoceritis is silence.[86] Berenger can know the way forward but not through reason alone, and not without renunciation. Reason depends upon intellectual traditions. Within such traditions, Berenger is a monster. Rational folk can dismiss his claims to humanness, and he may dismiss them himself. They are implausible. To live the truth, as he feels it, he must *give up or lose* his investment in *sakkayaditthi,* which is investment in his *self*. Truth is there, and is accessible, through intuition and experience, but not comfortably.

The Buddha was not political. But he lived simply. How we live, he taught, is inseparable from how we think. The smallest act of harm toward other beings causes agitation in the mind. It prevents concentration. It prevents access to truth. Martí's insistence, in the Montecristi Manifesto, on the "nature of ideas" was not without justification, given his profound understanding of imperialism. It explains Cuba's "unprecedented" history. To see it as a moral achievement is an easy way out for those who cannot, or will not grasp Martí's fervent anti-imperialism.

Emma Goldman said "Anarchism, then, really stands for the . . . free grouping of individuals . . . according to individual desires, tastes, and inclinations."[87] Such a formula can only result in slavery to habit patterns, which is enslavement to imperialism. Resisting rhinoceritis takes faith. But faith is energy depending precisely upon that faith, properly understood. It is a passage through dark water. The idea draws upon ancient traditions. Reading Martí, we see they are not so ancient after all, just unwanted and therefore dismissed, philosophically.

Notes

1 Lenin, "On the Question of Dialectics," 361.
2 E.g. Wilson 1999.
3 E.g. Kuhn, *The Structure of Scientific Revolutions*, 66.
4 E.g. Searle, *The Construction of Social Reality*.
5 Lenin, Conspectus of Hegel's *Science of Logic*, 189.
6 Martí, "Our America," 290.
7 Conde, "Ensayo introductorio," 36; Hart, *Ética, cultura, y política*, 49.
8 Rodríguez, *Pensar, prever, server*, 13.
9 Martí, "Our America," 292–93.
10 Ibid., 292– 93.
11 Sartre, "Preface," 15.
12 E.g. Babbitt, "America's Wars, Failure of Democracy: What Happened to 'There Are No Innocents'?"
13 See e.g. Babbitt, "Why it's so hard to understand what is happening in Venezuela?"
14 Martí, "Our America," 292.
15 Martí, "The Montecristi Manifesto," 343–44.
16 Martí, "Our America," 290.
17 Ibid., 288.

18 Rodríguez, "Una en alma y intento," 5.

19 E.g. Babbitt, "Cuba's Quiet Wealth: Why It's Needed."

20 E.g. Torres-Cuevas, *Historia del pensamiento cubano*, 329f.

21 It is important not to confuse the liberal idea of the "inner voice" or thinking "from the inside" with the idea of conscience. The "inner voice" is the voice of the self, the expression of a narrative of self-importance we struggle to make coherent throughout an entire life. Conscience, for most of us, tears that narrative apart. It breaks it down. In *Les Misérables*, Victor Hugo writes about Jean Valjean: "how many times had that implacable light [his conscience] . . . torn him apart, tortured him and broken him."

22 E.g. Boddhi, *Dhamma Reflections*, 125–7.

23 E.g. Hart, *The Art of Living: Vipassana Meditation as Taught by S. N. Goenka*, 18.

24 Gautama 2013.

25 Gautama *Mahāsatipatthāna Sutta*; Hart, *The Art of Living*, 156.

26 Martí, "Emerson," 49.

27 Rodríguez, *Pensar, prever, server: El ideario de José Martí*, 9.

28 Martí, "Emerson," 43– 44.

29 Brooks 2000, 134 cited in Taylor, *A Secular Age*, 477.

30 Taylor, *A Secular Age*, 479.

31 Martí, "Emerson," 50–51.

32 Martí, "Prologue to Juan Antonio Pérez Bonalde's Poem of Niagara," 49.

33 Ibid., 49.

34 Martí, "The Poet Walk Whitman," 187.

35 García Marruz 1968/2011: 406.

36 Rodríguez, *Pensar, prever, server*, 10.

37 Babbitt *Humanism and Embodiment: From Cause and Effect to Secularism*.

38 "Socialism and Man in Cuba," 207.

39 Ibid.

40 E.g. Gautama *Mahāsatipatthāna Sutta*, 7, 29.

41 *Dukkha* is often translated as suffering but means something more like dissatisfaction, the experience of never being completely happy, no matter how many desires are fulfilled. *Anattā* refers to selflessness. It is not the denial of agency. It expresses the substance-less nature of what is referred to as "self."

42 Cited in Gautama, *Mahāsatipatthāna Sutta*, xii.

43 Ledi Sayadaw, *Requisites of Enlightenment*, 73.

44 Ledi Sayadaw 2007, 62.

45 Ibid., 72.

46 Ibid., 64.

47 Boddhi 2005: 79f.

48 Martí. "My Verses," 57.

49 Babbitt 2014b.

50 Martí, "Our America," 296.

51 I use the term following Charles Taylor (2007) to refer to North America and Northern Europe. There is not much scholarship on Martí in the North Atlantic academic world in any case but almost none on Martí as a philosopher. 'To think is to serve' is referred to in the title of a book by Cuban Martí scholar Paulo Pedro Rodríguez (2012) but I have not seen it in English language discussions of Martí.

52 Marx, "The German Ideology," 223.

53 Castro, *Fidel and Religion: Castro Talks on Revolution and Religion with Frie Betto*, 149. I am of course aware of those who argue that Martí was a critic of communism and would have been a critic of socialist Cuba today. I have addressed these arguments in *José Martí, Ernesto "Che" Guevara and Global Development Ethics*. In short such arguments ignore Martí's metaphysical and epistemological views, which share almost nothing with liberal (capitalist) conceptions of essentially self-interested human beings, motivated by material incentives and employing predominantly instrumental rationality. When Martí's full philosophical picture is acknowledged, it is impossible to read him as a liberal proponent of capitalism.

54 Pedro Paulo Rodrguez and Cintio Vitier, renowned Martí scholars, suggest that even Latin Americans are not familiar with Martí's philosophical vision and its political implications (Rodríguez 2012c: 177; Vitier, "Martí futuro," 153–78).

55 Twentieth-century academic Marxists ignored Marx's dialectical materialism, which is his view of how we know through causal engagement. See Wood, *Karl Marx: Arguments of the Philosophers*, 266.

56 Martí, "Our America," 129.

57 Ibid., 290.

58 E.g. Vitier *Vida y obra del apóstol José Martí*, 211.

59 Martí, "Emerson," 128.

60 Ledi Sayadaw, *Manuals of Dhamma*, 256–7.

61 Ledi Sayadaw, *Requisites of Enlightenment*, 46–47.

62 Martí, "Prologue to Juan Antonio Pérez Bonalde's Poem of Niagara," 49.

63 Martí, "Emerson," 127.

64 E.g. Boyd, "Realism, Natural Kinds and Philosophical Methods." As I write this Donald Trump has just been elected U.S. president. Some argue that his election could have been foreseen if so many had not been drawn in for decades to lies about wars abroad and the benefits of globalization. The lies were known to be lies but had become a culture, presupposed in national image and daily life. E.g. http://www.counterpunch.org/2016/11/10/the-big-split/ (accessed November 10, 2016); http://www.counterpunch.org/2017/02/03/unspeakable-the-black-book-of-imperial-terrorism/ (accessed February 5, 2017).

65 Kitcher, *Abusing Science: The Case against Creationism*.

66 Kymlicka, *Liberalism, Community and Culture*, 12; Mills, "The Domination Contract," 102.

67 For instance, Veltmeyer and Rushton 2013, a (relatively) recent discussion of Cuba's conception of socialism and the contribution it might make to global development includes no discussion of Martí's philosophy.

68 Cited in Veltmeyer and Rushton, *The Cuban Revolution as Socialist Development*, 301.

69 E.g. Pink, "The Surprising Truth about Motivation."

70 Martí, "Wandering Teachers," 46–47.

71 Gott, *Cuba: A New History*, 238–40.

72 Gleijeses, *Conflicting Missions: Havana, Washington, and Africa, 1959–1976*, 300–327.

73 Ibid., 373.

74 Kissinger 1999, cited in Gleijeses, *Conflicting Missions*, 306.

75 Gleijeses *Visions of Freedom: Havana. Washington, Pretoria and the Struggle for Southern Africa, 1976– 1991*, 523–24.

76 Cited in Gleijeses, *Visions of Freedom*, 526.

77 Brouwer, *Revolutionary Doctors*.

78 E.g. Babbitt 2014a.

79 Wood (*Karl Marx: Arguments of the Philosophers*) and Hart (*Ética, cultura, y política*) point out that Marx's philosophy is not well-known, particularly his view of knowledge. Wood remarks that Marxist scholars ignored the 'mystical shell' of Marx's realism, naturalism and essentialism (*Karl Marx: Arguments of the philosophers*, 266).

80 E.g. Huish *Where No Doctor Has Gone before: Cuba's Place in the Global Health Landscape*, 150.

81 Lenin, "Conspectus of Hegel's *Science of Logic.*," 114.

82 Martí, "Our America," 128.

83 Ionesco, *Rhinoceros*, 102–3.

84 Ibid., 104.

85 Martí, "Our America," 290.

86 Cited in Merton, Rain and the Rhinoceros," 21.

87 Goldman, 62.

References

Babbitt, Susan. *Humanism and Embodiment: From Cause and Effect to Secularism.* Bloomsbury, 2014.

Babbitt, Susan. *José Martí, Ernesto "Che" Guevara and Global Development Ethics: The Battle for Ideas.* New York: Palgrave Macmillan, 2014.

Babbitt, Susan. "America's Wars, Failure of Democracy: What Happened to 'There Are No Innocents'?" *Global Research*. February 2, 2017. Accessed February 3, 2017. http://www.globalresearch.ca/americas-war-failure-of-democracy-what-happened-to-there-are-no-innocents/5572381.

Babbitt, Susan. "Cuba's Quiet Wealth: Why It's Needed." *Counterpunch*. September 2015. Accessed February 8, 2017. http://www.counterpunch.org/2015/09/30/cubas-quiet-wealth-why-it-is-needed/.

Babbitt, Susan. "Why it's so hard to understand what is happening in Venezuela." *Counterpunch*. August 8, 2017. Accessed August 13, 2017. https://www.counterpunch.org/2017/08/08/why-its-hard-to-understand-whats-happening-in-venezuela/.

Boddhi, Bhikkhu. *In the Buddha's Words: An Anthology of Discourses from the Pali Canon*. Boston: Wisdom publications, 2005.

Boddhi, Bhikkhu. *Dhamma Reflections*. Kandi, Sri Lanka: Buddhist Publications, 2015.

Boyd, Richard N. Realism, natural kinds and philosophical methods. In *The semantics and metaphysics of natural kinds*, edited by Helen Beebee and Nigel Sabbarton. New York: Routledge, 2010.

Brouwer, Steven. *Revolutionary Doctors*. New York: Monthly Review Press, 2011.

Castro Ruz, Fidel. *Fidel and Religion: Castro Talks on Revolution and Religion with Frie Betto*. Translated by the Cuban Centre for Translation and Interpretation, Trans. New York: Simon & Schuster, 1987.

Coetzee, J. M. *Disgrace*. London: Secker and Warburg, 1999.

Conde Rodríguez, Alicia. Ensayo introductorio: Para una teoría crítica de la emancipación cubana. In Roberto Agramonte, ed., *La polémica filosófica cubana 1838–1839*. Havana: Clásicos Cubanos, 2000.

Gautama, Siddhartha. *Mahāsatipatthāna Sutta: The Great Discourse on the Establishing of Awareness* Onalaska WA: Vipassana Research Institute, 2010.

Gleijeses, Piero. *Conflicting missions: Havana, Washington, and Africa, 1959–1976*. Chapel Hill, NC: University of North Carolina Press, 2002.

Gleijeses, Piero. *Visions of freedom: Havana. Washington, Pretoria and the Struggle for Southern Africa, 1976–1991*. Chapel Hill, NC: University of North Carolina Press, 2013.

Gott, Richard. *Cuba: A New History*. New Haven: Yale University Press, 2005.

Guevara, Ernesto "Che." "Socialism and Man in Cuba." In *The Che Guevara Reader: Writings on Guerilla Strategy, Politics and Revolution*, edited by David Deutschman, 212–220. New York: Ocean Press, 1997 (originally published 1965).

Hart Dávalos, Armando. *Ética, cultura, y política*. Havana: Estudios Martianos, 2006.

Hart, William. *The Art of Living: Vipassana Meditation as Taught by S.N. Goenka* New York: Harper Collins, 1987.

Huish, Robert. *Where no doctor has gone before: Cuba's place in the global health landscape*. Waterloo, ON: Wilfred Laurier University Press, 2013.

Ionesco, Eugène. *Rhinoceros*. Translated by Derek Prouse. New York: Penguin, 2000.

Kissinger, Henry. *Years of Renewal.* New York: Simon & Schuster, 1999.

Kitcher, Philip. *Abusing Science: The Case Against Creationism.* Boston: MIT Press, 1982.

Kuhn, Thomas. *The Structure of Scientific Revolutions* (2nd ed.). Chicago: University of Chicago Press, 1970.

Kymlicka, Will. *Liberalism, Community and Culture.* Oxford: Clarendon Press, 1991.

Ledi Sayadaw. *Manuals of Dhamma.* Igatpuri, India: Vipassana Research Institute, 1999.

Ledi Sayadaw. *Requisites of Enlightenment.* Kandy, Sri Lanka: Buddhist Publication Society, 1999.

Lenin, V. I. "Conspectus of Hegel's *Science of Logic.*" In *Collected Works, Vol. 38*, edited by Stewart Smith, translated by Clemens Dutt, 85–126. London, UK: Lawrence and Wishart, 1961 (originally published 1930).

Lenin, V. I. "On the Question of Dialectics." In *Collected Works, Vol. 38*, edited by Stewart Smith, translated by Clemens Dutt, 355–64. London, UK: Lawrence and Wishart, 1961 (originally published 1930).

Luz y Caballero, José de la. *La Polemica filosófica, Volume 5.* Havana: University of Havana, 1947.

Martí, José. "The Montecristi Manifesto." In *José Martí: Selected Writings*, edited and translated by Esther Allen, 337–345. New York, NY: Penguin Books, 2002 (originally published 1895).

Martí, José. "Wandering Teachers." In *José Martí Reader: Writings on the Americas*, edited by Deborah Shnookal & Mirta Muñez, 46–50. New York, NY: Ocean Books, 1999 (originally published 1894).

Martí, José. "Prologue to Juan Antonio Pérez Bonalde's Poem of Niagara." In *José Martí: Selected Writings*, edited and translated by Esther Allen, 43–51. New York, NY: Penguin Books, 2002 (originally published 1882).

Martí, José. "Emerson." In *José Martí: Selected Writings*, edited and translated by Esther Allen, 116– 29. New York, NY: Penguin Books, 2002 (originally published 1882).

Martí, José. "The Poet Walt Whitman." In *José Martí: Selected Writings*, edited and translated by Esther Allen, 183–194. New York, NY: Penguin Books, 2002 (originally published 1887).

Martí, José. "Our America." In *José Martí: Selected Writings*, edited and translated by Esther Allen, 288–296. New York, NY: Penguin Books, 2002 (originally published 1891).

Martí, José. "My Verses." In *José Martí: Selected Writings*, edited and translated by Esther Allen, 57. New York, NY: Penguin Books, 2002 (originally published 1913).

Marx, Karl. The German Ideology, part 1. In *The Marx-Engels Reader*, second edition, edited by Robert C. Tucker, 146–202. New York: Norton, 1978 (originally published 1932).

Merton, Thomas. "Rain and the Rhinoceros." In *Raids on the Unspeakable*, 9–26. New York: New Directions, 1967.

Mills, Charles. "The Domination contract." In *Contract and Domination*, edited by Carole Pateman and Charles W. Mills, 79–105. Cambridge, UK: Polity Press, 2007.

Pink, Dan. "The surprising truth about motivation." *RSA Animate*. 2010. Accessed November 19, 2013. YouTube video retrieved from http://www. youtube. com /watch ?v = u6XAPnuFjJc.

Rodríguez, Pedro Pablo. (2010). "Una en alma y intento": Identidad y unidad latinoamericana en José Martí, *De los dos Américas: Aproximaciones al pensamento martiano* (pp. 3–48). Havana, Cuba: Centro de estudios martianos.

Rodríguez, Pedro Paulo. *Pensar, prever, server: El ideario de José Martí*. Havana, Cuba: Ediciones Unión, 2012.

Sartre, Jean-Paul. Preface. In Frantz Fanon, *Wretched of the Earth*, trans. Constance Farrington, 7–31. New York: Grove Press, 1963 (originally published 1961).

Searle, John. *The Construction of Social Reality*. New York: Free Press, 1995.

Sweig, Julia. "Fidel's Final 'Victory.'" *Foreign Affairs* 1 (2007): 39–56.

Taylor, Charles. *A Secular Age*. Cambridge: Belknap Press of Harvard University Press, 2007.

Torres-Cuevas, Eduardo. *Historia del pensamiento cubano: Volúmen 1, Tomo 1*. Havana, Cuba: Editorial de ciencias sociales, 2004.

Veltmeyer, Henry, and Mark Rushton. *The Cuban Revolution as Socialist Development*. Chicago: Haymarket Books, 2013.

Vitier, Cintio. Martí futuro. In *Temas Martianas*, edited by Cintio Vitier and Fina García Marruz, 153–78. Havana, Cuba: Centro de estudios martianos, 2011 (originally published 1964).

Vitier, Cintio. *Vida y obra del apóstol José Martí*. Havana, Cuba: Centro de estudios martianos, 2006.

Wilson, Robert A., ed. *Species: New Interdisciplinary Essays*. Boston: MIT Press, 1999.

Wood, Allen. *Karl Marx: Arguments of the Philosophers: Second edition*. New York: Routledge, 2004.

9

The Ants and the Elephant: Martial Arts and Liberation Philosophy in the Americas

George Fourlas

The title of this paper, "The Ants and the Elephant," is inspired by the Dead Prez music video for one of their more popular tracks, "Hip Hop." Throughout the video martial artists train together to the sound of anti-colonial and anti-capitalist lyrics, culminating in the text flashing onscreen: "Together the ants . . . will conquer the Elephant."[1] "Hip Hop" is striking, it makes you move, and through explicit references to community organizing and the virtues of martial arts practice for realizing oneself with others, it inspires. In other words, the performativity of the video is at least partly rooted in the emphasis it places on a dialogic or communal ideal that is central to the martial artist's way of life and which many people crave in the absence of a meaningful community. Dead Prez's works stand with others in their amalgamation of martial arts and liberation themes.

The prevalence of liberatory and martial arts themes across counter-hegemonic representations is important because many people, including myself, have been influenced by these sorts of representations and find them meaningful in relation to the problem—violent domination—that is much bigger than hip hop; yet, the popular understanding and representation of the martial arts is that they are primarily violent. Thus, here I challenge this popular misunderstanding, and I argue that the martial arts as such are intended to be liberatory and that their violent manifestation is exceptional. In what follows I discuss the coexistence of both violence and peace-building in the martial arts, and I frame questions about the violent aspects through a distinction between competition and play. As I show, the liberatory potential of martial arts aligns with decolonial and liberatory philosophies of the Americas, making the development of uniquely South American martial arts form a bodily enactment of the Asian-Latin American philosophical conversation.

1. The two faces of the arts

In the lyrics to "Hip Hop," Dead Prez illuminate the challenges that many face in the effort to survive and find meaning in a world defined through violence. Though their focus is on the art of hip hop and how it has been appropriated and degraded, such that the ideals of hip hop are obscured, the problems faced in a violent world are consistent across experience (and part of the reason that it is bigger than hip hop). Dead Prez says, "You would rather have a Lexus, some justice, a dream or some substance? A Beamer, a necklace or freedom?" The lure of the self and its materialist manifestation is powerful, and despite the overwhelming and public suffering of the global majority many people choose the necklace over freedom. The martial arts also face this problem, having two sides, two faces: one form is a violent spectacle and the other is liberatory in its focus. In this section, I emphasize the violent side, while in the next I illuminate the liberatory and authentic aspect.

The violent spectacle of the arts is, unfortunately, better known, in part because professionalization has afforded gladiatorial displays and, as more people seek glory, the presence of schools that train students for purposes other than professionalization is diminished. And through the spectacle we find many examples of violent domination being enacted by individuals who identify as or are identified with martial arts. Such cases are increasingly common among Ultimate Fighting Championship (UFC) fighters. For example, Jonathan Koppenhaver (aka War Machine), who beat his ex-girlfriend and another man to within inches of their lives, is part of a frightening trend among mixed martial arts (MMA) fighters who are being arrested for domestic abuse at significantly higher rates than the U.S. national average.[2] In response to the increase in domestic violence among UFC fighters, Rener Gracie—who, along with his grandfather and father, helped create and disseminate Brazilian Jiu Jitsu throughout the world—suggests that there is a problem because the type of people who are taking up the sport already have internalized and normalized violence as a way of life, stating "You look at the potential of MMA and say, 'Holy cow I can make money fighting people and I can be famous and I can win a gold belt and be recognized and respected around the world for being one of the best for fighting? Where do I sign up?'"[3]

The commodification of violence is especially enticing for people who have few other options, and in our hyper-individualistic society this motivation is catalyzed as fighters strive to be godlike, lionized individuals. The audience is therefore also responsible for the reproduction of domination through their love of gladiatorial displays. The violent fetish is most apparent whenever a fight is too technical—i.e., both fighters demonstrate their art rather than merely attempting to destroy the other—and the broader audience complains, leading to a potential capital loss. Like other degraded practices, the media spectacle that feeds the bloodthirsty audience overshadows real martial artists and misrepresents what the arts are really about.

Similarly, it is increasingly difficult to find a martial arts school that opens its doors to all, with sliding scale payment options or guidance beyond the cultivation of physical techniques, and, at the same time there are more people looking to train because of the aforementioned violent representations. This is a dangerous combination, insofar as the degradation of the arts is becoming more common rather than less. A martial artist is lucky when able to find a school or an instructor that is not focused on money, winning, and only the violent aspects of the arts. Yet liberatory schools do exist and though outnumbered, their focus is clear and powerful. The well-operated dōjō (Japanese), dojang (Korean), or kwoon (Chinese) guarantees play and combats objectification. That is, the ethically oriented and thus liberatory training hall strives to build a strong and reflective community.

2. On authentic training: Situating martial arts in the liberation tradition

Despite the recent examples of martial arts being used for violent ends, the history of the arts is one of self-cultivation, resistance to violent domination, and liberation. The term "martial arts" references a range of historical practices that can trace their origins to various spaces in the territories now typically associated with Asia and occasionally with Africa and Eastern Europe. For example, the historical narrative of Okinawan Karate—comprised of a variety of styles that were introduced to the island by the Chinese—grounds itself as emerging at the moment when the indigenous Ryukyuan's were subjugated by Japanese forces and in desperate need of a defensive means because they were banned from keeping weapons. Karate means "open hand," and the style emphasizes striking, but the Ryukyuan's were largely agrarian and so their tools were not banned, since the occupying armies needed resources. Thus, practitioners of karate are often versed in wielding non-traditional weapons like boat oars (*eku*) or scythes (*kama*). The narrative starting point of Okinawan Karate is one of resistance to and struggle against domination, and karate is perhaps one of the most well-known styles in the world. And the Chinese forms that became karate are believed to have emerged throughout the mainland at the same time as Buddhism, affording groups like the Shaolin Monks, who practiced Wushu (Kung Fu), a way of overcoming the self as well as defending against bandits. Bushidō, or the way of the samurai that is rooted in reflection on death, was informed by Ruist, Shinto, and Buddhist thought, and was a means for the warrior class to find peace outside of the battlefield, as a way of reconciling the trauma of war, and freeing oneself from the impulse to reject virtue when one's survival is in question.

Along with a common lineage, the martial arts also share common values across disciplines and these values align with other liberatory projects in general. For example, one of the central values of these multiple martial practices is an emphasis on self-cultivation for the purposes of self-defense. A central organizing focus across all liberatory movements, including the martial arts, is the cultivation and maintenance of community.

From the Shaolin monasteries of the past, to present-day dōjōs in Rio de Janeiro or Brooklyn, martial artists have a strong communal history because that togetherness is where practitioners refine themselves. The martial arts cannot occur in a vacuum. Even those who focus on forms—i.e., kata (Jp.型 or 形), patterned movements meant to simulate a hostile encounter, but more importantly intended to help the artist discipline their bodily awareness—learn their style from one another and are critiqued, given feedback on things that would otherwise go unnoticed, by at least one other person. It is only through this practical relation that one's personhood is fully realized. As Enrique Dussel says, "the being face-to-face of two or more is *being* a person."[4] Dussel argues that all ethical discourse (which, for Dussel, is all discourse) must be subjected to or illuminated by the radical principle, or the community, which is realized through the face-to-face encounter.[5] The face-to-face is crucial because one cannot really know others or oneself without engaging in a communal relation. The community is the wellspring and horizon of meaning and the encounter is the path to realizing that meaning.

The encounter, however, is not a natural and unmediated event in our colonial world—that is, a world marked by increasing isolation and thus alienation, objectification (racism, sexism, classism, etc.), the normalization of violence as the primary means for solving problems or engaging with difference, and the universalization of hegemonic cultural norms (e.g. capitalism). Hence, to be a person in our violent present, to exist in the light of a reciprocal and thus ethical recognition, requires that communal conditions be intentionally cultivated.

And the martial arts afford these conditions both by claiming a communal space and through the adherence to tenets and virtues—that are common across most of the arts—such that we can understand a martial art insofar as it is rooted in the cultivation of said values. These include, but are not limited to, honesty, respect, discipline, self-control, flexibility/fluidity, and an emphasis on truth and justice.

A cursory examination of the underlying principles of any martial arts system will reveal some version of these specific tenets and more. In his "Twenty Precepts," for example, Shotokan Karate founder Gichin Funakoshi (1868–1957) emphasizes that "Karate is an aid to justice" and "the ultimate aim of karate lies not in victory nor defeat, but in the perfection of the character of its participants."[6] Practitioners of traditional taekwondo are taught the fundamental tenets of courtesy, integrity, perseverance, self-control, and an indomitable spirit. What is central to these values, however, is not that they linger in abstraction; rather, the meaning of these values is always realized as praxis, in the encounter, and thus all martial artists know these values not as textual dogma, but as communal relations that are enacted in every moment of the encounter.

The encounter among martial artists is unique in its intimacy and, for non-practitioners, phenomenologically mysterious. For many young men who take up the arts, it is perhaps one of the only spaces wherein they can be intimate with other people without that intimacy being intentionally sexual or violent. In Brazilian Jiu Jitsu, for example, people roll around on the floor, alternating between being locked between legs and sat on (mounted), etc. and remaining in near-constant contact. The goal of this exchange is not to subjugate or evoke an erotic feeling, but to learn about oneself with the other through play. More generally, sparring or the free-form deployment of an art in a controlled setting is especially interesting because it is an event wherein the boundary between self and other is fully blurred. The sparring encounter begins with a sign of respect, typically a bow or a fist bump. In sparring your movements become coordinated as a reflex; you know what is going to happen next, and it is in the moments that you are "in your head," thinking, and thus not present, that you are the most vulnerable to being caught—these are also the moments wherein you learn. Through sparring the artist comes to know the other without ever using words. The best example of this is the ability to sense the intentions of one's sparring partner. Even in no-contact sparring, persons frequently get hit and it is always clear if the strike was accidental or malicious. The martial artist knows the difference between an accidental strike, a playful strike, and a malicious strike, and that knowledge is something that can only be cultivated with others.

Of course, common values do not make the martial arts liberatory, but instead give them a liberatory potential. The potential to be liberatory is crucial, however, insofar as the martial artist is more likely than others to be moved by the message of liberation in part because the historical purpose of martial arts training was liberation from the self and liberation from the violence of others. Many pursue the arts because of their experiences with violence and oppression, so the liberatory potential of the arts is double: the arts, when properly realized, can both attract and refine an ethos and politics of liberation.[7]

There is also an obvious difference between the martial arts and the tradition of liberation thought in that most martial arts lack a Christian or Catholic element. Although many martial artists claim a certain spiritual experience, the spirituality of the arts is not tied to any one religious institution, and though some of the arts originally had a strong religious influence (i.e. Buddhism for the Shaolin), entering a training hall in the twenty-first century is not equivalent to entering a church and the religious influence will not be immediately obvious. The lack of a Catholic influence is ultimately irrelevant insofar as the message of liberation can be understood through the martial arts, as Ignacio Ellacuría emphasizes: "Liberation is a concept that represents the very essence of the revealed message and God's salvific gift to humanity. That message and that gift may be viewed from other points of view, but if they are not viewed from the perspective of liberation, they remain substantially reduced and often mischaracterized."[8] Often the message of liberation is not entirely clear, especially to the young person who frequently experiences violence. The cry of the oppressed is plural and echoes from strange places, and many who are moved to train are initially motivated by a desire to learn self-defense, though sometimes people do not hear the liberatory message and instead reproduce oppression.

The capacity to hear the message of liberation will also depend on the degree to which one is encouraged to intentionally reflect on one's practices, habits, and beliefs; thus, again, the relation between the liberatory praxis of the martial arts and liberatory thought is in many ways reciprocal, though within the philosophical tradition the material component is often overlooked, despite its being an equally important aspect of the liberation project. In other words, philosophies of liberation need practices like the martial arts, and the martial artist is given greater clarity through the various contributions made by theorists of liberation (i.e. philosophy).[9]

3. Grappling with(out) domination: Play, competition, and decolonial violence

Although the martial arts as such are intended to be liberatory, and their violent manifestation is exceptional, people may be initially attracted to training because they want to be able to fight. Many practitioners want to train because they have been threatened or hurt, and they want to be safe, happy, and free from the lingering oppression that is a life of violence.[10] Further, the uptake of the martial arts in popular culture has had a significant influence for many people, but young men are particularly moved by these images.[11] I have met many young men, especially young men of color, who grew up disempowered and watching Bruce Lee, *Dragon Ball*, the Ninja Turtles, and now the UFC; these men pursued training partly because of such influences. The underlying motivation for myself and for the many young men with whom I have discussed these themes—that is, what the arts as representation moved in us—has varied in details but the overarching common themes are a desire to transform, improve, and actualize a better situation for ourselves and our loved ones. There is a tension, however, between the two possible martial arts modalities: violence or liberation, which I will discuss in this section by unpacking a distinction between play and competition as modes of training.

Frantz Fanon states that "decolonization is always a violent phenomenon," but the nature of that violence for the transforming community is akin to exiting the cave for the first time and seeing light, which is distinct from the violence of domination that is definitive of colonialism and that more fully aligns with the common use of the term.[12] The common connection between the often harsh experience of transformation and the brutality of domination is pain, and that pain affects all involved parties before, during, and after decolonization. Decolonial violence is therefore faced with a choice between reproducing the same or realizing something new—both paths are painful, though one is a more familiar and thus seemingly easier pain. In the martial arts, the distinction between growing pains and violent domination, which I elaborate in this section through a discussion of play, ultimately rests on how martial artists understand the purpose of their training; that is, the martial artist must ask: who am I training for? Those who seek to dominate are self-interested and predominantly agonistic toward others, while those who tend toward liberation are interested in the possibility of creative meaning-making and collective development in all encounters, and are often agonistic toward the self—the latter aspect falling outside of the parameters of what would typically be understood as violence.

To further elaborate this distinction between training for liberation versus training to dominate, I think it helps to consider the role of play in one's training. The goal of play is to loosen tensions, test boundaries, experiment, and to have fun. As Hans-Georg Gadamer says, play is "the mode of being of the work of art itself," insofar as art and the work of that art is directed at creating meanings, or more precisely liberating meanings from a violently reified world—that is, a world which functions to keep meanings fixed.[13] Art enables a critical perspective, which is the first step in liberation, by drawing the participant in to an engagement that is unfolding and not yet determined. For the developing child, play is the primary mode of relational encounter with the world that is not yet known, which stands in wonder, and through which the mind or consciousness of the child emerges. The child learns how things work by playing with them. For the person who is aware and already influenced by the discourses that tell us how the world is, and thus limit play, however, the liberatory form of play is more difficult to enact because the already formed adult lacks the wonder and plasticity of the child. Thus, as Dussel puts it, "the first task of the ethics of liberation is to de-base (to destroy the basis of) the system in order to arrive at another basis which transcends the present system."[14] Proper training satisfies this condition in various ways and ultimately replaces the values of domination with a new modality: one that makes play possible.

For example, through martial play or training with others, one must learn to let go of the fear of losing to one's opponent because the goal of the engagement is not to win; rather, the goal of play in the martial arts is to learn about oneself and others through the encounter so that both parties will grow. Through martial play one learns one's style, one's weaknesses and strengths, and more importantly one learns about the other through a dialogical exchange that often involves no words. And one who continues to train also gradually lets go of those violent norms that are imposed upon us like a burning sun—specifically the self-centered ideal of individualism—and learns to live in the fire of domination without being completely consumed by it. The letting go of domination has various causes, but the most obvious is that the martial artist knows the consequences of real conflict and, having studied it, therefore prefers peace.

Competition, in contrast to play, is a closed dynamic wherein the goal is to dominate the other. Competition as such is violent. The competitor is taught to visualize the opponent, rather than actually engage with another, and to crush that projection. Competition should not be confused with being competitive. The best sparring partners are friends who push each other to transform, who work together for their collective betterment. Competition, however, often pits the artists against an unknown opponent with the incentive of reward (monetary, or just a shiny trophy to display in the school window). In competition, the relation and the practice is corrupted, and that corruption manifests itself in various ways—buying off the judges, attempting to undermine other competitors before the actual competition, or striving to really harm one's opponent. The difference between play and competition is that the goal of the former is collective meaning-making and intentional transformation—a reciprocal relation—which I take to be integral to liberation. The goal of the latter, competition, is individual elevation on the back of another—a relation of domination.

Here, the work of María Lugones is helpful for working out the distinction between competition and play. Lugones interprets the notion of play that is found in Gadamer, to whom I appeal above, as one that is fundamentally agonistic. Lugones defines agonistic play as follows:

> An agonistic sense of play is one in which competence is supreme. You better know the rules of the game. In agonistic play there is risk, there is uncertainty, but the uncertainty is about who is going to win and who is going to lose. There are rules that inspire hostility. The attitude of playfulness is conceived as secondary to or derivative from play. Since play is agon, then the only conceivable playful attitude is an agonistic one (the attitude does not turn an activity into play, but rather presupposes an activity that is play).[15]

I find Lugones's claim interesting because it attributes agonism in play as other-oriented and competitive, precisely what I am saying play is not. It may be true that play is sometimes agonistic—the root word agon meets both play and combat—but surely play is not exclusively agonistic. Further, I will not deny the possibility of an agonistic reading of play in Gadamer, but independent of his writing it seems to me that play includes all sorts of relational modes, including agonistic ones, because that is what play is about—testing, trying, not being too serious or sometimes acting really serious without having that act define your being, and always in a relationship that encourages this testing. Perhaps Lugones would disagree with me on this point, but it seems that play can and should sometimes be agonistic, because to foreclose the possibility of agonism in play would be to impose limits on play that undermine its very purpose. The point of play is that it is completely open-ended and the parameters of its unfolding are contextually determined, mutually agreed upon, or something that people figure out as they play. Indeed, when play exceeds the comfort of the participants, when things get out of hand, then playtime is usually over.

Similarly, in another essay by Lugones and Elizabeth Spelman, an additional distinction is made between individualist and communal forms of competition, both of which are rooted in how we conceive of excellence.[16] On the individualistic model, one is glorified as excelling in a particular activity because one has excelled over others. Lugones and Spelman say, "at the heart of the desire to excel in the context of opposition is the desire to excel not merely in some non-comparative sense, but to excel over others, to better them."[17] The communally oriented form of competition—which Lugones and Spelman note is closer to the Latin root of the word, *competere*, or "to come together"—attributes recognition of excellence to the "doing of excellent work" that is appreciated by a community and ultimately benefits a community.[18] And, in terms of the aspiring martial artist, I think they can be motivated to excel in both senses delineated above, while the form of competition Lugones and Spelman defend aligns with my understanding of being competitive—that is, pushing our comrades to improve or transform with us.

More importantly, many people enter a martial arts school for the first time because violence moved them; they have internalized the belief that being great means being greater than others, and it is crucial that a space exists where that violence, and thus the problematic notions of play and competition, can be exorcized and transformed. This is especially true for young men who, in a philopolemical society—a society with a cultivated love of war—are the most likely to act violently and are therefore the most in need of a space wherein they can reckon with that conditioning. In the post-colony, violent agonism is the norm for many relations and it is a way of knowing oneself, but it is not the only way and, when properly channeled, through playful training, that agonism can become a means to other relational modes of life. Indeed, the advanced and ethically oriented martial artists are often agonistic in relation to the self—who they are and who they want to be—and specifically to the parts of the self they want to change. But what it means to change oneself is a relational process that involves recognition and exchange.

The relational notion of play and competition that I am defending here does not occur in the complete absence of restraint. As noted above, there are the obvious constraints of play for an already socialized agent versus play for a developing child who does not yet know the world as rigid object. At the same time, play in the martial arts is a collective cultivation through a system, but I am not suggesting that play is possible only in the complete absence of restraint (an imaginary and impossible situation). The martial artist gains competence through play and not the other way around. The rules of play are internalized by playing, and once one has tinkered with the boundaries enough to know how to move within those parameters, then one can begin to play in a different way, with one's style as it is expressed through one's art.[19] Much like writing, the martial artist learns the system by playing in it, then once the structure of the art is known, the artists learns to play with the system itself; but in both cases the martial artist is able to learn about and transform themselves with others through play, and others recognize the excellence of the practice because it is done well and not because it stands on the corpses of fallen competitors.

So, again, adding to the initial distinction between the violence of domination and the pains of transformation, decolonial violence is a reckoning with domination, with the trauma that we live with; and ultimately it is a delicate process that can either reproduce domination or lead to liberation. Part of this process requires being honest about the violence that surrounds us, that tells us to define ourselves over and against others. The ethos of domination, violence, is cyclical or, as Bruce Lee puts it, karmic. And, Lee notes, "the way to transcend Karma lies in the proper use of the mind and the will. The oneness of all life is a truth that can be fully realized only when false notions of a separate self, whose destiny can be considered apart from the whole, are forever annihilated."[20] With the wrong training, the aspiring martial artist can become a conqueror rather than a liberator. But, in a school wherein the community is central and collective transformation is the way, violence is being studied so that its cyclical nature can be broken.

4. Martial arts and liberation in the Americas

The presence and transformation of the martial arts in the Americas represents an interstitial experience and, as I have argued here, also demarcates a way of knowing that is fundamentally liberatory. Steeped in the ceaseless violence that defines our colonized present, the uptake of martial arts practices is representative of a much larger shared experience of persons attempting to survive or even transcend violent domination in the pursuit of liberation and freedom. Many martial artists, throughout the Americas, transcend boundaries through the study of non-canonical texts, non-canonical readings of canonical texts, and through collective practices that are scarcely witnessed in Western academies. Rather than dismiss these ways of engaging and knowing the world as folksy, non-academic, or as mere ideologies of violence, I think it is crucial that they be given serious consideration as modes of resistance and creative meaning-making that are continuous with a larger liberatory tradition. Throughout this essay I have argued against the initial impulse to dismiss martial arts as violence in order to open a space where these practices and lifeworlds can be understood as valuable forms of knowledge systems that afford liberatory modes of being as part of an ongoing exchange that transcends and challenges colonial boundaries.

The history and transmission of the martial arts substantiates this claim, especially as they emerged and transformed in the Americas. Of the more important encounters is the introduction of judo to the Gracie family in Brazil by Esai Maeda. Maeda, according to the Gracie Academy's own record,

> befriended Gastão Gracie, an influential businessman, who helped Maeda get established. To show his gratitude, Maeda offered to teach traditional Japanese Jiu-Jitsu to Gastão's oldest son, Carlos Gracie. Carlos learned for a few years and eventually passed his knowledge to his brothers. Helio Gracie, the youngest ... was always a very physically frail child. Helio soon realized that due to his frail physique, most of the techniques he had learned from watching Carlos teach were particularly difficult for him to execute. Eager to make the techniques work for him, he began modifying them to accommodate his weak body. Emphasizing the use of leverage and timing over strength and speed, Helio modified virtually all of the techniques and, through trial and error, created Gracie/Brazilian Jiu-Jitsu.[21]

Brazilian Jiu-Jitsu, which empowers smaller practitioners to easily overcome larger opponents by redirecting and exploiting the opponent's force, is now widely practiced throughout Brazil, the Americas in general, and the world, and it has been particularly valuable as a means of self-defense training for women. Another example is capoeira, which was largely created by slaves in what is now Brazil and is often described as a fighting style disguised as a dance.[22] Also, the Black panthers emphasized martial arts practice and made traditional taekwondo training available to the community for similar liberatory meaning-making purposes.[23]

Beyond the style, in all of these examples the martial arts emerge and reproduce themselves as a communal activity wherein a tradition was developed and maintained allowing for shared meanings to be continuously formed, specifically in resistance to oppression and as a means of self-cultivation. The self-defense aspect of capoeira, for example, is not solely in the potential violent use of capoeira, but in the shared experience that the practice affords by giving the practitioners a meaningful sense of self in community and a means of protecting that meaning through a familial tradition.

And, there are many martial artists who fight in the UFC while maintaining their integrity as other-oriented persons but who do not receive as much attention because they do not satisfy the violent lust of the domination society. For example, Demian Maia, a black belt in Brazilian Jiu Jitsu, recently commented after a victory: "Fighting for me is a chess game. I'm not angry with my opponent. I just want to go in there and win without him hurting me or me hurting him."[24] Here Maia demonstrates the tension between being an exploited worker and also being a martial artist.

Although martial artists negotiate violence because we live in a violent world, the fundamental goal of the arts is to liberate the self and others from domination, and the motivation of many practitioners is rooted in the liberatory ideal. The Australian academic and independent political candidate Patricia Petersen discusses the moment that she was moved to train: "In some important respects, I was a doormat, and, as a result, suffered terribly from depression. What caused this vulnerability? Who knows? At the end of the day, it seemed much more important to deal with it than understand what had led to it."[25] Petersen tells us that by the time she received her blackbelt, she "felt like a feminist and acted like one," and that karate acted as the conditions of the possibility of her becoming a feminist.[26] Along similar lines, philosopher Michael Monahan discusses the transformative nature of training through Nietzsche's notion of self-overcoming. Though Nietzsche's self-overcoming is agonistic, Monahan rightly emphasizes that the agonistic process, when present in the martial artist, is not of central importance and is not just other-oriented. Monahan says, "the point of all this agonism (both with oneself and others) is not destruction for its own sake but rather the creation of something higher . . . the transcendence of given standards of value and the creation of something new out of the ashes of the old."[27]

The connection between martial arts practice and the history of imperial and colonial domination is not coincidental. And, throughout the formerly colonized world training halls will be found wherein martial artists are working on themselves and learning how to navigate the world so that violence is prevented and avoided at all costs. And, at this moment wherein professional fighting competitions are eclipsing the original meaning and purpose of the arts, it is exigent that we not only study the arts as unique epistemic forms, but that we also train to know the arts as a liberatory way of life.

Notes

1   Dead Prez, *Let's Get Free*.

2   Marc Raimondi, "HBO Unearths Trend of Domestic Violence in MMA," http://www.mmafighting.com/2015/7/21/9012669/hbo-real-sports-unearths-disturbing-rate-of-domestic-violence-in-mma.

3   Ibid.

4   Enrique Dussel, *Ethics and Community*, 9.

5   Ibid.

6   See, e.g., Funakoshi Gichin, *Karate-dō Kyōhan: the Master Text* and *The Twenty Guiding Principles of Karate: The Spiritual Legacy of the Master*.

7   This is not to suggest that martial artists do not contemplate violence and dwell on death—again, the Bushidō way, which many contemporary martial artists idealize despite not being samurai, is rooted in reflecting on one's own violent death. Yet, I think that the martial artist's realism and intimacy with violence, the awareness of the sort of agonism that is glorified in a philomolemical society—a society that has cultivated a love of war—is partly why it is so successful in bringing about the ends of local forms of peace and liberation. Of course, local liberation projects cannot fully transform the broader structures of domination on their own; rather, they can prepare for a broader decolonization and do their best to defend themselves in the meantime.

8   Ignacio Ellacuría and Michael Edward Lee, *Ignacio Ellacuria: Essays on History, Liberation, and Salvation*, 40.

9   The martial arts align with liberation thought in part because they are centrally focused on being completely present and aware of the interpersonal encounter and the praxis of that fundamental relationship—especially when it goes wrong. Further, by focusing on the collapse of sociality the martial artist learns the nuances of interaction with a heightened awareness and is better prepared to avoid or prevent social situations from collapsing into violence. The well-trained martial artist works to keep communal experience from devolving into violence. Similarly, the role that philosophical reflection can and ought to play in guiding training is various: critical thinking makes one aware of commodification, ethical reflection makes one aware of how actions impact others and learning about the self as a process of creation makes one attuned to how violence can be self-directed. Philosophy should be an explicit component of martial arts training today, but it need not be professional or academic philosophy.

10   For an example, I recommend reading Patricia Petersen's essay "Grrrrl in a Gi," discussed below.

11   See also Eric Francisco, "Hip-Hop's Favorite Anime," https://www.inverse.com/article/5753-how-rap-music-harnessed-dragon-ball-z-s-fighting-spirit.

12   Frantz Fanon, *The Wretched of the Earth*, 1.

13   Hans-Georg Gadamer, *Truth and Method*, 102.

14   Enrique Dussel and Eduardo Mendieta, *Beyond Philosophy: Ethics, History, Marxism, and Liberation Theology*, 138.

15   María Lugones, "Playfulness, 'World'-Travelling, and Loving Perception," 15.

16   María Lugones and Elizabeth Spelman, "Competition, Compassion, and Community: Models for a Feminist Ethos," 234–247.

17   Ibid., 236.

18   Ibid., 239.

19 Leah Kalmanson has pointed out to me that in Japanese this process is formally designated as "keep, break, leave" (守破離), which I had only heard expressed among practitioners of Kendo as Shu-Ha-Ri; but, I have learned the habit in an unnamed form through various schools and traditions, and this seems to be the general motivation for Bruce Lee's Jeet Kune Do.

20 Bruce Lee, *Tao of Jeet Kune Do*, 7.

21 "Gracie History," http://www.gracieacademy.com/history.asp.

22 Bira Almeida, *Capoeira: A Brazilian Art Form: History, Philosophy, and Practice.*

23 See, e.g., The Dr. Huey P. Newton Foundation, and David Hilliard, *Black Panther Party Service to the People Programs.*

24 Frank Curreri, "Demian Maia—Go Ahead, Punch Him in The Face," http://www.ufc.com/news/demian-Maia-Go-Ahead-Punch-Him-in-The-Face.

25 Petersen, "Grrrrl in a Gi," 93.

26 Ibid. p. 94.

27 Micahel Monahan, "The Practice of Self-Overcoming: Nietzschean Reflections on the Martial Arts," 40.

References

Almeida, Bira. *Capoeira: A Brazilian Art Form: History, Philosophy, and Practice.* 2nd edition. Berkeley, CA: Blue Snake Books, 1993.

Curreri, Frank. "Demian Maia—Go Ahead, Punch Him in The Face." *UFC*. 2011. http://www.ufc.com/news/demian-Maia-Go-Ahead-Punch-Him-in-The-Face.

Dead Prez. *Let's Get Free* [Recorded music]. New York: Loud Records, 2000.

Dead Prez. *RBG: Revolutionary But Gangsta* [Recorded music]. Sony, 2004.

Dussel, Enrique D. *Ethics and Community*. Eugene, OR: Wipf & Stock, 2008.

Dussel, Enrique D., and Eduardo Mendieta. *Beyond Philosophy: Ethics, History, Marxism, and Liberation Theology.* New Critical Theory. Lanham, MD: Rowman & Littlefield Publishers, 2003.

Ellacuría, Ignacio, and Lee, Michael Edward. *Ignacio Ellacuria: Essays on History, Liberation, and Salvation.* Maryknoll, NY: Orbis Books, 2013.

Fanon, Frantz. *The Wretched of the Earth.* Translated by Richard Philcox. New York: Grove Press, 2004.

Francisco, Eric. "Hip-Hop's Favorite Anime." *Inverse*. 2016. https://www.inverse.com/article/5753-how-rap-music-harnessed-dragon-ball-z-s-fighting-spirit.

Funakoshi, Gichin. *Karate-dō Kyōhan: the Master Text.* 1st edition. Tokyo: Kodansha International (distributed in the U.S. by Harper & Row, New York), 1973.

Funakoshi, Gichin. *The Twenty Guiding Principles of Karate: The Spiritual Legacy of the Master*, translated by John Teramoto. Tokyo and New York: Kodansha International, 2003.

Gadamer, Hans-Georg. *Truth and Method*. Translation revised by Joel Weinsheimer and
    Donald G. Marshall. New York: Continuum, 1995.

"Gracie History." 2017. http://www.gracieacademy.com/history.asp.

Lee, Bruce. *Tao of Jeet Kune Do*. Expanded edition. Valencia, CA: Black Belt Books,
    2011.

Lugones, María. "Playfulness, 'World'-Travelling, and Loving Perception." *Hypatia* 2,
    no. 2 (1987): 3–19.

Lugones, María and Elizabeth Spelman. "Competition, Compassion, and Community:
    Models for a Feminist Ethos." In *Competition: A Feminist Taboo?* edited by Valerie
    Miner and Helen Longino, 234–247. New York: The Feminist Press at CUNY, 1987.

Monahan, Michael. "The Practice of Self-Overcoming: Nietzschean Reflections on the
    Martial Arts." *Journal of the Philosophy of Sport* 34, no. 1 (2007): 39–51.

Peterson, Patricia. "Grrrrl in a Gi." In *Martial Arts and Philosophy: Beating and
    Nothingness*, edited by Graham Priest and Damon Young, 93–104. Chicago: Open
    Court, 2010.

Raimondi, Marc. "HBO Unearths Trend of Domestic Violence in MMA." *MMA
    Fighting*. July 22, 2015. http://www.mmafighting.com/2015/7/21/9012669/hbo-real-
    sports-unearths-disturbing-rate-of-domestic-violence-in-mma.

The Dr. Huey P. Newton Foundation, and David Hilliard. *Black Panther Party Service to
    the People Programs*. Albuquerque: University of New Mexico Press, 2010.

10

Legacies of Legitimacy and Resistance: Imperial and State Violence in South Asia and Latin America

Namrata Mitra

On a seemingly ordinary afternoon in London during the 1970s, the two main protagonists in Zadie Smith's *White Teeth* (2000) enter into an argument. Samad Iqbal, a Bengali Muslim from colonial British India, and Archibald Jones, a white man from England are the best of friends, and their relationship goes back to the Second World War when they had fought together on behalf of the British Army. At nearly every point he can, Samad is eager to claim his descent from Mangal Pandey. In 1857, Bengal, Pandey was one of the first casualties of the failed "mutiny" within the British Army. He had tried to shoot a British officer but his gun jammed. He was hung for treason. South Asians, of course, prefer to remember the "mutiny" as the First War of Independence and Mangal Pandey as a revolutionary hero. Nevertheless, on this afternoon, Archibald is growing somewhat irritable by his friend's repetition of this story yet again. Today, he comes armed with a citation from the OED (Oxford English Dictionary), the definitive authority of all English words. Smith walks us through the scene:

> Pande's only claim to fame, as Archie was at pains to point out, was his etymological gift to the English language by way of the word "Pandy," under which title in the OED the curious reader will find the following definition:
> Pandy /'pandi/n. 2 colloq. (now Hist.) Also – dee. M19 [Perh. F. the surname of the first mutineer amongst the high-caste sepoys in the Bengal army.] **1** Any Sepoy who revolted in the Indian Mutiny of 1857–9 **2** Any mutineer or traitor **3** Any fool or coward in the military situation.[1]

As we see in this excerpt, the colonized revolutionary, becomes "a traitor," "fool or coward in any military situation" in the history and language of the colonizer.

Our entire systems of language, culture, and historical knowledge are embedded in our power relations with others.

The relation of the colonizer and the colonized is one in which the colonizer's language, laws, and conception of political legitimacy prevail during the period of colonization. However, the colonial framework for laws and political legitimacy does not end its sphere of influence when the colonizer is forced to leave. As we will see in the case of South Asia and Latin America, laws, grounds for state violence, and racial identities created by the colonizer are passed on to colonial national elites, who, even after driving out the imperialists, have on various occasions iterated the colonizer's harmful worldview and political practices.

The aim of this essay is to set up a dialogue among political thinkers in South Asia and Latin America in order to unpack the complex legacy of colonization. Despite the significant difference in their timeline, with Iberian colonization of the Americas starting in the late-fifteenth century, and British colonization in South Asia in the mid-eighteenth century, postcolonial/decolonial scholarship from both these regions wrestles with a shared legacy of European colonialization and contemporary state violence. This essay will examine some of the ways in which the colonizers' claims to the legitimacy of their rule, and their deployment of large-scale violence, have been perpetuated by the formerly colonized but now politically independent states. The goal of tracing the influences of the colonizer in political thought and practice in contemporary state action, is to locate possible resources for disrupting nationalist echoes of colonial frames of political thought, particularly the colonial legitimation of violence against the colonized people.

This essay is divided into three sections. The first section offers a brief glimpse into the present condition of state violence in South Asia and Latin America. The second section focuses on the colonial origins of such violence. It draws on Ranajit Guha, Dipesh Chakrabarty, and Anibal Quijano to demonstrate how colonial and nationalist investments in ideas of "progress," "modernity," and "consent" function to legitimize their rule and render their coercive methods invisible. The third section stages a comparative study of Quijano's analysis of the place of race and Chakrabarty's absence of the discussion of race in their respective analyses. While the construction of race occupied a central place in the justification of the colonization of South Asia, its analysis is commonly neglected in comparison to other systems of social oppression such as caste, gender, religion, which were deployed to legitimize imperial rule. Accordingly, this section explores the politics of race in South Asian colonization and the conditions of possibility for silence around it. The fourth section invites us to imagine other possible ways of telling the story of our pasts. This chapter is anchored in South Asian historiography, philosophy, and literary theory with the aim of unraveling the discursive conditions and legitimizing grounds of state violence.

1. Postcolonial state violence: A reckoning

In August 1947, British India was partitioned into the newly independent states of India and of Pakistan. In the process, over a million people were massacred and nearly twelve million people were displaced. The religious majority groups on either side of the border raped and/or murdered those trying to flee to the other side. The heaviest casualties of violence in Pakistan were Sikhs and Hindus, and in India they were Muslims. At the time, accounts of massacres and sexual assaults were rarely framed as the culmination of an ongoing series of violent acts based on economic, religious, and caste-based interests. Instead, early representations of partition violence, in literature[2] and in history,[3] were most commonly framed as spontaneous bursts of "madness" interrupting an otherwise rational and calm series of political events. Within such a framework, the newly emerging state was assigned the status of a "sane" institution to restore order.

In fewer than three decades another partition followed, between East and West Pakistan, more commonly dubbed the Bangladesh Liberation war in 1971, through which was produced the independent nation state of Bangladesh. As Gyanendra Pandey says, partitions are brutally violent events, yet school history textbooks invariably frame partition and violence as two separate events rather than the same. That is, the political formation of two nation states is presented as one event, and the violence as another separate event in the background. However, for those who experienced the violence, partition and violence were not two different events; rather "Partition was violence, a cataclysm, a world (or worlds) torn apart."[4] Yet it has been central to Indian nationalist historiography that the experiences and fragmentary accounts of the violence and trauma are assigned the status of "memory" and decoupled from the story of the two emerging nation states as an event of secular, modern, progress which is assigned the status of "history." The dichotomy of history and memory is based on the assumption that history is constructed out of "official" and more "reliable" archives about the people as a collective, whereas memory is an unreliable repository of subjective, changeable, and often unarticulated records. In the last seventy years of their existence, the new states of India, Pakistan, and Bangladesh have violently suppressed political dissent and dubbed dissenters and religious minorities the "enemy within." The state's account of events is invariably assigned the status of history in school textbooks. How does the state legitimize its domination and its violence against civil opposition?

Subaltern studies writers such as Gyanendra Pandey and Sumit Sarkar have both shown the different ways in which the Indian state places middle-class, upper-caste Hindu interests as a primary guide for state action (or inaction). Sometimes middle-class Hindu interests are unmarked, such as when the state legitimizes its actions in the name of "progress and modernity,"[5] and at other times Hindu interests are more directly marked, such as when the state enacts laws to protect "Hindu sentiments"[6] or for a "Hindutva Nation" (a nation founded on Hindu principles).[7] In contemporary India, both these forms of legitimation for state action coexist simultaneously. If the former drives a wedge between middle-class and working-poor Hindu interests then the latter consolidates Hindus as a class across economic divisions forged against religious minorities, particularly Muslims. The narrative of national "progress" to justify military and police actions is frequently deployed in cases where the Indian state has seized natural resources and displaced indigenous groups, such as in Bauxite-rich Orissa and in the Narmada dam project. Meanwhile, any opposition to the state's land seizers is usually framed in mainstream discourse as involving ethnocentric, self-interested, and anti-national activities, which are then contrasted to the disinterested and therefore fair work of the state. In a stunning case of inconsistency, the state has also sought to justify its actions on the explicit grounds of the Hindu majority interests. Over the course of this year alone, the state's justification for the amended beef ban laws targeting Dalits ("untouchable/outcastes") and religious minority groups have been articulated in terms of Hindu interests. Several regional states in India have recently instituted a ban on beef consumption, transportation, and possession which specifically targets dietary and ritual practices of religious minorities and Dalits. The official justification for this ban is to prevent "hurting [Hindu] religious sentiments." While the former set of justifications ("national interests" and "progress") aim to preserve the interests of economic elites (urban middle class and rural rich), the latter set of justifications ("religious sentiments") has been in the service of upper-caste Hindus. While both sets of laws and practices have been in the service of upper-caste, middle-class Hindus, in the former case, Hindu upper-caste interests are conflated with the "national interest," whereas in the latter, Hindu interests are stated as the explicit justification for state action. How did we get here? Two centuries of colonization have had a long-lasting effect on the "independent" colonies. Colonizers instituted various policies and practices for the continuation of their power, such as establishing colonial laws that legalized imperial/state violence in the colonies, framing imperial interests as universal human interests, and opposition to imperialism as self-interested, illegitimate, and irrational. Long after the colonized regions acquired statehood, these modes of control, suppression of dissent, and violence are reproduced and developed in new ways, such as in the case of South Asia discussed above. Similarly, one of the long-lasting effects of European colonization in Latin America has been on the framing of state violence.

The logic and legacy of colonialism in Latin America have on various occasions been manifest in the twentieth-century state's treatment of indigenous groups. Over the course of the civil war in Guatemala (1960–996), the military adopted a divide-and-rule policy to overcome indigenous resistance against the state. Jennifer Schirmer shows how the military ensured the complicity of some Mayan groups in state-led massacres of other Mayan groups. The military's aim was to break the resistance by forging alliances with some communities against others, "thereby producing fissures within indigenous communities, possibly for generations, as 'insurance' against another insurgency."[8] The state's action was carried out in three stages: first the military implied the threat of total destruction of some indigenous communities; then the communities had to "choose" between either fighting against the government or with the government against other communities; and finally, the military propaganda adopted Mayan phrases, numbers, and symbols to create images of the "Sanctioned Maya" or the "good" Maya who identified with the state over the local traditions, unlike the "bad" Maya.[9]

The legacy of colonial violence shaped the tactics of military action against indigenous and exploited labor in El Salvador. During the 1930s, the Salvadorian Military Government sought to suppress indigenous opposition by forcing them to "choose" between two options: assimilate or be killed. In 1932, the governmen-led massacres, since dubbed *La Matanza* or The Killing, have had the long-lasting effects of trauma and the cultural annihilation of indigenous groups.[10] Indigenous groups stopped dressing in traditional clothes, speaking their languages, and began concealing their identities and cultural heritage. The pogrom had rendered them invisible to the extent that the El Salvador government for years later claimed that "it had no more Indians in its population."[11]

Colonization never ended for most indigenous groups in Latin America. Patricia Seed illustrates this claim through a comparative study of indigenous land rights in former colonies. According to the 1988 finalized draft of the Brazilian constitution, indigenous groups do not possess the mining rights of lands historically occupied by them. A previous ratified draft had placed severe restrictions on the state's ability to mine, in order to protect indigenous land relations. However, the daily newspapers broadly represented such restrictions as the loss of state sovereignty. In response, the final draft constitution ensured that the state acquire control over all mining within its borders. However, since the 1980s, several Latin American countries have tried to disrupt the reproduction of the colonial orientation to landownership and imperial frames of denying recognition to indigenous groups. As though seeking to address past wrongs, various Latin American countries granted tribal ownership rights to indigenous groups.[12] At the same time, over the past three decades, neoliberal state economic policies have allowed multinational oil corporations to displace indigenous groups and leave the land polluted, which is an eerie reproduction of imperialism in South Asia by the East India Company.

The next section explores the genealogy of the legitimation of state violence. The language and ideology of state rule and state violence in South Asia and Latin America bear a complicated relation to their colonial histories. On the one hand, the modern nation state draws heavily on the ideologies of imperialism to frame any opposition to its governance by appealing to categories of "progress" and "modernity," while on the other hand the state claims its political legitimacy precisely because it is not a foreign imperial ruler but one that is native and elected democratically by its own citizens. Accordingly, the next section of this essay explores the ways in which the legacy of colonialism shapes the justifications offered for state violence. I am particularly interested in critically unpacking the ways in which the legitimation of state rule and violence in South Asia and Latin America iterate and challenge legitimation of imperial rule.

Subaltern studies and decolonial studies emerging from South Asia and Latin America are particularly valuable resources for tracing these questions. They are invested in exploring the discursive conditions of possibility for the state's legitimation of violence and the vilification of any opposition to itself. More specifically, what makes it possible for the state to sanction violence against its opposition in the name of "progress"?

2. Ideologies of colonial domination in Latin America and South Asia

As Ranajit Guha tells it, a small group of South Asian historians watched with alarm at the rise of state violence during the 1970s and 80s. Despite increased state aggression, its effects on the people were not entering into historical record or historical analysis.[13] One of the main problems with the academic trends in

British Indian and later South Asian history until the 1980s is that it emerged from elite perspectives (British colonial elitism and then bourgeois national elitism) and left out the "domain of Indian politics in which the principal actors were not the dominant groups of the indigenous society or the colonial authorities but the subaltern groups constituting the mass of the laboring population and the intermediate strata in town and country—that is, the people."[14] What, asks Guha, motivated an elite monistic view of history in colonial British India and later independent India?

The nineteenth-century British government vociferously claimed that it was a liberal, democratic institution, whose legitimacy to rule was grounded in the consent of its citizens. However, as critics of the political liberalism in the late-twentieth century[15] have amply demonstrated, liberalism's investment in "consent" has served to create an illusion of equality in Europe (and North America) while rendering structural domination on the basis of sex and race invisible (since forced subordination of marginalized groups is conflated with their "consent"). Therefore, while it may seem eminently clear that the British government's claims of consent-based governance in nineteenth-century Europe was entirely a fiction, it nonetheless did not curb the government from claiming that its rule in Europe was democratic and consent-based. The imperial government was forced to confront the irreconcilable contradiction of being both a purportedly consent-based democratic institution (in Europe) and a patently autocratic institution (in South Asia). One of the ways to gloss over this political contradiction that could potentially undermine its legitimacy to rule as a democratic institution was to present imperial rule in South Asia (the Raj) as a system established with the consent of its South Asian subjects much like it ostensibly was in Europe. Accordingly, British colonial rule in South Asia was repeatedly framed in terms of "the rule of law," based on hegemony, in which persuasion and consent, not coercion, became the means of rule.[16] As it was a common trend until the 1970s for Cambridge scholars of history to frame the Raj as hegemonic rule, one of the early aims of subaltern studies historians was to demonstrate this as false by drawing attention to the lack of evidence of consent sought during British Indian rule.

Indian nationalists, in the early-twentieth century, recognized the value of dominance acquired through hegemony (i.e. persuasion outweighing coercion) over structures of dominance without hegemony (i.e. coercion outweighing persuasion). In his book titled *Dominance Without Hegemony* (1997), Guha shows the ways the in which the Indian bourgeoisie, under colonial rule, garnered support for their particular opposition to British rulers by presenting colonial nationalism (from the 1880s to 1947) as a movement with a hegemony that represented "universal" interests of all South Asians under their rule. Movements such as the Swadeshi Movement (1903–1908) and The Non-Cooperation Movement (1920–22) were mobilized with the promise of mass participation and consent.[17]

Peasants, unskilled laborers, and women from the working class and the middle class took up the colonial nationalist movements in new and unpredictable ways. The movements were successful because they were mobilized by various disenfranchised groups within the codified terms of their cultures; they were cast in local idiomatic terms, the prevailing gods in different regions were invoked to assist with the movement, and in some cases the nationalist movements themselves were framed as conceived and directed by Gods. However, far from recognizing and acknowledging these different manifestations of the political mass movements, dominant narratives of colonial nationalisms and later of India-Pakistan independence, either entirely exclude them or subordinate them to a monolithic story of the political and economic elite. What is the effect of such historical erasures in the service of an elite history of nationalism? Subaltern studies thinkers focus on two major areas of the harm of such historical erasures on postcolonial historiography. First, while marginalized and subordinated groups were actors and codesigners of nationalist movements under colonization, in the dominant historical narratives they are cast as uncritical, unthinking executers of a plan conceived and mobilized by the political elite.[18] This hierarchical structure is reproduced in the writing of the nation even after independence, such as in history textbooks, contemporary media coverage, and policymaking. Second, even though nationalist movements aimed to acquire political modernity, Marxist historians such as Eric Hobsbawn and Sumit Sarkar identify them as premodern movements, since they were religious and political at the same time. Various local groups invoked gods to inspire and direct the movements. They did not speak with the linguistic markers of class consciousness. According to Marxist historians this meant that the peasant uprisings are not a modern but a premodern struggle that still needs to advance to its next teleological stage of secular, political modernity.[19]

How does framing history into specific periods or stages, such as modern and medieval, and then assigning them characteristics based on binaries such as "progress or backward" and "religious or secular" become the basis of legitimizing colonial rule and national elitism? According to Dipesh Chakrabarty's analysis, the justification of imperial rule is embedded in the structure of historicism and the transition narrative of development from one period of history to the next, such as from medieval to modern, which is characterized by the transition from feudalism to capitalism. This transition narrative is not value-free but imbued with increasing positive value as it "progresses" from its former stage to its subsequent stage.[20]

Narratives of historical progress were roundly championed in ideas of universal history during the Enlightenment. Consider Immanuel Kant's essay aptly titled "Idea for a Universal History with a Cosmopolitan Purpose" (1784). In it, he locates a singular teleological end for the all of nature and of mankind, in which it is nature's purpose to eventually establish a cosmopolitan world order or a civic union among all men. Moreover, the task of discovering and ensuring that we proceed toward political modernity as the teleology of all of nature and man, in Kant's view, falls on philosophy. Consider the imperative in the Ninth Proposition of the essay according to which "[a] philosophical attempt to work out a universal history of the world in accordance with a plan of nature aimed at a perfect civil union of mankind, must be regarded as possible and even as capable of furthering the purpose of nature itself."[21] Here, Enlightenment thought is assigning historiography not just a descriptive role of analyzing or "work[ing] out" the historical processes but a prescriptive one aimed at expediting or "furthering the purpose of nature."[22] The promise of teleological history gripped European Enlightenment thought, particularly the idea that philosophy should guide universal world history to its purposed end of political modernity. Herein, though, lies the issue: if we, all over the world: colonizer and colonized, Europe, Asia, Africa, and Latin America are racing toward the same teleological end of political modernity, then some are more ahead than others. In that case, those who have progressed the most and are closest to mankind's shared purpose become entitled to instruct the colonized on how to walk the same path.[23]

The British justified imperialism in South Asia on the grounds of historical teleology before and after the first War of Independence in 1857 (dubbed "The Sepoy Mutiny" in dominant British historical narratives). The East India Company regarded their routine land annexations and trade expansions in South Asia as a fair exchange for their self-assigned burden of assimilating Indians to European culture, science, and politics. The stated goal was to bring the colonies from the premodern stage of darkness to the light of modernity. Perhaps the most famous exemplification of this is Thomas Macaulay's "Minute" on Indian education to the British Parliament (1835) in which he makes a case for the British to educate a class of Indians on European culture. This new class of persons, "Indian in blood and colour, but English in tastes, in opinions, in morals and in intellect" would help educate and assimilate all other Indians to the standards of European culture and science:

> We [the British] must at present do our best to form a class who may be interpreters between us and the millions whom we govern, – a class of persons Indian in blood and colour, but English in tastes, in opinions, in morals and in intellect. To that class we may leave it to refine the vernacular dialects of the country, to enrich those dialects with terms of science borrowed from the Western nomenclature, and to render them by degrees fit vehicles for conveying knowledge to the great mass of the population.[24]

As various subaltern studies writers have shown, the growth of political liberalism and democratic theories in Europe, particularly in England, did not seem to contradict the growth and consolidation of the British Empire through the nineteenth century. According to Chakrabarty, it was historicism that enabled the compatible coexistence between political liberalism and imperialism. For instance, John Stuart Mill ("On Liberty" and "On Representational Government") could declare self-rule as the best form of government and at the same time claim that Indians and Africans "were *not yet* civilized enough to rule themselves."[25] Mill consigned the British colonies to the "imaginary waiting room of history" and let it fall to the colonizer to rule and educate the colonized on how to becomes civilized in the "future" and to wait patiently till they reach the stage of modernity.

The classification of people and places based on historicist constructions of "eras" and "periods" such as "modern" and "medieval" with distinct assigned characteristics such as "rational" or "superstitious" was also one of the main organizing principles of Iberian colonial domination in Latin America. As Anibal Quijano shows in the context of Latin American colonization, these historicist categories were transposed and codified into new racial categories such as "European," "Indian," "black," and "mestizo." That is, black and Indian were constructed as racial categories that were permanently situated in the state of nature, whereas European was constructed as a "civilized" racial category that had long overcome the state of nature through a complex consent-based social contract. Iberian colonizers granted themselves imperial legitimacy on grounds of their "natural" racial superiority and "naturally" given right to dominate. If Chakrabarty asserts that the justification of British imperialism in South Asia was that the colonizer was needed to bring the colonized "forward" into the stage of European modernity, then Quijano claims that Iberian colonizers granted themselves imperial legitimacy on grounds of their "natural" racial superiority and "naturally" given right to dominate, which was demonstrated by their advanced stage in history. Accordingly, a comparative study between these two explanations of imperial justifications must force us to ask: was race absent in the imperial ideology in South Asia or is it absent from discussions of imperialism and nationalism in South Asia? If race as a category of postcolonial analysis in South Asia is repeatedly absent, how can we account for the silence? I will explore possible explanations for the silence race in Chakrabarty's analysis of European historicism shortly after unpacking the place of race in Quijano's analysis of Latin American colonization. To return to Quijano's analysis, the new racial hierarchy in Latin America was instrumental in formalizing exploitative labor practices into law, within which Europeans were the only group to receive wages for labor, while Amerindians were subject to colonial serfdom and black Africans were bought and sold as slaves. In the case of Iberian imperialism, the concepts of race and historicist progress are constructed through each other.

Quijano shows how world capitalism was made possible by the intertwined racial and economic structures of colonial Latin America. Early colonial settlers forced Amerindians to work until they could do so no longer and then killed them. Bartolomeo De Las Casas's account of early Spanish settlers in the Americas offers a vivid instance of sexual violence, torture, forced labor, and massacres in the service of imperialism. To the settlers, Amerindians were expendable labor. Yet, not wanting the total annihilation of Amerindians, European colonizers reassigned Amerindians as serfs under the colonial feudal system. However, colonial feudalism had very little in common with its European counterpart. While the serfs in both contexts were required to provide non-waged labor to their feudal lords, unlike in the European system, colonial feudal lords neither promised Amerindian serfs protection nor designated land to them for cultivation in lieu of wages.[26] Africans were introduced within this racial system as "blacks" and assigned the status of slaves. Those identified as mestizos were allowed to apply for jobs occupied by European non-nobles only after the eighteenth century. Colonial law formalized the difference between European labor and non-European labor as waged labor and non-waged labor.

Quijano focuses on two aspects of the new economic system: first, how the colonial system of slave and serf labor relied on the Eurocentric construction of race and racial difference and second, how Europeans ushered in the first phase of world capitalism by structuring their exploitative labor practices toward the formation of world trade. In the matter of the former claim about race as the basis of labor laws, the settlers attributed "scientifically" created racial identities and racial differences to natural origins whose effects were supposedly manifest in cultural differences. In what would soon become a common trope in European liberalism, the colonizers traced their political and cultural history starting from a "primitive" state of nature to the "advanced" stage of political modernity. Looking around at their newly conquered colonies, they placed the subjugated people into categories close to the historical stage of the state of nature while maintaining willful ignorance of their own part in creating these identities and situating them in historicist "primitive" categories. Instead, the imperialists framed their socially constructed racial difference as a natural fact, which in turn became the grounds of justifying colonial domination. Accordingly, the implications of Quijano's latter claim are far-reaching. Imperial rule was commonly legitimized on grounds of the historical "advancement" of Europe from the stage of feudalism to the stage of capitalism. Therefore, to show that world capitalism was forged and spread through the colonial forms of feudal-capitalism undermines the prevailing claims of imperial legitimacy, which relies on the neat separation between "premodern feudalism," located in the colonies, and "modern capitalism," located in Europe.

3. Visibilities of race: A point of comparison in different colonies

According to prevalent academic narratives, British imperialism in South Asia was legitimized by claims of educating Indians and assimilating them into Enlightenment culture, such as that which was propagated by Macaulay, while Iberian imperialists ensured the erasure and prevention of literacy practices among Ameridians on grounds of racial difference. They were "condemned to be an illiterate peasant subculture stripped of their objectified intellectual legacy."[27] While Quijano draws our attention to the troubling dualities in historicism (e.g. modern-secular, feudal-capitalist) *and* racial identities (e.g. European-Indian, white-black) in the structure of colonial Latin America, Chakrabarty only focuses on the deployment of historicist categories in British imperialism in South Asia. Their analyses overlap at some points, particularly around the claim that the colonization of Asia was markedly different in its aims and atrocity than in Latin American colonization. For instance, Quijano claims that the Occident-Orient binary at work in Asian colonization produced a form of "repression [that] was much less intense in Asia" than the effects of the European-Indian and European-black binary in Latin America. Similarly, Chakrabarty claims that there needs to be a distinction made between the form of colonization in which European white settlers aim to destroy native lives and culture such as in the Americas and Australia, and colonies in which "the idea of 'self-rule' was promulgated right from the beginning," such as in South Asia.[28] Both thinkers assert that European imperialists based their methods of colonization on what they perceived was the level of "civilization" or "primitiveness" of the natives they encountered. Drawing on a correspondence between South Asian novelist Amitav Ghosh and Chakrabarty, a little later in the essay, I show what underlies these commonly held assumptions about the differences between South Asian and Latin American colonization, particularly that one was somehow less violent than the other, or that Iberians condemned the colonial natives to perpetual servitude while the aim of the English was to help South Asia become fit for democratic governance at some point in the future. Both colonial regimes were designed for the perpetual subordination of the colonies and the exploitation of their labor and resources. Moreover, as Ghosh points out, the commonly held belief that South Asian colonial experience was less brutal is sustained by the continued historical erasure of mass transportations of low-caste and poor South Asians who were regarded as dispensable labor on new British imperial expansions across the Global South. However, since Quijano examines the structure of race in Latin America and Chakrabarty does not enter the category of race into his analysis, the comparison between the two analyses appears to yield the following difference: British imperialists insisted that South Asians were "not yet" ready for self-rule because they were yet to be educated on how to become modern and less "oriental," while Spanish and Portuguese colonizers condemned Amerindians and Africans as being forever "primitive" and who could never be assimilated into European culture. Oddly enough, Chakrabarty does not address how Enlightenment ideas about race may have shaped and regionalized ideas about social contract theory itself. That is, he appears to hold that Enlightenment ideas about race and political ideals were two separate spheres of thought in which ideas about race may have been contingently limited and may have contradicted the Enlightenment's universal concepts of equality and liberty. He does not contend that "scientific" and "anthropological" writings about race worked in tandem with ideas about political modernity to legitimize colonization, which would imply that imperial claims to bring political modernity to the colonies (at any point in the future) were always a ruse and never sincere.

Soon after the publication of *Provincializing Europe*, South Asian writer Amitav Ghosh, whose historical novels are mostly set in British colonies in the Global South, wrote to Chakrabarty to inquire about the absence of race in his analysis, which he added is a common omission among South Asian historians.[29] Ghosh asserts that despite the silence on the subject, race had always been a major component in shaping the colonization of South Asia and was always intertwined with Enlightenment claims about the spread of social reform and modernity in its colonies. He argues that colonial governance had always been "rule of law + R [race]," that is, laws and their application depended on whether they involved the British or Indians.[30] An exemplary illustration of this can be found in the opposition to the Ibert Bill (1883) which would for the first time allow Indian judges to try Europeans in Indian courts. Jenny Sharpe shows how opposition to the bill relied on narratives of Indian men raping English women during the first War of Independence/ "Sepoy Mutiny" in 1958. Despite magistrates appointed to investigate the widely circulated reports of mass rape during the rebellion, there were no reported cases of sexual assaults of Englishwomen by Indian men. These new constructions of hypersexualized predatory Indian men were very specific racialized images deployed to specific political ends. Public opposition to the continuation of British rule in South Asia, especially in England, was routinely countered through the circulation of racialized images with common tropes of predatory Indian men and/or helpless Hindu widows about to be burned on their dead husbands' funeral pyres and thus needing to be saved from Hindu men. Drawing on another example, Ghosh argues that the British approach to racial difference in India was guided by skin color and not their observations of the state of "civilization" or "primitiveness," as was asserted by both Chakrabarty and Quijano. Even though dark-skinned South Indians had a long tradition of martial arts, the British insisted on appointing lighter-skinned North Indians to the military and assigning South Indian Tamil men to less valued labor, such as having them "shipped out to clear new colonial territories."[31] Moreover, during the Second World War, under the continuous shelling of bombs, the British, despite the state of emergency, spent much time ensuring that they created separated "white" and "black" routes in Northern Burma for the civilians seeking to flee.[32]

The correspondence between Ghosh and Chakrabarty exposes some long-standing beliefs about British legitimation of their rule that have been insidiously passed down to Anglophone South Asians, including those in postcolonial studies. At one point, Chakrabarty sums up the chief difference between Ghosh's position and his own by saying that it is based on whether one holds that Enlightenment conceptions of freedom and political modernity are undone by its conceptions of race. After all, Enlightenment thinkers spoke of freedom, equality, modernity, white racial superiority, and non-white racial inferiority all in the same breath. As Chakrabarty says, it really "boils down to this: how seriously do we take the ambiguity that lies at the heart of liberalism, the ambiguity caused by the tension between the universal applicability that it claims for itself and the unacknowledged racism that runs through it?" (Ghosh and Chakrabarty; 155). For Ghosh there is no ambiguity here. If anything, liberalism has relied on its ideas of racial hierarchy to justify imperial rule as a permanent political condition. If Chakrabarty thinks that British liberal thinkers held that South Asians were "not yet" ready for self-rule until they learned the ways of political modernity, then Ghosh says the timeline was actually "not yet forever" because of their conception of race.[33] At this point, Ghosh's understanding of South Asian colonization begins to read a lot more like Quijano's analysis of the function of race in the legitimation of Latin American colonization.

Race, even though unacknowledged, occupied an important place in the legitimation of the Raj. However, why has the invisibility of race been perpetuated in South Asian writings since independence? Until I received my editors' comments on the last draft of this essay, I shared the same lacuna about the place of race in South Asian colonization. As someone who is trying to unpack the conditions for the continuation of the silence about race in South Asia's past and present, while having participated in it, I will explore three possible explanations. First, India has a long and public record of colorism whose harms include widespread discrimination, punishing beauty standards, cultural stereotypes, and institutionalized violence against darker-skinned groups. However, this is usually explained by South Asians in terms of caste, regionalism, and ethnicity rather than race. In fact, the translation of the Sanskrit term for caste, *varna*, is color. This raises the following question: is colorist discrimination based on caste and region that was also widely prevalent during the Raj and common in contemporary India the same as racism, or is there a difference? While the effects and harms of the two are very similar, the grounds on which the two are legitimated are very different; casteism draws on ancient religious Hindu texts for justification, whereas racism in the nineteenth century was grounded in secular science, which sought to classify measurable physiognomic differences as indices of differences in character, intelligence, ability, and culture. European racism in the nineteenth century appealed to the scientific method to establish its truth claims. It also fulfilled a specific political role in imperialism. If teaching natives on the ways of political modernity was why the British came to South Asia, then racial differences ensured that the South Asians were incapable of learning and self-governing and so the British had to stay for longer, nay, forever. As Ghosh argues, liberalism developed both concepts of equality before the law and scientific arguments about racial inferiority which worked together, "rule of law + R," to make colonization into a permanent enterprise. Caste-based discrimination, while as damaging and harmful, asserted its permanence based on Hindu cosmology. It neither appealed to the scientific method nor did it function as a counterweight to ideas of political modernity. Therefore, to conflate caste-based colorism with racism overlooks the grounds on which they seek legitimation and their epistemologies, even though the outcomes of the two systems are similar. As Ghosh, in his novel *The Sea of Poppies*, illustrates, racism did not challenge the caste system but rather sat atop casteism during the Raj. Through the story of a civil court case in which the British rulers seize the land of a Hindu Brahmin *zamindar* (landowner) in the name of justice and fairness, he shows how "rule of law + r" does not disrupt the caste system but rather establishes the British as the new Brahmins situated above the existing Brahmins on an intact caste system.

The subject of race is often met with a troubled silence, especially by those South Asians who worked closely with the British and who started identifying with British Indian institutions such as the military and education. This brings us to the second reason why analysis of racism under British rule seems to be mostly absent in historical documents and historiographical analysis by South Asians, even though stories of them are more common in South Asian fiction. To identify with the institutions which bore the promise of political modernity publicly but continually treated Indians as racially inferior may have been puzzling and painful. Ghosh recounts a difficult moment in his father's career in the British Army when a white South African officer racially abused his father, who did not speak of this incident or other racist encounters within the army until the last few days of his life. Hundreds of thousands of Indians served in the British Army to maintain the empire across the Global South through the First and Second World Wars. In fact, toward the end of the Second World War, the British Empire started losing hold over its territories due to a resistance group that broke away from the British Army and called itself the Indian National Army.

Since the late-nineteenth century, South Asian universities began offering higher education degrees in subjects such as English literature, philosophy, math, and the sciences. Most children of upper-caste, rich families went to college to receive degrees in these subjects. For many colonial South Asians who participated in various European institutions and identified with European culture, the experiences of racism were alienating, distressing, and nearly impossible to articulate in the language of the colonizer. As Walter Mignolo asserts, and as we saw with the etymological discussion of "Pandy" in Smith's *White Teeth* earlier in this chapter, languages are specifically shaped to express the interests and knowledge of the group and region from which they emerge and where they circulate. "Knowledge-making presupposes a semiotic code (languages, images, sounds, colors, etc.) shared between users in semiotic exchanges ... Knowledge-making is entrenched with imperial/colonial purposes, from the European Renaissance to the US neoliberalism."[34] Languages emerge from specific socio-cultural, power-based systems and its limits are that of the systems and the interests which they are designed to articulate. White racial superiority was and continues to be embedded in European languages to the extent that the very use of the language easily reproduces images and social concepts affirming that Europe is superior to Orient, white is superior to brown and black.

Many Hindu upper-caste nationalists fighting to oust the British in the nineteenth and twentieth centuries adopted racist worldviews. The third possible reason for silence about race in South Asian political public discourse is complicity with European racist worldviews. While Indians were routinely abused by Europeans on the basis of race, they were nevertheless placed above black Africans in the racial hierarchy. Many South Asian nationalists came to see themselves as Aryans based on a hypothesis put forward by nineteenth-century Orientalists. Consider the story of Mahatma Gandhi, renowned pacifist, anti-colonial dissenter, and later dubbed the "father of the [Indian] nation," who traveled to South Africa in his early twenties to work as a lawyer. He spent the next two decades in the country. However, after being subjected to racist treatment by white colonizers in South Africa, Gandhi campaigned for Indians and black South Africans to be segregated, such as being assigned separate entrances to the post office in Durban, so that Indians would no longer be subjected to the same treatment as that of black Africans. He spoke of black Africans in racist tropes common in European anthropological writings. In trying to make the case that Indians should be treated more like white South Africans rather than be placed in the same racial category as that of blacks, he says using the derogatory term *kaffir*, "ours is one continual struggle against a degradation sought to be inflicted upon us by the Europeans, who desire to degrade us to the level of the raw kaffir whose occupation is hunting, and whose sole ambition is to collect a certain number of cattle to buy a wife and then pass his life in indolence and nakedness."[35] These lines could have been lifted out of any major European Enlightenment thinker's writing on race. Gandhi clearly held racist views on black Africans and sought to end racism against Indians by reenforcing racism against black South Africans. The legacy of racism against black Africans remains alive in contemporary South Asia and is most commonly manifest in daily discrimination and violence against African college students, as documented by national newspapers in the last few years.

Comparisons between Latin American colonization and South Asian colonization yield some insight into the ways in which race is an overt organizing principle in one and a covert principle in the other. In the case of Latin America, the function of race was to formalize slavery and other forms of unwaged labor in the establishment of the colonies. The self-proclaimed racial superiority of the European colonizers was itself the justification for rule. In South Asia, the legitimation of rule was grounded in historicist claims about the stage of political modernity and its rule of law yet to come. Meanwhile, the ideology of racial hierarchy ensured that the natives would never be ready to self-govern. Jenny Sharpe's discussion of the circulation of gendered and racialized images of predatory South Asian men and South Asian women who needed rescuing in the aftermath of the 1957 rebellion shows the ways in which the construction of race offered a counterweight to liberalism's language of freedom and equality of all men before the law.

4. Concluding remarks: Disrupting colonial legacies of historiography and violence

While South Asian subaltern studies scholars interrogated the frameworks of colonialism and nationalism during the 1970s, Enrique Dusserl discusses a parallel move well underway within the Latin American philosophy of liberation, one of the aims of which was to reconstruct indigenous histories. As he identifies it, the major harm of Hegelian dialectical history is that the fragmentary narratives about the victims of European oppression appear before the holistic narratives of European history only as minor obstacles to be subsequently negated and absorbed into the next dialectic movement. So dualisms such as "center-periphery," "dependence-liberation," "exploiters-exploited" exist only till one half of the dualism "should overcome" the other.[36] Dusserl makes a case for alternative historical narratives of marginalized groups that resist negation and assimilation. As he claims, it is only when marginalized groups can reconstruct colonially erased historical narratives that new political visions and demands for rights become possible. This rallying cry has since been taken up by contemporary political philosophers writing with the specific aim to decolonize or disrupt the intellectual and epistemic legacies of colonization.

One such proposal is by Gyanendra Pandey who appeals to the "fragment" as a possible narrative form which defies assimilation to holistic narratives of the nation as the preferred genre for writing subaltern histories.[37] In the legacy of colonial historicist narrative structures, the new nationalist narratives do not treat the state as a historically contingent entity but rather an absolute entity emerging at the teleological end of history. Most school history textbooks in India end with the events in 1947 as the moment of Indian independence.[38] The violence, particularly sexual violence and the trauma of partition are either subordinated to the narrative of independence or are entirely erased from school textbooks. The fragment, which Pandey suggests as a resource, refers to a part that cannot be assimilated into whole historical narrative, but rather ruptures it.[39] As an illustrative example, he discusses poems written by a Muslim survivor of an organized Hindutva massacre in Bhagalpur in 1989. The poet's articulation of pain, trauma, and loss of trust in the world cannot be absorbed into a totalizing narrative of the nation as a cohesive whole designed for the interests of all the people it claims to represent. The images of the riots and their aftermath in these poems also unequivocally refuse to comply with the imperatives of historicism, particularly the demand to frame one historical stage yielding to the next stage of greater progress.

What would it look like to seek those unassimilable fragments in the stories of ourselves to continue disrupting the overarching historicist narratives, such as images of race in contemporary South Asian past and present; religiously inspired movements in "secular modernity;" and the particular, not universal, interests of the contemporary nation states?

Notes

1   Smith, *White Teeth*, 209.

2   Didur, *Unsettling Partition: Literature, Gender, Memory*; Marangoly George (2013) 173–202.

3   Pandey, *Remembering Partition: Violence, Nationalism and History of India*.

4   Ibid., 7.

5   Pandey, *Routine Violence: Nations, Fragments, Histories*.

6   In May 2014, a "cow protection law" passed in various states was amended to ban beef consumption, transportation, and possession. The only justification offered for this law is the safeguarding of "Hindu sentiments" This law particularly targets religious minorities and Dalits whose diet includes beef. Since 2015, there have been many instances of Muslims and Dalits being lynched by militant Hindu "cow

protectors" (*gau rakshak*) and lately by non-affiliated Hindus. The relatives of those killed and survivors of the assault have claimed it was buffalo meat, not cow meat. (BBC)

7   Sarkar, *Beyond Nationalist Frames: Postmodernism, Hindu Fundamentalism, History.*

8   Schirmer 2002, 52.

9   Ibid., 63–66.

10   Maybury-Lewis 2002, 351.

11   Ibid.

12   Paraguay in 1981, Bolivia in the 1990s, and Ecuador in the 1980s (see Peru 1979; Columbia 1991; Seed 2001, 136).

13   Guha 2000, xi–xiv.

14   Guha "Introduction," xiv–xv.

15   Carol Patemen, *The Sexual Contract*; Charles Mills, *The Racial Contract.*

16   Guha "Introduction," xviii.

17   Guha, *Dominance Without Hegemony: History and Power in Colonial India*, 104.

18   Ibid.

19   Chakrabarty, *Provincializing Europe: Postcolonial Though and Historical Difference*, 31.

20   Ibid., 32.

21   Kant, "Idea of Universal History with a Cosmopolitan Purpose," 51.

22   Ibid.

23   Chakrabarty, *Provincializing Europe*, 9.

24   Macaulay 1835.

25   Quoted in Chakrabarty *Provincializing Europe*, 8.

26   Quijano, "Coloniality of Power, Eurocentrism, and Latin America," 186–87.

27   Ibid., 189.

28   Ghosh and Chakrabarty, "A Correspondence on Provincializing Europe," 151.

29   Ibid., 154.

30   Ibid., 148.

31   Ibid., 153.

32   Ibid., 149.

33   Ibid., 148.

34   Mignolo, "Epistemic Disobedience, Independent Thought and Decolonial Freedom," 176.

35   Gandhi quoted in B. Chakrabarty, *Confluence of Thought: Mohandas Karamchand Gandhi and Martin Luther King Jr.*, 74.

36   Ibid., 343.

37   Pandey, *Routine Violence*, 66.

38   Pandey 1997, 3.

39   Pandey, *Routine Violence*, 66.

References

BBC News desk. "India BJP Leader Says Muslims Should Stop Eating Beef." *British Broadcasting Corporation*. October 16, 2015. Accessed September 1, 2016. http://www.bbc.com/news/world-asia-india-34546960.

Chakrabarty, B. *Confluence of Thought: Mohandas Karamchand Gandhi and Martin Luther King Jr.* New York: Oxford University Press, 2013.

Chakrabarty, D. *Provincializing Europe: Postcolonial Though and Historical Difference,* Princeton, NJ: Princeton University Press, 2000.

De Las Casas, B. *A Short Account of the Destruction of the Indies,* New York: Penguin, 1999 (originally published 1552).

Didur, J. *Unsettling Partition: Literature, Gender, Memory.* Buffalo: University of Toronto Press, 2006.

Dussel, E. "Philosophy of Liberation, The Postmodern Debate, and Latin American Studies." In *Coloniality at Large: Latin America and the Postcolonial Debate,* edited by Mabel Moraña, Enrique Dussel, and Carlos A. Jáuregui, 335–349, Durham, NC: Duke University Press, 2008.

Express Web Desk. "Beef Row: Where it is Illegal and What the Law Says," *Indian Express,* 27 July 2016. Available Online: http://indianexpress.com/article/india/india-news-india/beef-madhya-pradesh-video-cow-vigilantes-gau-rakshaks-2938751. (Accessed 1 September 2016).

Ghosh, A. and D. Chakrabarty. "A Correspondence on Provincializing Europe." *Radical History* 83 (Spring 2002): 146–72.

Guha, R. *Dominance Without Hegemony: History and Power in Colonial India,* Cambridge: Harvard University Press, 1997.

Guha, R. "Introduction," *A Subaltern Studies Reader: 1986–1995,* New Delhi: Oxford University Press, (1997) 2007.

Kant, I. "Idea of Universal History with a Cosmopolitan Purpose." In *Kant's Political Writings,* edited by Hans Reiss, translated by H.B. Nisbet. New York: Cambridge University Press, 2003 (originally published 1784).

Khan, Y. *The Great Partition: The Making of India and Pakistan.* New Delhi: Penguin, 2007.

Mignolo, W. "Epistemic Disobedience, Independent Thought and Decolonial Freedom." *Theory, Culture & Society* 26 (7–8 2009): 159–181.

Mills, C. *The Racial Contract.* Ithaca, NY: Cornell University Press, 1997.

Pandey, G. *Routine Violence: Nations, Fragments, Histories.* Stanford, CA: Stanford University Press, 2006.

Pandey, G. *Remembering Partition: Violence, Nationalism and History of India.* New York: Cambridge University Press, 2001.

Patemen, C. *The Sexual Contract.* Stanford, CA: Stanford University Press, 1988.

Quijano, A. "Coloniality of Power, Eurocentrism, and Latin America," In *Coloniality At Large: Latin America and the Postcolonial Debate,* 181–224. Durham, NC: Duke University Press, 2008.

Rosemary, G. M. "Partition Literature and the 'birth' of National Literature." In *Indian English and the Fiction of National Literature*, 173–202. New York: Cambridge University Press, 2013.

Sarkar, S. *Beyond Nationalist Frames: Postmodernism, Hindu Fundamentalism, History.* New Delhi: Permanent Black, 2002.

Sharpe, J. *The Allegories of Empire: Figure of the Woman in the Colonial Text.* Minneapolis, MN: Minnesota University Press, 1993.

Smith, Z. *White Teeth.* New York: Vintage, 2009.

Index

aesthetic monism 143
Ahmed, Sarah 5
Al-Andalus 15
Alexandria 53–4
Algeria 88–9
Amano Teiyu 8, 129, 129–42
    background 129–30, 147 n.1
    and creativity 130–6, 147
    and moral education 136–7, 138–42,
      146–7
    theory of education 136–8, 146–7
Amerindians 227
anarchy 175–93
Anchieta, Joseph 72
Anderson, Arthur 160, 169 n.21
anti-colonial philosophy 9, 217–35
anti-materialism 40, 52–3, 65 n.24
Anzaldúa, Gloria 115
aptness 155
Arabs, in Spain 76
Argentina 47, 91
Aristotle 8, 160, 167, 170 n.23, 170 n.34
Aryan mysticism 27
Aryan-German race, formation of 55–6
Aryans and Aryanism 21, 27, 34–6, 41, 42,
    46, 55–6, 59, 64, 233
Asia
    Spanish and Portuguese colonial ties
      73
    as victim 34
Asian philosophy
    cultural traditions 4
    status 3
Asiatic despotism 27
Ateneo de la Juventud 7
Ateneo de la Juventud 14, 18, 26, 48–9
Atlantis 34, 35, 36, 42, 44, 56–7, 59
authenticity 5, 183–5
awareness, disciplined 180
Aztecs, the
    and aptness 155
    and the good life 156, 157–9, 167

    and the human condition 157
    middle way 8, 155–68
    and practical wisdom 163–4, 165

Babbit, Susan 8
Balmont, Konstantin 17
Bangladesh 219–20
Bangladesh Liberation war, 1971 219
Baralt, Rafael María 85–6
Barreda, Gabino 18
Battista Belzoni, Giovanni 77
Bautista Alberdi, Juan 83
Bedouin 85
Being, philosophy of 132
Bello, Andrés 81–2, 82–3, 88
Ben-Ezra, Josafat 75
Berdyaev, Nikolai 25
Bergson, Henri 18, 47, 57–8
Bergson, Mina 58
Besant, Annie 45–6, 50
    Esoteric Christianity 53–4
betweenness 8, 107, 109–11, 113–16, 117,
    121–2
Bhagavad Gita 20, 21, 24–5, 39
    Spanish translation 48, 49
Black panthers, the 212
Blavatsky, Helene 41, 48, 50, 91
    historical narrative 42–6, 57, 60, 64
    Isis Unveiled 42, 43, 62
body, and mind 175–7, 183
body, the 110, 127 n.86, 137
    and mind 175–7, 183
Bolívar, Simón 75, 75–6, 78, 79, 93 n.32
Borrell, José Roviralta 48
Brasseur de Bourbourg, Abbot Charles E.
    35, 36, 42
Brazil 8–9, 77, 221–2
    martial arts 201–13
breastfeeding 8, 105–23
    colonial logic 119–20
    liminality 121–2
    Lugonian reading of 116–20, 120–3

political aspects 106, 120–3
in public 123
public backlash 106
rates 106
British Army 232
Buchenau, Jürgen 17
Buddha
    cause-and-effect relationships 177,
        179–80, 182–3, 191–2, 192
    dhamma 179–80, 191
    fact/value distinction 186
    and loss 191
    political implications 192–3
    and reality 179–80
    teachings 180
    universals 175
Buddhism 18–19, 23–4, 49, 180, 185–6
Buenos Aires 47, 77, 78, 84
Bulwer-Lytton, Edward, *The Coming Race*
    36, 43
Bushido 214 n.7

Cantares Mexicanos, "Flower-Song" 158
capitalism 26, 27
Cárdenas, Lázaro 22
Carter, Robert 108, 109, 109–10
Caso, Antonio 7, 14, 49
    conception of society 19–20
    conception of spirituality 30 n.39
    discussion of the *Bhagavad Gita* 24–5
    "*El Oriente y el Occidente*" ("The Orient
        and the Occident") 14, 20–5, 28
    El peligro del hombre (The Peril of Man)
        19
    interests in Buddhism and Hinduism
        18–19, 23–4
    *La existencia como economía, como
        desinterés y como caridad* 19, 26
    *La persona humana y el estado
        totalitario (The Human Person and
        the Totalitarian State)* 14, 18–19
    and personhood 19, 20
    and phenomenology 28
    political stances 26
    and positivism 18
    and the role of the state 20
    students 28
    two souls view 26–7, 28
Castro, Fidel 184, 189, 190

cause-and-effect relationships 175–7,
    179–80, 182–3, 185, 186–7, 191
Cecilio del Valle, José 78
Center of Psychological Studies of San
    Pedro 21
Centers of Disease Control 106
Chakrabarty, Dipesh 1, 4, 5, 218, 224–5,
    228–9, 229–31
change, and loss 190–1
Chapman University 106
Chaves, José Ricardo 20, 48
Chichen-Itza 36
Chile 82–3
China
    comparative philosophy 4
    early treatment of 3–4
    Egaña and 81
    Han dynasty 4
    Marx and 27
    studies in colonial America 72–3, 77
Christianity 28, 34, 42, 53–4
Científicos, the 16, 18
civilization, journey of 77–8
Clarification of the Kokutai 139
class struggle 23–4
Clavijero, Francisco Javier 89
Colombia 78
colonial logic
    breastfeeding 119–20
    human/non-human dichotomy 115–16
colonial matrix of power, the 14, 28
colonial nationalism 223–4
colonialism 177–8
    historical narratives 234–5
    ideologies of domination 222–8, 228
    legacy of 217–35
    and race 228–34
    and state violence 219–22
communication, political nature of 117–18
communism 26
comparative philosophy 1, 2–4, 5, 8
competition 208–11
Comte, Auguste 16, 18
Conde, Antonio 76
Confucius 74, 81
    aims 156–7
    Analects 160–1, 164
    and aptness 155
    Doctrine of the Mean 161–2

ethics 165
  and the good life 156–7, 159, 167
  and moderation 8, 155–68
  and practical wisdom 164–5
Conink, Juan Ramón 72
conscience 139
consent 218, 222–8
cooperation, spirit of 137
Cousin, Victor 39
creativity 130–6, 147, 182
Creole Enlightenment 73–4
Creole groups, supremacy of 71
Cristero Rebellion 22
Cuba 8, 175–93
Cuban Revolutionary Party 178
Cueva, Mario de la 18
cultural chauvinism 4
cultural imperialism 14
culture 134, 144

dao, the 156, 166, 168 n.6
Darwin, Charles 16, 35–6, 54–5
Davis, Asahel 35
Dawson, Raymond 161
De Las Casas, Bartolomeo 227
de Mora, José Joaquín 76
de San Martín, José 75
de Vidaurre, Manuel Lorenzo 76
Dead Prez 201–13, 202
death 214 n.7
decolonial studies 222
decolonization 9, 207, 211, 217–35
Denis, León 44–5
Descartes, René 188
despotism 80–1
development, transition narrative 224–5
dhamma 179–80, 191
Díaz, Porfirio 16, 17
Dibble, Charles 160, 169 n.21
disorientation 6
domestic violence 202
dori 131, 134
Dussel, Enrique 28, 204, 234
dynamic right 143

East, the 5–6
East India Company 222, 225–6
East-West dialogue 3, 5
East-West Philosophers' Conferences 3

Echeverría, Esteban 84–5
Edinburgh Review, The 35
education 8, 129–47, 191
  Amano's theory of 136–8, 146–7
  and creativity 130–6, 147
  examinations 137–8, 147
  influence of nature 136
  moral 136–7, 138–42, 146–7
  reform 142
  role of 137
  status 141–2
  Vasconcelos's theories and practices
    144–6, 147
Egaña, Juan 81
el espíritismo (spiritism) 20–1, 38–9, 40, 64,
    65 n.24
El Salvador 221
El Sol de Cuzco (newspaper) 77
Ellacuría, Ignacio 206
Emerson, Ralph W. 39
Enlightenment 73, 84–5
  Creole 73–4
  historical narratives 34–5
  and race 229, 230
epistemology 8
Escuela Magnético-Espiritual (Magnetic-
    Spiritual School) 47
ethics 107–9, 110–11, 117–18, 155–68
Eurocentrism 2, 3, 77, 86–7
Europeanization 82–4, 90
evolutionism 33, 35–6, 43, 49–50, 54–5

fact/value distinction 185–7
factual claims 185
faith 183, 193
Fanon, Frantz 177–8, 207
Fernández, Cristina 189
Fernández de Lizardi, José Joaquín 74
Fiengo, Nicola 77
Figueira, Dorothy M. 34, 37, 47
Florentine Codex 155, 157, 159, 168 n.1,
    169 n.13
"Flower-Song", *Cantares Mexicanos* 158
Fourlas, George 8–9
France 34, 44–5, 52
Francia, García 79
freedom 135, 136, 176, 180–2, 187, 188,
    230
French Revolution, the 16

friendship 110
Frye, Marilyn 111
Funakoshi, Gichin 205

Gacía, Telésforo 90
Gadamer, Hans-Georg 208, 209
Galeón de Manila, the 73
Gandhi, Mahatma 233–4
Gasquet. Axel 84–5
Gasset, José Ortega y 28
gender 116
    decoloniality 118
    definition of women 122
German Idealism 25
German phenomenology 28
German Romanticism 39
German vitalist Orientalism 25
Ghosh, Amitav 229, 229–31
Gobineau, Arthur de 55
Goldman, Emma 193
Gómez, Antonio 74
González de Mendoza, Juan 72–3
good life, the 156–9, 167
Goodrick-Clarke, Nicholas 56
Gott, Richard 189
Gracie Academy 212
Gracie, Rener 202
Greece 88, 167
Guatemala, civil war 221
Guevara, Che 176–7, 178, 182
Guha, Ranajit 218, 222, 223–4

Haddox, John 19
Haeckel, Ernst 49–50
Hansen, Chad 164–5
happiness 166
Hara de la Torre, Raúl 91
harmony 162
Havana, University of 188
Hawaii, University of 3
Hegel, G.W.F. 2, 3–4, 16, 27, 86, 234
Herder, Johann Gottfried von 27, 34
Hess, David 20–1
hierarchies 176, 224, 227
Hinduism, Caso's interests in 18–19, 23
hip hop 202
Hispanic Orientalism 13
historiographical terms 2
historiography 219, 222–8

history
    and creativity 133–4
    philosophy of 87
    stages 16
    study of 1–2
    transition narrative 224–5
Hobsbawn, Eric 224
Huehuetlatolli (Discourses of the Elders)
    163
human condition, the 157
human freedom 18
human perfection 139
human reason 131
human/non-human dichotomy 115–16
Hurricane Katrina 190
Husserl, Edmund 18, 28

Ibert Bill (1883) 230
Illich, Ivan 190
Ilustración Espírita 40
immigration, Latin America 78, 83
imperialism 26, 177, 178–9, 192, 222
    and capitalism 27
    justification of 225–6, 228
    and race 226–8, 228–34
    U.S. 47
India 15, 63
    Blavatsky and Olcott visit 41
    British Army service 232
    British rule 223–4, 225–6, 229–32,
        233–4
    comparison of Mexico with 21
    cow protection law 235–6 n.6
    German Romanticism and 39
    historical narratives 235
    ideologies of domination 223–4
    influence on the Americas 33–64
    partition 219–21, 235
    and race 229–32
    racism 233–4
    in Theosophy 42–6
    Vasconcelos' understanding of 50–3
Indian National Army 232
indigenous populations 27, 116, 221–2,
    227–8
individual consciousness 108
individualism 131–2, 135
individuals, relationality 108
Inés de la Cruz, Sor Juana 72

inner voice 194 n.21
Inoue Tetsujiro 130
Ionesco, Eugène 175, 191–2, 192
Isabelle, Arsène 86

Jacinto Zavala, Agustín 8
Jacolliot, Louis 62
James, William 58
Japan
    Meiji Restoration 15, 91
    studies in colonial America 72–3
Javier, Francisco 73
Jefferson, Thomas 81
Joseph, Gilbert 17
Judge, W.Q. 41
justice 19–20

Kalama Sutta 183
Kalmanson, Leah 215 n.19
Kant, Immanuel 2, 225
Karate 203–4
Kardec, Allan 20–1, 38–9, 40–1, 44, 48
Kendo 215 n.19
Keyserling, Hermann von 23, 25, 28
Kim, David 3
kinds 176
Kircher, Athanasius 72
Kissinger, Henry 190
knowledge
    and loss 191
    and power 13, 178
    production 13, 233
knowledge-making 233
Koppenhaver, Jonathan 202
Koran, the 81
Kumarajiva 4
Kushington, Julia 13, 15
Kyoto circle 130
Kyoto Philosophy 130

La Matanza 221
La Revue Spirite (The Spiritist Magazine)
    38, 40–1
Lachapelle, Sophie 44
Lacunza, José 87
Lacunza, Manuel 75
languages
    colonial 217–18, 232–3
    study of 75, 90

Larrazábal, Antonio 74
Latin America
    Europeanization 82–4, 90
    immigration 78, 83
    Orientalism in 7, 71–92
    Orientalization 85–7
    reaction against the Orient 82–9
    and Western civilization 71
Latin American philosophy, dilemma of
    4–5
Latin American School of Medical
    Sciences 190
Latinism 64
Lau, D.C. 161
Le Plongeon, Alice 36, 42
Le Plongeon, Augustus 36–7
Ledi Sayadaw 183, 186
Lee, Bruce 211
legitimacy
    colonial domination 222–8, 228
    political 218, 222
    state violence 219–22
Lemuria 43, 44
Lenin, Vladimir 26–7, 175–6, 179
li 165
liberalism 143, 226, 231–2
    rise of 7–8, 89–90
liberation
    human 178
    paths to 111–13
    political 181
liberation philosophy 8–9, 201, 234
    martial arts tradition 203–6, 214 n.9
    message 206
    values 204
libraries 145
liminality 8, 107, 109–11, 113–16, 117,
    121–2
List, Guido, *Die Bilderschrift der Ario-
    Germanen* 55–6
Littlejohn, Ronnie 2–3
llaneros 85–6
López, Vicente 75, 87
López, Vicente Fidel 88
loss, and change 190–1
love 62
Lugones, María 8, 106, 107
    account of liminality 113–16, 117
    on competition 210

on decoloniality of gender 118
and liberation 111–13
and modernity 119
on play 209
"Purity, Impurity, and Separation" 112
reading of *Aidagara* 117, 120–3
and resistance 111–13
"Structure/Anti-Structure and Agency under Oppression" 111
Luz y Caballero, José de la 175, 177, 178, 178–9, 192

Macaulay, Thomas 225–6, 228
McCarthy, Erin 108, 109
Madero, Francisco I. 13, 14, 20–1, 48, 49
Maeda, Esai 212
Maffie, James 170 n.34
Mahasatipatthana Sutta 180
Maia, Demian 212–13
Mandela, Nelson 190
Marchard, Suzanne 25
Mariátegui, José Carlos 91, 176
Martí, José 40–1, 45, 176–7, 177, 178, 180–2, 183–5, 189, 190, 191, 192, 193, 195 n.51, 195 n.53, 195 n.54
martial arts
  communal history 204
  competition 208–11
  and decolonization 207, 211
  degradation 203
  liberation tradition 203–6, 207, 211–13, 214 n.9
  liberatory schools 203
  meaning-making purposes 212
  motivation 207
  performativity 201
  popularity of 8–9, 201–13
  restraint 210–11
  spiritual experience 206
  training 208–11
  and transformation 211–12
  underlying principles 205
  understanding 201
  values 204, 205–6
  violence 202–3, 204–5, 207–11, 211–12, 213, 214 n.7
Marx, Karl 27, 111, 179, 184–5, 196 n.79
Massis, Henri, *Defense de l'Occident (Defense of the West)* 23

master narrative, the 1, 4
materialism 35–6, 40–1, 52–3
Mayans, the 17, 36–7, 42, 56, 221
Mazgaj, Paul 23
mean, the 155–68
  and aptness 155
  central features 155
  definition 160
  and the good life 156–9, 167
  and moderation 160–3
  and practical wisdom 163–5, 166
  realization 161–2
  role of 160–3
  understandings of 160–3
meaning-making 212
Meghiya Sutta 182
Meiners, Christoph 2
memory 113
Mencius 165, 168 n.6
Mendieta, Eduardo 16
Mendoza, Adalberto García de 28
Merton, Thomas 190
Mexican Communist Party 26
Mexican Orientalism 13–28, 48
  in Caso's writings 20–5
  emergence of 15–20
  Odalisque-Mania 15
  patterns of 25–8
  terms of 26
Mexican Revolution, the 16–18, 21, 26, 47, 49, 90
Mignolo, Walter 14, 28, 232–3
Mill, John Stuart 226
mind
  and body 175–7, 183
  and self 188
Miranda, Francisco de 80–1
Mitra, Namrata 9
moderation 8, 155–68
  and aptness 155
  central features 155
  definition 160
  and the good life 156–9, 167
  and the mean 160–3
  and morality 8
modernity 86, 119, 218, 222, 230, 232, 235
Monahan, Michael 213
Montecristi Manifesto, the 178, 193
moral education 136–7, 138–42, 146–7

morality, and moderation 8
Moreno, Mariano 79
Moscardo 72
Müller, Max 36
Muñoz Chimalpáhin, San Antón 73
muralismo 145–6

Nagami, Isamu 118
Nagy-Zekmi, Silvia 13
national culture 18
National Socialism 22, 27, 55
nationalism 22, 26–7, 147
    colonial 223–4
nationalist movements 224
nation-building 26
nature 136, 190
Nazi racism 55
negation, of negation 132
neltiliztli 158–9
neocolonialism 1
Neo–Platonism 49
Nervo, Amado 25, 49
neutrality 1
New England Trasncendentalists 39
New School movement 147
Nietzsche, Friedrich 18, 24, 47, 213
ningen 108–9, 110–11, 117, 119, 120,
    120–1
Nishida Kitaro 129, 130, 132–4, 135,
    136, 142, 148 n.6, 148 n.9
Non-Cooperation Movement 224
Northern Africa 15
Novoa, Adriana 7

Obama, Barack 189
Occidental personalism 24
Occidental philosophy, Christian tenets 14
Odalisque-Mania 15, 21
Okuda, Kazuhito 108
Olcott, Henry Steel 41, 42, 47
oppression 111, 115
Orient, the
    construction of 5–6
    definition 71
    Eurocentric view of 86–7
    extent 71
    function of 77
    influence over America 84
    lessons of 75–6

as metaphor for oppression 90
    reaction against 82–9
    role of 78
    Spanish and Portuguese colonial ties 73
Orientalism 4
    definition 15
    Enlightenment 73
    European 84–5
    expansion in the Americas 47
    Hispanic 13
    and knowledge production 13
    in Latin America 7, 71–92
    Mexican 13–28, 48
    popularity 33
    renewal 47
    texts 37
Orientalist mysticism 27
Orientalization, Latin America 85–7
orientation 5–6
Orozco, José Clemente 145
Ortega, Mariana 112–13, 125 n.45
Ottoman Empire 81

Páez, José Antonio 85
Pakistan 219–20
Panama Canal 78
Pandey, Gyanendra 219, 220, 235
pantheism 24
Park, Peter K. J. 2
Paz, Octavio 13, 25, 64
pedagogical philosophy 8, 129–47
personality belief 185–6
personhood 19, 20
Peru 76
Petersen, Patricia 213
phenomenology 28
Philadelphia (journal) 47
Philosophical Polemic of 1838–40 178–9
philosophy, history of 2
Pitts, Andrea 7
Plato 34, 35, 43, 46
play 208–11
political economy 77
positivism 7, 16, 18, 90
postcolonialism 9, 217–35
    state violence 219–22
power 116
    and knowledge 13, 178
practical wisdom 163–5, 166

progress 218, 222
Prothero, Steven 41
provincialism 4
provincialization 1, 3–5
Purcell, Sebastian 8
Pythagoras 38, 45–6

quan 165
Quijano, Anibal 28, 218, 226–8, 228–9

race
    construction of 218
    evolutionary archetypes 49–50
    evolutionism 35–6
    Germanization of metaphysics 55–6
    hybridization 61
    and imperialism 226–8, 228–34
    invisibility of 231–2
    metaphysical interpretations 36–7
    metaphysics of 33–64
    mission in Latin America 54–63
    place of 218
    search for origins 34–7
    taxonomies 2
    Theosophy and 42–6, 50
    Vasconcelos view of 54–63
    visibilities of 228–34
racism 44, 55, 232, 233–4
Ramaswany, Sumathi 44
Ramos, Samuel 28, 64
rationality 2
Ravaisson, Félix 40
reality 111–12, 112–13, 125 n.43, 140, 179–80
reason 185, 187–8, 191, 192
reason, sense of 131, 134–5
relationality, individuals 108
relationships, networks of 109–10, 117
Reyes, Alfonso 49
Ribot, Théodule-Armand 39–40
Riepe, Daniel 39
Río de la Plata 77–8, 86
Rivail, Hippolyte Léon Denizard 20–1, 38–9
Rivera, Diego 145
Rocafuerte, Vicente 76
Rodó, José Enrique 18
Rodrguez, Pedro Paulo 195 n.54
Rodríguez de Francia, Gaspar 76, 79
Rojas, Roque 38
Rome 88

Roy, M.N. 26–7
Rudbeck, Olof 34
rule of law 223, 232

saddha 182–3, 192
Said, Edward 13, 14–15, 71, 83–4
sakkayaditthi 185–7, 192–3
Salazar Bondy, Augusto 4–5
Samkhya 46
Sarkar, Sumit 220, 224
Sarmiento, Domingo F. 39, 86, 87–9, 90, 95–6 n.59
Sartre, Jean-Paul 177–8
Schirmer, Jennifer 221
Schopenhauer, Arthur 18, 24
Schwab, Raymond 83
science 185, 187–8
Seed, Patricia 221–2
self, the 188
self-formation 133
self-identity 133
self-overcoming 213
self-rule 229
semiotic code 233
Shaolin Monks 204
Sharpe, Jenny 234
Sierra, Justo 18
sincerity 131
Sinophilia 73–4
Siqueiros, David Alfaro 145
Sismonde of Sismondi 82
slaves and slavery 227, 234
Smith, Zadie 217–18, 233
social reform 62
social responsibility 18
social rites 165, 167
Société Parisienne des Études Spirites 38
South Africa 189
Spain 15, 177
    Arabs in 76
    Orientalization 85–7
Spanish Inquisition 78–9
Spelman, Elizabeth 210
Spence Hardy, R. 35
Spencer, Herbert 16, 18, 28
Spengler, Oswald 23
Spinoza, Baruch 24
spiritism 20–1, 38–9, 40, 44–5, 46, 64, 65 n.24

spiritual evolution 60
spiritual freedom 181–2
spiritualism 33, 37, 40, 41, 48, 64, 65 n.24
Spiritualistic Realism 40
spirituality, Caso's conception 30 n.39
Spranger, Eduard 144
state, the, role of 20
state violence 218, 219–22
Stehn, Alexander 18
subaltern studies 222, 223–4
Summit of the Americas, 2015 189
Swadeshi Movement 224
Sweden 34
Sweig, Julia 189

Tablada, José Juan 25
Taboada, Hernán G. H. 7–8
taekwondo 205
Tagore, Rabindranath 21, 23
Taylor, Charles 195 n.51
Tenneman, Wilhelm 2
Tenorio-Trillo, Mauricio 15, 17, 27
Teotihuacan 157
Theosophical Society 41, 45, 47
Theosophist, The 58
Theosophy 7, 17, 41, 42–6, 47–8, 50, 54, 55,
    56, 57–8, 64
Theravadan Buddhism 8
thinking 175–7, 177, 183–4, 187–9, 191
Third-Worldism 91
tlalticpac 157–9
Tokyo circle 130
Torres-Rodríguez, Laura J. 13–14, 15, 21,
    22
totalism 132, 135
Tott, Baron de 80–1
Trincado, Joaquín 47
Trump, Donald 195 n.64
Turner, Victor 113–14, 115

Ueda Shizuteru 130
unfreedom 180–1
United States of America
    breastfeeding 119–20
    and Cuba 177, 189–90
    cultural imperialism 14
    imperialism 47
    influence of Theosophy 46
    reaffirmation as a chosen people 45

spiritualism 37
    Trump elected president 195 n.64
Universalópolis 62
universals 175, 178–9
Ureña, Pedro Henríquez 49
Uriccoechea, Ezequiel 90

Vallenilla Lanz, Laureno 86
value-claims 185
values 139, 140, 204, 205–6
Varela, Felix 175, 177, 178, 192
Vargas Tejada, Luis 75
Vasconcelos, José 7, 8, 13, 14, 21, 22–3, 26
    "A Dynamic Theory of Right" 143
    aesthetic monism 143
    anti-materialism 52–3
    background 142
    conception of culture 144
    The Cosmic Race 33, 54–63, 64
    and creativity 147
    educational practice 145–6
    Estudios indostánicos 49, 54, 57, 64, 144
    exile 54
    historical narrative 57, 59–60, 64
    and human nature 50
    political theory 143
    project 51, 54, 62–3
    racial narrative 54–63, 63–4
    and religion 53–4
    social theory 144
    theory of education 129, 142–6, 144–5,
        147
    Theosophical intuitionism 58–9
    understanding of India 50–3
    worldview 143
Venezuela 74
violence 202–3, 204–5, 207–11, 211–12,
    213, 214 n.7
    state 218, 219–22
virtue 138, 155, 156–9, 161, 163, 167
virtue ethics 8, 155–68
Viswanathan, Gauri 50
Vitier, Cintio 195 n.54
Vivekananda, Swami 21
Volney, Conde de 76, 78–80, 93 n.37
Voltaire 34, 73

Wall Street Journal 189
Watsuji Tetsuro 8

aidagara 107, 109–11, 116–20
and communication 117–18
criticism of 117
ethics 107–9, 110–11, 117–18, 123
Guzo Saiko (Revival of Idols) 118
Lugonian reading of 116–20, 120–3
and modernity 119
Rinrigaku 105–23
West, the
provincialization 1, 3–5
situated nature of 5
Western colonial logic 107
Western civilization, Latin America and 71
Westernization 107
Wilkins, Charles 39

Williams, Bernard 167
Wolf, Allison 8
women, colonial definition 122
Wood, Allen 196 n.79
World War I 232
World War II 22, 55, 142, 230, 232

Xuanzang 4

Yasuo, Yuasa 110
Yu, Jiyuan 162, 165
Yucatán peninsula 36–7

Zavala, Lorenzo de 79–80
Zea, Leopoldo 89
Zirión, Antonio 28